Hard Fought Victories

Women Coaches Making a Difference

Sara Gogol

Wish Publishing
Terre Haute, Indiana
www.wishpublishing.com

No part of this book may be reproduced, stored in a data base or other retrieval system, or transmitted in any form, by any means, including mechanical, photocopy, recording or otherwise, without the prior written permission of the publisher.

LCCN: 2001093602

Proofread by Heather Lowhorn
Cover designed by Phil Velikan
Cover photography of coaches provided by (top to bottom) University of Pittsburgh Sports Information Office, Old Dominion University Sports Information, University of New Hampshire Sports Information, Fresno State University Sports Information, and Notre Dames Sports Information Office. Trophy photo by arrangement with Photodisk.

Printed in the United States of America
10 9 8 7 6 5 4 3 2 1

Published in the United States by
Wish Publishing
P.O. Box 10337
Terre Haute, IN 47801, USA
www.wishpublishing.com

Distributed in the United States by
Cardinal Publishers Group
7301 Georgetown Road, Suite 118
Indianapolis, Indiana 46268
www.cardinalpub.com

To all the women coaches who have done
so much for girls and women in sports

Muffet and Murphy McGraw

Acknowledgements

I am deeply grateful to the many current and former coaches who took time from their busy working lives to do one or more interviews with me. Although I could not include all their stories within this book, all of the coaches' perspectives helped give me insight into the many challenges and rewards of a coach's life and to what a difference women coaches have made.

In addition to the coaches who preferred to remain anonymous, I want to thank Vivian Acosta, Jenny Allard, Beth Anders, Lisa Beckett, Erica Blanco, Beth Bozman, Beth Bricker, Debbie Brown, Joan Broderick, Linda Carpenter, Sharon Chiong, Cindy Cohen, Deitre Collins, Jody Conradt, Laurie Corbelli, Kristy Curry, Chris Davis, Lori Dauphiny, Andrea Durieux, Jorjean Fischer, Lisa Fisher, Marianna Freeman, Stephanie Gabbert, Stephanie Gaitley, Judi Garman, Judy George, Pat Griffin, Sally Harmon, Jan Harville, Holly Hatton, Betty Jaynes, Karen Kay, Beverly Kearney, Pat Kendrick, Dana Kusjanovic, Donna Lopiano, Teri Mariani, Marcia McDermott, Muffet McGraw, Shannon Miller, Jeannie Milling, Digit Murphy, Julie Orlowski, Jane Paterson, Mary Jo Peppler, Paula Petrie, Marlene Piper, Rhonda Revelle, Cecile Reynaud, Stephanie Schleuder, Chris Shelton, Karen Smyte, Katey Stone, Angie Taylor, Ellie Trussell, Shannon Tuttle, Tara VanDerveer, Barb Viera, Traci Waites, Marian Washington, Joann Wolf, Noleana Woodard, Margie Wright, Martha Yates and Jenny Yopp. Many of these coaches also provided valuable referrals to other coaches.

My thanks to Vivian Acosta, Linda Carpenter, Mary Jo Kane,

Donna Lopiano, Marlene Piper and Stephanie Schleuder for sending me materials in addition to doing interviews with me. Numerous sports information directors and administrative assistants helped with photos and interviews. I want to especially thank Barb Kowal from the University of Texas and Cindy Vinyard from the University of Kansas, who were both very helpful. Thanks as well to George Wolfe and Bruce Henderson for helping inform me about coaching overall; to Edward Gogol for sending articles; to Kay Porter for her thoughts; to Sandy Vivas for her perspectives on Stephanie Schleuder and volleyball coaching; to Dorothy Turchi for her helpful suggestions; and to Julie Allen for her help with research. I am grateful to Holly Kondras for her interest in this project, her support in many ways, and for having the vision to found Wish Publishing. Finally, my thanks to Elaine Carter for her daily encouragement and caring and for listening to so many stories about coaches.

Sara Gogol
Portland, Oregon
November 1, 2001

Sara Gogol teaches English and women's studies at Portland Community College in Portland, Oregon. She is the author of two previous books on women's sports: Katy Steding: Pro Basketball Pioneer, *and* Playing in a New League: The Women of the American Basketball League's First Season.

Table of Contents

Jody Conradt

Introduction

Marlene Piper is a friendly woman, a Canadian native with a lilting British Columbia accent, who has coached volleyball for many years at several American universities. When we sat and talked in her small office filled with team photos and other coaching memorabilia, Marlene told me a great deal about the coaching profession. Then shortly afterward, she sent me an article and a note. "Most wonderful to meet you," she wrote. "Not sure where your coach adventure will take you with this upcoming book, but you will enjoy the process, I am sure. Coaches are an awesome group, eh?!!"

After speaking with more than 60 current and former coaches across the country, I find that Marlene Piper's words ring true. Coaches are remarkably interesting people. At least that certainly has been true for the women coaches at colleges across the United States whom I interviewed for this book. They're a lively group of women who are articulate, very competent, sometimes humorous and typically just plain nice. They have personalities and backgrounds that vary widely, of course, as do their personal experiences with sport. But they share a strength, a love of competition and a genuine caring for and connection with the athletes they teach.

"It is wonderful that you are focusing on a professional population that gets overlooked and unrecognized by the media because we, as women coaches, are constantly in the shadows of our male counterparts," cross country coach Sharon Chiong e-mailed to me. I appreciated her supportive message and agreed with her comment. Just as women's sports in the

United States still receives far less attention than men's sports, women coaches as a group have received relatively little attention. And yet they play important roles within the area of female sports.

The job that women college coaches do is not an easy one. In spite of the huge increase in sports opportunities for girls and women, the sports world, by and large, is still defined as male turf. With most college athletic departments run by male athletic directors and no separate organization representing all women's college sports, the percentage of women who coach college teams is actually lower than in the past. In fact, women coaches provide good examples of women succeeding within a male-dominated field of work.

Women college coaches have witnessed, worked for, and not infrequently fought for many of the key changes in opportunities for women's sports. Regardless of their age, they are all, in a sense, engaged in pioneering opportunities for girls and women. They also are important role models for the female athletes they train. They show their athletes on a daily basis strong women leaders who have often themselves been excellent athletes.

The women coaches who took time from their busy schedules to talk with me gave me fascinating looks into the demanding and rewarding college coaching profession. Since I've never been a coach myself—my experience teaching and sometimes mentoring my community college students is the closest I can come personally—I looked at the coaches' lives from the perspective of an outsider. But listening to the coaches' stories, I thought I could understand, in part at least, what it was like to breath in the sweat of countless practices and to experience many kinds of wrenching defeats and thrilling victories.

These coaching "chronicles" were told to me by women who practice their profession or formerly coached at colleges and universities across the United States—at prominent Division I universities with well funded athletic programs, at universities where athletics overall or the coach's particular sport receive fewer resources, at Division III schools where both the level of competition and the balance between sports and academics differs from that at Division I colleges. The women I interviewed coach or coached a wide variety of sports. Many of the women are head coaches, but some are assistants. Some of the coaches are retired, others are middle-aged, others are relatively new to the coaching profession.

"I believe in empowering women," soccer coach Stephanie Gabbert told me. That seems like a good description of the lives women coaches lead. The coaches whose voices fill this book not only empower the young women they work with but are powerful women themselves. This book tells their collective story.

Photography Credits:
Interior photography: page iv provided by Notre Dame University Sports Information; pages viii, 2, 9, 68 and 72 provided by University of Texas Sports Information; page 15, provided by Willamette University Sports Information; pages 22 and 27 provided by University of Delaware Sports Information Office, pages 31 and 202 provided by Portland State University Sports Information; page 37 provided by Kansas University Sports Information; pages 42 and 242 provided by Cal State-Fullerton University Sports Information; pages 51 and 115 provided by Brown University Sports Information; page 55 provided by Syracuse University Sports Information; page 62 provided by University of Nebraska Sports Information; pages 75 and 148 used with permission of AP Sports Worldwide; page 83 provided by University of Minnesota-Duluth Sports Information; page 92 provided by Macalester College Sports Information; page 106 provided by Joann Wolf; page 127 provided by Fresno State University; page 134 provided by Arizona State University Sports Information; pages 144 and 186 provided by Texas A &M Sports Information; page 152 provided by Purdue University Sports Information; pages 162 and 222 provided by UNLV Sports Information; pages 164 and 237 provided by George Mason University Sports Information; pages 175 and 196 provided by Mills University Sports Information; pages 178 and 235 provided by Harvard University Sports Information; page 193 provided by Old Dominion University Sports Information; page 213 provided by Illinois State University Sports Information; page 232 provided by Georgia Tech University Sports Information; page 244 provided by University of Michigan Sports Information; page 247 by Iowa State University Sports Information.

If there is an error in these credits, the publisher will gladly correct it in subsequent editions of the book.

Hard Fought Victories

It was the last day of the 1999 NCAA Outdoor Track and Field Championships, held at Bronco Stadium at Boise State University. And it had come down to the last women's event, the mile relay. That's what would decide which one of three top teams, Texas, UCLA or USC, would win the women's championship.

For University of Texas head track coach Beverly Kearney, that last race was one more challenging event in a challenging meet. With the Texas women last year's champions and the team favored to win this year too, Bev and her athletes faced a barrage of media attention. Press cameras of all types recorded the moves of Texas athletes.

Bev Kearney is a forthright person who expresses her own feelings and encourages others to do the same. She's the kind of coach who works to keep the lines of communication open with her athletes. But at the 1999 nationals, women who would normally talk to their coach, who would tell her if they were feeling nervous about an event, instead kept those feelings inside because there were so many cameras focused on them. With the high level of media scrutiny and the intense pressure athletes felt, perhaps it wasn't surprising that on the previous days of the meet, some of Bev Kearney's athletes hadn't performed as well as expected. "Oh my God, we're in trouble," Bev had said to herself sometimes. Then another of her athletes would perform better than she'd hoped. Throughout the three days of the meet, she felt like she was on an "emotional roller coaster."

1

Beverly Kearney

The night before the final day of the meet, the entire Texas women's team met in a hotel room. At that point Texas held only a slender three-point lead. With all her athletes focused on her, Bev Kearney expressed her faith in them. "It's not over," she said. "The only thing that we can do right now is to simply do the best we can..." It was a sports cliché, of course, and yet the young women on Bev's team surely knew how heartfelt their coach's advice was and trusted in her words.

The next day, as Beverly watched from the stands, her athletes prepared to run the mile relay. Runners found their lanes on the terra-cotta colored track, and positioned themselves in the starting blocks. Then both runners and spectators heard the announcement: the outcome of the entire meet would depend on this race. Beverly knew that already, but it was new news—one more piece of pressure—for her runners.

They could handle the pressure, Bev thought to herself. They'd been in exactly the same situation last year at the outdoor nationals, where a Texas victory in the 4 x 400 relay had won them a national championship. But as Bev sat alone in the stands, she still felt nervous. There were so many things that could go wrong in a relay race: a lane violation, a false start, a bump with the baton. "No matter how good your team is," she recollected, "You're on pins and needles till they cross the line."

"Go, go, go," Bev kept thinking as the race unfolded. As it turned out, nothing did go wrong. And just at the end, as the last Texas runner broke clear of the pack, Bev even had a moment to look back at the other relay finishers.

As her anchor leg runner crossed the finish line, well ahead of the runners trailing her, Bev rose to her feet. She raised her arms in triumph, opening them outward as if to both salute and embrace her athletes, pumping her arms in triumph. "Yes, yes, yes, yes!" she shouted, as television cameras focused on her, the joy of the victory overwhelming her. She made a telegenic picture of a coach at a moment of triumph for herself and her athletes.

———◆———

Joyous victories and bitter defeats are a staple of athletic competition. Although Bev Kearney's exuberant reaction to her team's victory made it into television coverage, often the focus of attention in sporting events is on the athletes who run the races or score the goals or hit the home runs. Their participation is, of course, often intrinsically dramatic. Yet the lives of coaches as well as athletes are a story worth following. Coaches are the ones who lead their teams and teach their athletes and in any number of ways make sports competitions possible.

With many well-funded college sports programs in the United States, intercollegiate varsity sports offer both a high level of competition and professional opportunities for many coaches. Within the college coaching profession, male and female coaches do similar jobs and have much in common. However, for women coaches, the victories they celebrate occur within a sports landscape still different in many ways than the one occupied by male coaches of men's varsity sports. For this reason, women collegiate coaches are an especially interesting group to consider.

The far greater media coverage that men's sporting events typically receive, as compared to women's sporting events—in spite of the media focus on Bev Kearney's team—is one part of this gender-divided picture. Although college sports are viewed as an important part of the national sports scene, those are usually male college sports. With women's college basketball growing in popularity, a fairly small number of coaches of women's college basketball teams, such as Tennessee coach Pat Summitt and Stanford coach Tara VanDerveer, have anything approaching national name recognition. They'd never win a match-that-coach contest when compared to men's basketball coaches Bobby Knight or Mike Krzyzewski.

Media attention, or the lack of it, is only one part of the scene. If men's and women's college sports were mapped topographically, men's collegiate sports overall would take place on a level surface, reflecting the history of solid support for those sports. In contrast, the terrain occupied by women's college sports would appear much hillier, and at times mountainous, reflecting a very different history.

Throughout the earlier part of the twentieth century, women were thought to be too frail for rigourous sports competition, an attitude which only changed significantly during the later part of the twentieth century. The female physical education teachers who worked with girls and young women—the foremothers of today's women coaches—were themselves trained away from an emphasis on competition. For boys and men, on the other hand, vigorous training and competitive sports have long been highly valued. The sports world, like the world of the military, has been defined as male territory. References to "killing" the opposition or not "playing like girls" reveal the connection between sports, the military and masculine gender identity. Such language also reinforces the idea that both sports and the military, like the high-level ranks of the corporate world and other male-dominated work areas, have traditionally been areas where no girls are allowed.

As a group, women collegiate coaches have fought long and hard to carve out a place for themselves and their female athletes within the male-dominated world of sports, just as women have done in the military or in the corporate world. In the United States, we have of course seen a revolutionary change in the levels of female sports participation within the last generation or so. Spurred in part by Title IX, the 1972 federal law prohibiting discrimination based on gender in educational institutions receiving federal funds, high schools and colleges across the country have provided far more opportunities than in the past for female athletes. While only 300,000 high school girls competed in sports in 1971, by 1996 the number of girls competing had grown to 2.4 million! At the collegiate level, while 90,000 women participated in college sports in 1981-82, 163,000 women took part in 1998-99. These days, young women on college sports teams have typically grown up participating in sports. And women college coaches have also benefitted from Title IX, the younger coaches as athletes themselves and all coaches from the increased training their athletes have had.

But women college coaches still face plenty of uphill terrain. Virtually no women coach men's collegiate sports. As the ongoing study by R. Vivian Acosta and Linda Jean Carpenter reveals, by the year 2000, less than 2 percent of women coached men's college teams, a scanty percentage that has basically remained the same for the last 30 years. And as women's sports have gained in stature, paradoxically the numbers of women college coaches have greatly declined. As coaching women's teams has become more prestigious and as salaries have risen, more men have been attracted to the field. In 1972, over 90 percent of women's college teams were coached by women. In contrast, by the year 2000, although opportunities for college women to participate in sports continued to rise, the number of women who held head coaching positions for women's teams declined to 45.6 percent, a figure which represented an all-time low!

"Today, women coaches and administrators are (an) endangered species," wrote Donna Lopiano, Executive Director of the Women's Sports Foundation. Part of the reason for the abysmally low numbers of women coaches, Vivian Acosta and Linda Carpenter believe, is due to a positive change: the increased amount of career options for women. Yet discrimination against female coaches is also surely a factor. "You still hear the phrase," Linda Carpenter commented, "'Well, I'd hire a woman but I'm not going to hire someone who's unqualified.' And the second part of that phrase says that in their mind women are unqualified."

In fact, however, many women college coaches are not only competent professionals but pivotal figures within the female sports revolution. Across the country, women college coaches today work with talented athletes who compete at high levels of their sports. Across the country, women college coaches are serving as important role models and teachers for today's young women.

Typically these coaches were involved in sports themselves; some, in fact, were world-class athletes. The same is true for many male coaches, of course, and many of the men who coach women's teams do excellent jobs of training and inspiring their athletes. Yet however skilled and well-intentioned these male coaches may be, their relationships with their female athletes are inevitably different from that of female coaches. A female coach who has herself been an athlete provides a direct life example that females can achieve in sports. In spite of the huge growth in girls' and women's involvement in sports in the United States, this is still an important lesson.

Some male college sports have been justly criticized for their abuses, including the practice of using athletes as hired gladiators with little regard for these athletes' academic performance. Coaches in quintessentially macho sports such as football have not infrequently encouraged or even forced athletes to play through injuries and to risk further injuries for the good of the team. While some female coaches are also guilty of such abusive practices, many women college coaches, as do many male coaches, do their jobs with high levels of integrity and responsibility toward their athletes. Because of their shared experiences, some women coaches argue, they are more able than male coaches to empathize with the feelings of female athletes. Over and over women coaches describe their relationships with their athletes as the most important part of their job, far more important than their win-loss records.

The jobs that women coaches do have a significance beyond the sports world. They provide models of women in positions of leadership not only for their athletes, but for fans, girls who attend the camps many coaches lead, and for others as well. They provide examples of women taking on and doing well at tough jobs, in the same way that women in the military or women corporate executives do. Like the coaches of men's teams, women college coaches manage substantial budgets, face the pressures of maintaining winning teams and of recruiting top athletes. Unlike coaches of men's teams, female coaches face the additional difficulties of working within college athletic departments that are mostly controlled by male athletic directors and where women's sports often receive unequal funding.

Many women coaches have fought difficult battles for equitable treatment for their athletes, battles that have been directly responsible for some of the progress made in women's collegiate sports. Women coaches have also fought for more equitable treatment for themselves as professionals, yet today they often cope with working situations where they typically have little job security. And just like female athletes, female coaches cope with stereotypes, such as the still prevalent belief that women in sports, like women in the military, are lesbians. Minority coaches, such as African-American female coaches, face an extra level of prejudice. All-in-all, women coaches face numerous difficulties, yet they also reap the rewards of victories of many sorts.

———◆·◆———

Beverly Kearney has made a coaching career out of teaching and inspiring athletes to do their personal best. At 42 years old, she has won numerous honors. Her teams at both the University of Texas and the University of Florida have won national championships. "People have tried to tell me I'm a very powerful coach, one of the most powerful coaches in the country," Beverly admitted. Undeniably, she is both an excellent coach and a strong, articulate person with a clear vision of what's important to her. However, like many women coaches, she prefers to place the focus on her athletes rather than herself.

"True success is about empowering another individual," Beverly asserts, "about them believing in themselves instead of you. That's the key to success."

Beverly has high standards both for herself and for her athletes. For herself, she is constantly striving to improve as a coach while maintaining a demanding, far more than 9 to 5 work schedule, the kind of schedule many women coaches keep, which often leaves her juggling many demands on her time. She asks for and expects nothing less than personal bests from her athletes. She is a teacher with the highest of expectations for her pupils, expectations that include fostering independence and personal strength. "The only person that has the ability to create or destroy anything in your life is you," Bev tells her athletes. Day after day, she works to build a foundation of trust between herself and the young women on her team, so that she can help them accomplish their personal goals.

The life lessons Bev teaches, along with the caring she extends to her athletes, have often borne fruit. In 1999, Nanceen Perry, one of Bev's star runners, strained a hamstring the week before the conference meet at the end of May. Bev wouldn't allow Nanceen to run at that meet and risk losing her chance to run at the national championship, held early in June. The conservative strategy paid off, and Nanceen received a medical OK. But right before the national championships, she sought out her coach. "Coach, I'm scared," she told Bev. "I'm not scared of the competition. I'm scared I'm going to get injured."

Kearney emphatically rejects a win-at-all-costs philosophy. She would never break the bonds of trust between herself and her athletes by pushing an athlete beyond what's best for that athlete. But she's an intuitive person who knows when to push an athlete to achieve at the highest level. "You're OK. You're gonna be all right," Bev assured her runner. Because of the relationship Bev had built with Nanceen, the young woman trusted in her coach. In four days and six races, she achieved personal bests.

The trust and confidence Bev inspires helped her team at the 1998 Outdoor Track and Field Championships as well, when Texas was well behind their opponents. "Do we have a shot at winning?" Bev's athletes asked her at a team meeting.

Bev is honest as well as inspirational. "It's a long shot," she told her team.

"What do we have to do to win?" the young women asked her.

Beverly Kearney's answer was simple: "You've got to win, you've got to win, you've got to win," she told the young women, looking in turn at each one of her athletes. "We've got to win five out of six events to win the championship."

The weather on the last day of the nationals, 40 degrees with heavy rain, couldn't have inspired anybody. Athletes would take off gloves and blankets just before their events. Texas won in spite of the weather, and afterward, members of the press asked Bev Kearney's athletes about their team meeting, "Didn't that feel like pressure?" the press inquired about Bev's no-nonsense advice.

Bev Kearney

No way, was her athletes' basic response. "We expect to win," they told the reporters. "We would have been upset if she told us to get second or third."

Beverly Kearney knows whereof she speaks. She knows firsthand the importance of having a role model to provide, as she puts it, a "map" for one's personal journey. Fittingly enough, it was another woman coach who helped provide that map for Bev Kearney.

Bev grew up with low expectations. "I never imagined I'd have a real job, let alone a job in coaching," she recalls. With her father in the Air Force, Bev grew up moving around the country, living in California, Nebraska, Mississippi, Kansas, and graduating from high school in Brandon, Florida. Bev's mother, Bertha, was an alcoholic who died in Bev's senior year, the same year that Bev left home after her father told her and her siblings that they would be on their own after high school.

Coach Joan Falsone, at the time head track coach at Hillsborough Community College in Tampa, came to Beverly's rescue. Since she was no longer living at home, Bev hadn't known about some scholarship offers for college basketball, but Joan Falsone, who had watched Bev's performance in high school

9

track, offered her a track scholarship.

In fact, Joan Falsone provided Beverly far more than just a scholarship. "She became like a second mom to me after my mom died," is how Beverly described her relationship with Joan. On varying occasions, the older woman provided both Bev and her brother Derick with food they would otherwise have done without. After Bev received a track scholarship to Auburn University, Joan supplied her essential items blankets and irons. And after college, it was Joan who encouraged Bev to get a masters degree, and to inquire about graduate assistantships in track coaching. "She kept telling me I was smart. She kept telling me I was talented. She kept pushing me to do better. She was a very loving, caring person," Bev recalled.

Joan Falsone encouraged Bev to become a coach, and Joan, whom Bev still talks with frequently—"I'm like her daughter now," Bev says—became a key role model for Bev as she rose rapidly through the coaching ranks. Perhaps most fundamentally, Beverly maintained Joan's concern for all aspects of her athletes' lives.

After one season as a graduate assistant coach at Indiana State University, and two years as head coach at the University of Toledo, Bev was offered a big step up, to a position as top assistant track coach for the powerful track and field program at the University of Tennessee. Many people expected her to fail at that job. "I think I had three strikes against me," Bev commented. "I was a female, I was African American, and...I was 25 years old."

But Bev didn't fail. Her first summer on the job, she put miles on her car driving to see numerous coaches, asking them for tips on training and anything else she needed to do to be successful. Six athletes coached by Bev won NCAA titles and 12 were honored as All-Americans. In 1988, Beverly accepted the position as head coach at another powerful track program, the University of Florida.

When Bev encourages her athletes to overcome obstacles and to offer no excuses for personal failure, she is once again speaking from experience. At the University of Florida, she encountered what she referred to as "rudeness," which was caused, she feels sure, at least in part because she was African-American. At coaching meetings she attended, many other coaches ignored her. Other coaches "badmouthed" her in recruiting. "Don't go there," they would tell potential recruits. Bev couldn't coach, she couldn't recruit, she wouldn't win, was many people's attitude.

Deeply involved in her new coaching job, Bev didn't always notice the prejudice she faced. Yet all that negativity still took its toll on her. "There were a lot of times I just went home and cried," Bev remembered.

In spite of the tough times, Bev became a remarkably successful coach. At the University of Florida, her team won first and second place at NCAA meets, and Bev was recognized as 1992 NCAA Indoor and Outdoor Coach of the Year. When the University of Texas women's athletic director, Jody Conradt, offered Bev the position as head track coach at Texas, Bev at first turned her down, then accepted the job due to a strong feeling that Texas was the place for her to be. At the University of Texas, Beverly inherited a track program in need of rebuilding and in 1998, her track team won NCAA Indoor and Outdoor National Championships.

It was at the University of Texas where Beverly started a mentorship program for African-American athletes. After she realized that some of the athletes on her team who aspired to careers as doctors, lawyers, etc., had never met any African-American females in those professions, she set up a program that provided African-American professional women as mentors for athletes. Another motivation for the mentoring program was undoubtedly Bev's strong sense of history, her awareness of a larger world beyond athletics, an awareness that includes her own role as an African-American female coach. "When I get tired or I get down...," she explained, "I think of all the great leaders that pioneered and opened doors for me.... I think of the civil rights movement and how many people gave their lives for me to have the opportunity to get an education.... I think about all the women that fought for Title IX for us to have an opportunity in athletics."

Kearney herself has made good use of those opportunities

in her coaching career. But what she's all about as a coach goes far beyond achievements on the track. Like many other women coaches, Bev is well aware that as coach she's a role model and teacher for her athletes. A key goal for her is to help develop the young women in her care as strong, self-confident people who will succeed academically at college and overall in life. "I hope that through me," Bev said simply, "and the things that they see me accomplish in my life, considering where I've come from, that it inspires them that they can achieve that and even more."

In fact, Beverly Kearney's current and former athletes provide eloquent testimonials that the example and inspiration she provides have greatly affected the lives of the women in her care. She keeps these testimonials in scrapbooks, and reads through them when she needs a reminder of how much the work she does matters.

"I attribute my success thus far, not only as an athlete but as a person as well," one athlete wrote Bev, "to your belief in me at a time when I did not believe in myself."

———

While female coaches such as Beverly Kearney at the University of Texas's nationally prominent athletic program are very much in the public eye, other coaches do their important work in relative obscurity. Such is the case for Paula Petrie, head women's basketball coach and senior women's administrator at Willamette University in Salem, Oregon.

Paula Petrie is a friendly person who smiles easily, communicates enthusiasm for her sport, and has an obviously good rapport with her players. On a rainy late afternoon in late February, 2000, a day when gray rain clouds hovered low over the red-brick Sparks Center, the campus gymnasium, Petrie and her players were hard at work. Inside a roomy gym decorated with the Willamette colors—maroon, yellow and orange—the thud of baskeballs against the polished wood floor made a constant drumbeat as the players ran through drills. At midcourt, Paula, clearly an athlete herself, made sharp, strong passes to her players. Slightly later she directed three player weaves where the young women had only 12 seconds to get down the floor and back. Much later on, practice involved a full-court scrimmage.

Paula's voice was clear, ringing, slightly hoarse. A coach's voice. "Nice run," she encouraged one young woman. "Yes, yes," she shouted after a sweet outside shot, clapping to encourage the player.

This Wednesday afternoon was the last of two full practices before the Willamette players ended their regular season with two home games, since the team wouldn't be going on to postseason play. Yet they seemed focused, obviously working hard in practice. Paula had talked to them yesterday about how they wanted to end their season. "It's your choice," she had told the players.

In today's practice, Paula was serious yet never nasty, at moments projecting something of an older sister demeanor. For Paula Petrie as for Beverly Kearney, teaching is something she sees as an important part of her job. Rather than just shouting out instructions, as a stereotypically authoritarian coach would do, Paula often asked the kind of questions that encouraged players to think about the game. "Who's going to jump out to switch on this screen?" she asked at one point.

Towards the end of the practice, during a full-court scrimmage with the shot-clock running, some of the players lost their focus. "Use the clock," Paula shouted to the team on offense, wanting them to prepare for an end-of-game situation. First the players on one end ignored her advice, shooting far too quickly, then players at the other end made the same mistake.

Paula blew her whistle to stop the action. "What did I just say?" she demanded. "We just lost the stinking game because you weren't listening." Although anger is an emotion many women still find hard to express openly, Paula had no trouble expressing her feelings. Her voice was loud, her frustration clear.

"Down and back," she told the young women, directing them to sprint from one end of the court to the other and back as a physical reminder of the high standards she holds them to. After the players ran, play resumed quickly and the practice game ended on a positive note. Paula smiled at a beautiful outside shot made right at the buzzer. "Good job, you guys," she said warmly to her players as they formed a huddle.

The players know that "I'm like a tea kettle which finally boils over," Paula commented after the practice. A highly competitive person and a former high-level athlete who competed on the U.S. national team in field hockey, sometimes coaching at the Division III level can frustrate her. Since NCAA Division III colleges don't offer athletic scholarships, Paula can't recruit the kind of elite athletes Beverly Kearney can attract to her program at the University of Texas. "You're not going to get 12 students of the game at this level," Paula assessed realistically. On the other hand, she appreciates the balance Division III offers student athletes. And as is true for Bev Kearney, Paula Petrie is obviously a coach who is deeply engaged in her profession.

Paula came to the coaching job at Willamette by a somewhat circuitous route. She grew up just outside of Philadelphia, played three sports in high school—field hockey, basketball and lacrosse—and in the summer she added softball. When she was a senior in high school, college scholarships for girls were just beginning to come out, and Penn State offered Paula a scholarship in either field hockey or basketball. In tune with the philosophy of athletic specialization, a philosophy new to women's college athletics, Penn State wouldn't allow Paula to play both sports.

"I cried all the way home and said I couldn't choose," Paula remembered. Instead she went to the University of Delaware without a scholarship to play basketball and field hockey. By the end of her sophomore year she was an All-American in field hockey and had made the U.S. national field hockey team. Since she now needed to train year round, she gave up basketball. Then when she didn't make the final squad for the 1980 Olympics, she knew she'd reached another decision point. "I've got to get on with my life," she thought.

She began her coaching career in high school, coaching varsity field hockey, junior varsity softball, and serving as an assistant coach for basketball. After she received a master's degree in sports management at the University of Massachussetts, Paula

14

took a job as field hockey and lacrosse coach at Drexel University in Philadelphia. There she encountered the catch-22 which has faced many other women coaches. In spite of Paula's coaching abilities and love for both sports, without an adequate budget or competitive facilities, the results were predictably negative. Recruiting was tough—"It became like a meat market to me," Paula described. Lopsided losses were frequent. Her lacrosse team might lose by 23 to 1, 20 to 2. "It just got to a point where I couldn't handle getting beat all the time and getting beat badly," Paula remembered.

Paula Petrie

As many women coaches have done, Paula fought for more equitable treatment. She especially wanted more scholarships and better athletic facilities. And as with many other coaches, Paula's battles came with a personal cost. Even though she had been hired to rebuild the field hockey program, the athletic department consistently refused to support her. They wouldn't even cut the grass on the hockey field short enough for playing. Finally, Paula had had enough. She walked into the athletic director's office and resigned. The toughest part of all was telling her players that she would no longer be their coach. Yet Paula felt that the players understood that she had to stand behind her personal beliefs.

After a couple of noncoaching jobs, experiences that helped convince Paula that she was hooked on coaching, and another stint at high school coaching and PE teaching, Paula's career path took a turn she described as "totally bizarre." After the women's basketball coach at Lewis and Clark College in Portland, Oregon, resigned, Paula received a call about the position.

"Why me?" Paula wondered. She flew out for the interview thinking that Lewis and Clark wouldn't hire her. She didn't, after all, have any experience coaching college basketball. Of course, she had just worked at a basketball camp at Lewis and Clark. And it probably didn't hurt that Paula's oldest brother, Geoff Petrie, was then general manager for the Blazers. "The next thing I knew," Paula recalled, laughing at the memory, "they called me and offered me the job. So I took it. Kind of crazy."

At 33 years old, Paula crossed the country to a new coaching job—which was a definite adjustment. At the first basketball practice, when only 12 girls showed up, Paula kept waiting for more players to appear. In field hockey, a squad would have about 20 or 25 girls. "Where is everybody?" Paula asked her athletes. They laughed in response. "No, Coach, this is it," they told her.

Paula liked coaching basketball, she found. When she had the chance to move on to the head women's basketball coach position at Willamette University, she seized the opportunity since Willamette put more emphasis on athletics than Lewis and Clark.

Willamette University is a fairly good fit for someone with Paula Petrie's high energy level. The energy part is important, because at the Division III level, as opposed to the Division I level, coaches often are assigned non-coaching jobs as well. In addition to Paula's responsibilities as head women's basketball coach and the activities classes she teaches during the school year, she's also the assistant athletic director, a.k.a. "senior women's administrator" in NCAA lingo. "Everyone calls me SWA," is Paula's own joking description. But she doesn't joke about the fact that as head coach at a Division III college, she's essentially "a one-person show." Unlike in a well-funded Division I program, Paula can only hire part-time assistant coaches, and since they receive only a low stipend, Paula can't expect them to do more than help her at practices and games. All the other coaching jobs—the recruiting, phone calling, scouting, fundraising—fall on her shoulders.

But coaching jobs at all levels have many similarities. As is typical for college coaches, Paula's work day is a long one.

During basketball season, her busiest time, she usually arrives on campus between 9:30 or 10 a.m., a schedule that works for her since so many basketball events occur in the evening. During the day her responsibilities as coach and senior women's administrator keep her busy. Her basketball practices typically run from 4–6 in the afternoon, and she often then goes on to watch a high school game, or a junior college game, or perhaps to watch another team whom her team will play soon. When she finally gets home, about 8 or 8:30, she may call some high school girls who are potential recruits. Or she might sit and watch a videotape of a Willamette game or a game played by one of their opponents. Often she doesn't eat dinner until 10 p.m. "It's why they invented microwaves," Paula joked, adding that Mark, her significant other, does most of the cooking during the basketball season.

On weekends, when Paula's teams play most of their games, her schedule gets even busier. Too wired up to sleep, she might stay up late watching game videos after a Friday night game. Typically she gets up early the next day and meets her team about mid-day to do the final preparations for their Saturday night game.

As with any head coach, recruiting is a time-consuming job for Paula. During the 1999-2000 season, she flew to a high school basketball tournament in San Diego so she could watch potential recruits. She was in the stands at eight in the morning for the first game, at nine at night for the last game. "I couldn't have had enough coffee in those two days," Paula remembered. "You have no idea what it's like sitting in a bleacher all day long."

Like many women's basketball coaches, Paula can feel frustrated by NCAA rules, clearly motivated by abuses in men's college basketball, that restrict her contact with the women on her team. Until October 15th, she can't work with her athletes at all, for example. "It's the one thing I struggle with in terms of philosophy of Division III," she stated. "If Division III is about teaching, then why not let us teach during that time?" she questioned. She feels "handcuffed" by rules that don't allow her to teach her athletes to the best of her ability. But Paula appreciates the Division III philosophy that emphasizes the student in "student athlete." At Willamette, athletes often compete in more than one sport and coaches recognize that academics can at times take precedence over athletics. During the 99-2000 season, one of Paula's players was in the college band and missed one basketball practice a week. Another player arrived late to practice because of a science lab. Paula accepts the kind of schedule conflicts that would be unthinkable at a Division I college and recognizes the benefits for her players.

Another plus for Paula at Willamette is that as senior women's administrator she can advocate for positive change for women's sports. Until recently, for example, Willamette provided a full-time baseball coach and first-class facilities for its baseball team, while its softball coach was only part-time and the team lacked a field of its own. As senior women's administrator, Paula went to the athletic director about the situation. "We're sitting on a time bomb," Paula said, referring to the obvious inequity. Soon afterward, Willamette constructed a good softball facility and changed the softball coach's status to full-time.

Moments like those, where she personally can get involved with furthering women's sports, are rewarding to Paula. But like many women coaches, what she describes as most rewarding is her relationships with the young women athletes she teaches. She enjoys watching her players grow as people during the four years she typically coaches them. And she knows that she's made a difference in that growth: "The things that they've learned over the four years, the sweat and the effort they've put into it, and the ups and downs, that will help them wherever they go."

If someone were to make a generational map of women college coaches, at 42 years old, both Beverly Kearney and Paula Petrie would fall roughly in the middle. They are young enough to have received, or been eligible for, athletic scholarships to college. They coach at the college level at a time when funding for women's sports, although still not equitable, has greatly increased from past levels and when women coaches are hired as specialists whose main job is to lead particular teams.

Coaches younger than Paula and Beverly have experienced far more direct benefits of Title IX in their own athletic careers. Older coaches and retired coaches, on the other hand, have lived through a longer span of the history of girls' and women's sports. They have seen more radical changes between past and present. But women college coaches of all ages have been eye witnesses to the development on women's intercollegiate sport. And more than perhaps any other group, they have been centrally involved in the changes. They have worked and battled for positive change, nurtured their athletes, served as key role models and advocates for the young women in their charge.

"It's a vicarious life here as a coach," University of Oregon assistant track coach Sally Harmon described. "You live through your athletes' success and you're breathing their pain daily." Women college coaches stand on the sidelines of basketball courts, shouting instructions to their team, voices often growing hoarse with the effort. They wave runners forward in softball games, make crucial decisions about who to substitute in the final minutes of soccer games. They teach and inspire young women across the country.

What does it mean to be a competitor? What are the rewards of running another sprint when your legs are rubbery and your breath burns in your chest? How does it feel to play hard and strong, to put your body on the line as you run full tilt toward both the ball and your opponent? How do you balance the joy of victory and the sadness of defeat? How do you fight for what you believe, on and off the field?

Women college coaches have experienced these emotions, lived out the answers to these questions. Many women coaches are former athletes, competitive women who have themselves faced and overcome the kind of challenges sports can offer. Winning games and matches and other competitive events matters to these coaches, as does the personal growth they both witness and nurture in their young women athletes. Within the still far from equitable college sports scene, women coaches have fought hard for fair treatment for themselves and their athletes.

As a group, women college coaches are strong people, powerful and empowering women. The many kinds of victories they have achieved have not come easily.

Long Time Coming

After 27 years as head volleyball coach at the University of Delaware, Barbara Viera was officially hanging up her coaching whistle. The press conference to announce her retirement was held at the Bob Carpenter Center on February 15, 2000. In addition to members of the press, many of Barb's University of Delaware coaching colleagues were in attendance at the event.

At 60 years old, Barb was looking forward to retirement. She planned to replace her old motor home, to follow the many personal interests that coaching had left her little time for. She placed a high value on the personal freedom she'd have. "If somebody comes along and says, 'Let's go to Tibet tomorrow,'" she described, "I can say, 'Yeah, that sounds good, I'm gonna do it.'"

And yet in spite of Barb's enthusiasm for the major life change she was making, there was also sadness. She was leaving behind years of hard work, numerous colleagues and friends, a volleyball program she'd spent much of her lifetime building. And she was taking something with her too: a personal history that went beyond the purely personal, a history she feared would be lost. In her years as a coach, Barbara Viera had both witnessed and been deeply involved in the huge changes within the world of women's sport.

At her retirement press conference, Barb spoke to the assembled reporters, coaches and other colleagues. "My only regret in my career," she told them, "is that I didn't have the opportunity to participate (in sports) that the young women have today."

Barbara Viera

"I hope that these women realize how lucky they are," Barb added. Privately, however, she wondered if they did. "I think a lot of them do not know from whence we come," was her personal conclusion.

Barbara Viera's own life story makes a good example of that history. She grew up in Westport, Massachusetts, where both her parents were factory workers. Although Barb was interested in sports from an early age, her sports opportunities were limited, as was typical for girls at the time. In junior high, when she at least could play sports in physical education classes, she made an important decision: teaching physical education would be her career. In high school, where Barb played field hockey, basketball, volleyball and softball, her career aspirations were strengthened by a high school physical education teacher whom Barb described as "a very strong mentor in my life. I wanted... to be like her as a coach and teacher."

But sports for girls weren't emphasized during the '40s and '50s, and Barb was a bright enough student—she was valedictorian of her high school class—to attract her teachers' attention. "Many of my teachers actually tried to steer me away from physical education," Barb recalled, recognizing the irony. Physical education, her teachers felt, "wasn't good enough for my talents." In spite of that advice, Barb majored in physical education at the University of Massachusetts. But during her undergraduate years, 1959 to 1963, she ran up against the obstacle she once more described as her "only regret." In the late '50s and early '60s, there were no intercollegiate teams for women at the university, only sports clubs that young women could participate in. As a player on the field hockey club, Barb would take part in sports days and play days, events deliberately designed to reduce competition. "You'd play maybe 15 or 20 minutes..." Barb described with some sarcasm, "and then you'd have a little social hour where you'd have the punch and the cookies." It's a bittersweet memory that Barb laughed about as she remembered. "I lived it," she commented.

The history that Viera lived came from very different assumptions about females and sports than are prevalent today. As historian Susan Cahn described, in the 19th and early part of the 20th century, while male sports activities went along with "an ideal of virile, athletic manhood," females were viewed as "the physiologically inferior sex, weakened and ruled by their reproductive systems." Women were viewed as too delicate to take part in rigorous sports although some degree of exercise was viewed as healthy for females. In the late 19th and early 20th centuries, women collegiate physical education instructors began to establish themselves as a professional discipline, basing their approach to female sports and exercise on the cardinal virtue of "moderation." Women were to be protected from the excesses of male sports, such as overly strenuous competition, commercialization, and too great a focus on winning.

Women collegiate physical educators, the foremothers of today's women college coaches, were most able to implement their own vision of female sports within colleges and universities. Throughout the first half or so of the 20th century, women physical educators by and large accepted the prevailing ideas about female athletic limitations and set about implementing their own female-centered model of women's sport. It was a nonelitist vision—sports should be enjoyed by all women not just by the outstanding athletes. Sports should build ethical values, women physical educators believed, and create comraderie between participants. Women physical educators established the play days common in the early to mid 20th century, where women from several schools would attend an event, and then the players from various schools would all be mixed together into improvised "teams" that would then play against each other as best they could. A slightly later variation, the sports day, allowed college teams to directly compete but de-emphasized both winning and losing, and didn't allow coaching during competitions

Although women physical educators had what they viewed as their students' best interests at heart, and while play days and sports days surely satisfied the needs of some girls and young women, others were deprived of the chance to achieve at the highest level they were capable of. "It wasn't enough for me," Barb Viera recalled. "I wanted to be more competitive, and I did not see this as being at the competitive level that...I needed as an athlete."

Barb met with some of the same frustrations when she started her coaching career at the junior high level. Although teams would maintain their school identity while competing, physical education teachers were required to officiate for other games at the same time their own teams were playing, and so were unable to coach their own teams. Barb moved on to Wilson High School in Connecticut in 1966, where her schedule was typical for the time. She coached four sports, including volleyball, in addition to her duties as a full-time teacher. Then after receiving her master's degree and doctorate from Springfield College, she took the job she would ultimately hold for the rest of her working life, as coach and physical education instructor at the University of Delaware.

Although Barb coached field hockey in her first year there, ultimately she chose volleyball as the sport on which to concentrate her coaching energies. Fittingly enough for a woman who would herself go on to become a role model and mentor for numerous young women, Barb made her decision due to an outstanding women physical education instructor at the University of Massachusetts, Ruth Totman. "She was the one who really put the fire of volleyball in my heart," Barb recalled. In fact, Ruth Totman was a pioneer herself who had started the women's physical education program at the university. Barb Viera was a member of the first class of young women who graduated from the University of Massachusetts as physical education majors.

Barb began her collegiate coaching career at an exciting time for women's sports. In the '60s and '70s, finally intercollegiate sports competition for women was first becoming acceptable and then actively being promoted. That didn't mean, however, that conditions were anything close to those of today. At the University of Delaware, when Barb began coaching, women's varsity teams had only begun three years ago. Barb's first-year volleyball budget was the impressively low sum of $500. "Now don't spend it all in one place," was the joke Barb remembered.

In the early days of Barb's coaching career at Delaware, with little money available, the team would travel in Barb's car, and sometimes in cars furnished by players. They went to play teams driving distances away, distances engraved in Barb's memory—an hour to Baltimore or Philadelphia, two hours to Washington, DC. When the team travelled to weekend tournaments, they made the most of their time, playing Friday night and all day Saturday. In contrast to the plush accomodations typical of today's college road trips, players would sleep six to a motel room, bedding down on the floor and anywhere else possible. At the yearly tournaments held at Brooklyn College, the team would bring bedrolls and sleep in the gym, or in dance studio rooms, with breakfast-in-the-gym served to teams the following morning.

In spite of their limited budgets, Viera and other women college coaches didn't have to do their work in isolation. In 1971, the Association for Intercollegiate Athletics for Women (AIAW) was begun, a women-run group that worked to increase opportunities for women's intercollegiate sports. As Joan Hult described, the organization was built around a "women's model" that "held to a vision of student first, athlete second and emphasized the sporting experience rather than the outcome on the scoreboard and the resulting commercialization." Between 1971 and 1982, the AIAW grew in membership. It conducted championships in many sports and provided an important forum for women coaches.

Barb Viera was deeply involved in the AIAW, especially in her regional branch, the Eastern Association of Intercollegiate Athletics for Women (EAIAW). She served on committees and helped plan and select the teams for the eastern region championships. Every year the EAIAW held a several day meeting, not just for volleyball coaches but for coaches of all women's sports. Coaches planned for championships and talked about common issues such as athletic scholarships, which the AIAW agreed to allow after 1973. And beyond that, the yearly meetings provided a way for women coaches from various colleges and sports to meet each other and work together for their common interests.

AIAW championships, while lacking the funding currently available for NCAA championships, were still memorable events that offered the opportunity for numerous women to experience post-season competion. One year the University of Delaware hosted the EAIAW regional tournament. In the opening ceremony, Barb Viera recalled, all the teams marched into the gym in uniforms, holding placards announcing their team's name, forming a multi-colored collage of female athletes.

But the very success of the AIAW, and the parallel success of Title IX in increasing funding for women's college sports, helped contribute to the AIAW's demise. The rich and powerful NCAA, which previously controlled only men's collegiate sports, began to see women's collegiate sports as a threat to men's sports. After mounting an attack on Title IX, the male-run NCAA used its power to drive the AIAW out of business.

As Mary Jo Festle described in *Playing Nice*, the larger amount of money the NCAA could offer—its annual budget of 20 million contrasted to the AIAW's one million—appealed to many colleges. Although not all women coaches and administrators opposed NCAA championships for women, many AIAW members rallied in support of their own organization. In 1980, after the NCAA voted to run its own women's championships, a move towards NCAA control of women's sports, the AIAW assembly held an emergency session. "This is not consent of the governed," the AIAW's Peg Burke said about the takeover attempt, comparing it to a rape. In January, 1981, at the NCAA convention that again voted to offer championships in women's as well as men's collegiate sports, the University of Iowa's Christine Grant spoke eloquently in protest: "Obviously it was not persuasive to you that by your actions women...students and professionals were losing control of their own destinies...it was a conviction

Barb Viera

of those most closely associated with women's athletics, that your actions will do untoward damage. ..."

The end of the AIAW did in fact have a significant impact on women college coaches. They had lost an organization whose main purpose was to advocate women's college sports. The AIAW, Barb Viera recalled, was "an organization which was of women, for women and run by women. ...We were the ones who were making the decisions about how the tournaments were going to be run, we were selecting the teams." Beyond the personal disappointment she felt at the end of the AIAW, she realized over time that there was no longer a place for women coaches of all sports to join together and work on their common concerns.

The new NCAA-run, post-Title IX era for women's college sports has brought many changes for coaches. "I think the one thing that has changed more than anything else is the amount of paperwork that a coach has to do," Barb Viera commented. In 1984, when volleyball celebrated its centennial, she wrote an article comparing the past and now and listed the 58 different forms she used as a coach each year to conform to NCAA regulations. Player attitudes were another change. In her early days as a coach, Barb Viera would tell her more recent players, "I would give the kids a new pair of knee pads and they would be ecstatic." More recently, she noticed, she would distribute an assortment of attire and equipment to players—"bags and kneepads and warmups and four outfits and shoes and socks," but the players' response would be quite different. "Is that it coach?" they would ask. "So that's the difference" between then and now, Barb summed up.

Other changes for women college coaches concerned Barb as well. While she had tenure as a faculty member at the University of Delaware, nowadays numerous coaches, she explained, "are being hired not as faculty but as professionals," a status which denies them the job security of tenured faculty. "They can be let go on a moment's notice," Barb commented, adding that "that's happened to a lot of female coaches."

But as Barb approached her retirement, most of what she felt was positive. She received numerous cards, letters, e-mails and phone calls, thanking her for the coaching work she'd done, telling her about the positive impact she'd had on people's lives. "I can't begin to tell you how much you shaped my life and the person I am today. You were a great inspiration to me," one former player wrote. "Who else will dedicate her life to a program, care for and nurture the athletes, work with enthusiasm to develop volleyball in the state, and be modest about her accomplishments?" an e-mail writer questioned.

As Barb began to clean out her office, she felt at times overwhelmed by the sentiments expressed by numerous well-wishers. Yet she valued the chance to think back on her entire coaching career. "When you look at it," she said, "my career has really paralleled this outstanding development we have for women's sports and women's athletics... For me to have really been a part of that I feel has been been a wonderful experience."

Other older and retired coaches echo Barb Viera's perspectives. Vivian Acosta and Linda Carpenter, both professors emerita of physical education and former coaches at Brooklyn College, remember being paid to teach but not to coach, a typical situation for women. When she coached gymnastics in the '60s and early '70s, Linda described, in her first season the man who coached men's gymnastics was given seven release hours from teaching each semester. Linda, in contrast, received a thank you note!

At the same time period, Vivian Acosta coached women's basketball, softball, volleyball, field hockey, and finally badminton for men and women. Like Linda, Vivian coached her teams without any extra pay and, for the most part, without the release time which male physical education instructors received for coaching. "What is wrong with this picture?" Vivian began to question after several years. "Why is it that the men get all this release time and we don't?" she asked her department chair. "That's just the way it is," the woman replied. "Well, shouldn't we do something about it?" Vivian asked. "Well, not yet, not yet," the department chair answered. It was a maintain-the-status-quo approach typical of the era.

Retired physical educator and coach Ellie Trussell began teaching and coaching at Sonoma State University in 1965, when all that existed at Northern California colleges was "the germ of a woman's athletic program." Coaching in those pre-Title IX, pre-athletic scholarships-for-women days, Ellie experienced the positives—"the players were there just because they loved to play"—and the negatives—"the frustrating part was they had very little skills background, and you had to start with the very basics... so you were working at a very much lower level." On road trips, coaches sometimes supplied the money themselves for team meals. Ellie recalled "driving home in the middle of the night because you can't afford to stay over" and "always scrounging for money."

"Our women coaches were doubly special," Donna Lopiano, Executive Director of the Women's Sports Foundation, wrote about women coaching pre-Title IX. "As a rule, they were paid absolutely zero for their efforts as...coaches which they were privileged to do on top of full-time teaching loads. Yet, they approached their involvement in sport with a love, enthusiasm and positive attitude..."

Willamette University volleyball coach Marlene Piper shares the enthusiasm other older coaches express for the coaching profession. "It's been a wonderful ride for me," Marlene commented. At 57 years old, an age when many women coaches in her generation had already retired, Marlene continued to coach, taking a year by year approach—"not a five-year plan"—for how much longer she would continue in her profession. "Keep working as long as you love it," some of her peers have advised her, and Marlene clearly does love being a coach.

A warm, easily approachable person, Marlene Piper is also someone with plenty to say about women in coaching and the college sports scene. Like Barb Viera, Marlene Piper has coached enough years that she has a long perspective on women's college sports. She can see well beyond women's college athletics nowadays, back to the very different way things were when she began coaching.

Marlene grew up near White Rock, British Columbia in the '40s and '50s, at a time when for a girl interested in sports, it was a distinct advantage to live in Canada rather than the United States. As a Canadian girl, Marlene competed in organized sports from early grade school, in contrast to girls around her age from the U.S., who typically received few or no competitive sport opportunities. From an early age as well, Marlene had the kind of naturally competitive personality characteristic of many other women coaches. She remembers crying after losing a foot race in the second grade, and hustling to be first at the school bus stop so she'd have the chance to open and shut the bus door for everyone else.

At the University of British Columbia, where Marlene began her undergraduate education, she competed in basketball and track. She also was a member of the Canadian National volleyball team and an international track competitor with the Vancouver Olympic Club. But when Marlene came to the United States in 1965 to continue her undergraduate education at Oregon State University, she immediately noticed the scarcity of competitive sports for college women, with golf, tennis, and swimming the only options.

Marlene rebelled against the same widely prevalent attitude about women's sports competition that Barb Viera encountered, that competition was basically unladylike. "Well, this is so fun. We're just having tea and crumpets, and it doesn't matter if you win or lose," was how Marlene satirized the play days mentality. "Winning is important," Marlene thought. "Why are we playing these games then?" she questioned, if not to compete seriously.

Marlene Piper

In the late '60s, Marlene began her coaching career at the junior high level, then taught and coached at the high school level, and in 1969 accepted a job coaching volleyball at Portland State University. Actually, Marlene felt most qualified to coach basketball, but her lack of strong volleyball credentials seemed unimportant when she was interviewed for the PSU job. "I was hired as a volleyball coach because it didn't mean anything anyway," Marlene commented ascerbically. Women's sports "didn't matter" at the time.

In her 13 years at PSU, Marlene performed the wide variety of job duties typical of the time period. She taught classes, coached volleyball, and sometimes coached track and softball as well. She moved on to the University of California at Berkeley, coaching there for four years, then spent six years at the University of California-Davis, and in 1994 finally accepted a position at Willamette University in Oregon. At the end of the 1999 season, after 30 years of coaching, Marlene's number of total wins put her in the rarified coaching air of being one of the four top active women volleyball coaches regardless of division.

After so many years of coaching, Marlene has vivid memories of the way things used to be. In the '70s, when she started coaching at PSU, women athletes on the volleyball, basketball, and softball teams all wore the same uniforms, because the women's sports budget was so small. Not only was there no athletic training room for women, the location of the men's training room, inside the men's locker room, led to a bizarre scenario. If a female athlete sprained her ankle, for example, the athletic staff would literally put a bag over the young woman's head, then lead her through the men's locker room into the training room.

"You were kind of pioneers in a way," Marlene characterized herself and other women coaches at the the time. Although she and other women coaches only received "this little pittance" of money, they worked together against the still prevalent attitude that women's sports weren't really needed, that cheerleading was a more appropriate activity for females.

In spite of the hardships of her early years of coaching, like Barb Viera, Marlene Piper remembers a kind of group spirit among female coaches that doesn't happen in the same way now. Unlike today, when coaches of a particular sport such as basketball typically network with other coaches of that sport, the AIAW brought both women coaches overall and women athletic administrators also together. During the AIAW days, Marlene commented, "I think there was a camaraderie of working together." While the AIAW both encouraged and directed intercollegiate competition for women, the type of competition men had long enjoyed, in many ways the organization continued to follow a women's model of sport. The AIAW, as L. Leotus Morrison documented, believed that women should run women's sports, giving women "power over their sports lives."

Marlene Piper, like many other women coaches, felt strongly about the loss of their own organization. In December, 1981, the last AIAW national volleyball championship tournament took place at Florida State University. By then, Marlene and other volleyball coaches already knew that because of the NCAA takeover, this season would be their final one within the AIAW. Marlene described the NCAA action as comparable to "an abusive relationship" and a "total hostile takeover" of a company. For Marlene and her volleyball coaching peers, the sudden and forced change, the loss of their own professional organization was "devastating. ...We were stunned that you can just be wiped out."

For women's collegiate volleyball, that last national championship represented one last hurrah for post-season competition run by women. Twenty-four women's volleyball teams, from colleges across the country came to Tallahasee, Florida. At the time, the FSU campus was decorated with yellow ribbons commemorating young women killed by Ted Bundy, an eerie addition to the overall atmosphere. But within the FSU main gym, where the tournament was held, the atmosphere was electric, focused solely on women's volleyball.

In the final game, PSU went up against the University of Texas for the AIAW national volleyball championship. The match went to the full five games, with Texas finally beating PSU 17-15 in the fifth game to win the championship. Even though her own team lost in the end, Marlene didn't see it as a defeat for the young women on her team. They were winners, in a sense, in a bittersweet moment of collegiate sports history just before women coaches and athletic directors lost the women-run professional organization that represented them. "I just felt so proud of the women and the accomplishments they made," Marlene said about her team. They had fought long and hard, just as had the women's athletic organization that supported them. And like the AIAW, they "didn't go down without a battle."

───◆───

Hard fought battles and hard work were simply part of the job for numerous longtime coaches. Basketball coach Marian Washington, for example, never could have succeeded in her profession if she'd been someone who backed away from hard work. As a college freshman in the '60s, a time when virtually no athletic scholarships were available for women, Marian worked the graveyard shift at a factory that made plastic cups. Her body aching from standing all night on the concrete factory floor, Marian admired the "toughness" of the "longtime employees that just seemed to get through every day." Since Marian also carried a full load of classes and competed in several sports, she found that she eventually had to quit the factory job because her grades were suffering due to her marathon schedule. But Marian Washington is most certainly not a quitter. By June, 2001, she had completed 28 seasons as head coach of the University of Kansas women's basketball team. During her long tenure as coach, and also as the Kansas women's athletic director from 1974 to 1979, Marian worked hard to build the Kansas women's basketball program and to advance all women's sports there.

In 1969, Marian was waiting at an airport along with the rest of the U.S. national women's basketball team when she and a teammate and close friend began discussing their possible futures. They would become college coaches who would compete against each other, the two women envisioned. Since Marian herself was an excellent athlete, the coaching profession must have seemed like a logical choice. Marian competed on national teams in both basketball and track and field, one of the first two African-American women to do so in basketball, was recognized as an All-American, and played on the the West Chester State women's basketball team that won the first women's national championship in 1969.

In 1972, as a graduate student at the University of Kansas, Marian also served as an assistant basketball coach, and in 1973, she accepted the position as head women's basketball coach. In 1974 she became the director of athletics for women, started up the women's track program, and even coached the women's track team for a year. During her early years in coaching, Marian continued to compete on U.S. national teams in basketball and track. She also raised her daughter, Josie, as a single mother. "When you're young, you've got...an enormous amount of energy," Marian recalled. Her numerous commitments certainly must have demanded the full amount of that energy.

As was typical of that time period, one challenge Marian faced was the low level of support for women's athletics. When Marian began coaching, there were no full time women coaches, only physical education teachers who would agree to coach and perhaps receive a small stipend for their efforts. The playing schedules were limited, "little more than a sophisticated intramural program," and the competition was often limited to regional opponents. When Marian's basketball team did travel, they would bring their own food, and drive to games in "caravans of four or five cars." Did Marian herself do plenty of driving? "Oh, yes," she quickly replied. In the '70s, she described, "one of my biggest trips was to Plainview, Texas," where Kansas played against Wayland Baptist. "I think I can remember because I drove it," Marian recalled. It took her 19 hours of driving to get from Kansas to Texas.

In her position as women's athletic director, Marian kept working to build the women's sports program. In 1975, she provided the first scholarships for female athletes at the University of Kansas. Amounting to only a few hundred dollars, these were nothing like the full scholarships of today, but they did represent progress at a time when athletic scholarships for female athletes were just beginning to appear nationwide. Progress didn't come easily, though. Marian encountered the common negative attitudes about women in sports: that athletic scholarships weren't necessary for women, that women athletes were inferior to male athletes and so didn't deserve as much support. And eventually, after Title IX began to have more of an impact, Marian had to deal with the now familiar argument that the growth of women's sports would undermine men's sports. "There was always a fight there," Marian commented.

It was a fight that other women in college sports were also waging. But for Marian there was an extra challenge. "As an African-American woman in the position of coach and athletic director, Marian explained, "you never knew why people were against you. You didn't know whether it was personal. You didn't know whether it was because you represented women. You didn't know whether it was because you were colored, ...a black woman." But it was perfectly clear to Marian that racism added to the things she had to struggle against, as did the fact that hardly any other African-American women were athletic administrators and only a small number of black women were coaches.

Marian's strong religious faith helped her persevere, as did her sense that she was someone with the ability to help other people and to help bring about change. "The fact that we had to constantly justify, validate [the women's sports program] was an ongoing challenge for me," she described, "as an athletic director, as the women's basketball coach, as a mother of a daughter. And yet I was always hopeful. I truly believed that I could help to bring about change in people's perception and respect and appreciation for women in sports."

As athletic director and as a coach, Marian worked to raise money for the women's sports program. Kansas women coaches ran sports camps as one way of bringing in funds. But while some colleges across the country began to significantly increase funding for their women's sports programs, the piece-meal approach to fundraising began to seem like a losing battle. Although Title IX did not require it, at many colleges the men's and women's athletic departments began to merge, with Kansas one of the last holdouts. "I always was afraid of being submerged," Marian commented, which is exactly what did happen in many cases, with male athletic directors heading most combined departments. Yet Marian also realized that women's sports at Kansas needed more funding to compete successfully, and the men's athletic administrators at Kansas insisted that if they were going to fund women's sports, they needed to "have some control," Marian quoted. The end result was that men's and women's sports at Kansas did merge, with 1979 being Marian's last year in the position of athletic director for women.

By June, 2001, Marian Washington could look back on many winning seasons and numerous conference championships during her long tenure as head women's basketball coach at the University of Kansas. On February 20, 1999, she received her 500th career win when her team beat the University of Oklahoma, a victory that placed Marian in a small group of men's and women's basketball coaches with that many wins and an even smaller group who had achieved those numbers while continuing to coach at the same university. Numerous other coaching honors have also come Marian Washington's way. She was recognized as the Big Eight Coach of the Year in 1992 and 1996,

Big Twelve Coach of the Year in 1997, and as the Black Coaches Association Coach of the Year in 1992 and 1996. In 1991, at the NCAA women's basketball finals, Marian received the prestigious Carol Eckman Award, which honors a coach who has shown high personal values and integrity.

Marian Washington

In 1983, as the coach of the U.S. Select Team, Marian had achieved another first, becoming the first African-American woman to coach a U.S. national women's basketball team against international competitors. Then in 1996, Tara VanDerveer, head coach for the women's basketball Olympic team, asked Marian to be an assistant coach. "It was a real blessing," Marian described, and "a tremendous experience." It was also a chance for Marian to work with a team of immensely talented players. "As a coach, if you're fortunate, you have one of those elite athletes every so often. To be surrounded with a team full of elite athletes," Marian commented, the laughter in her voice expressing how special the memory was, "is a most amazing experience."

Other rewarding experiences for Marian have been seeing her daughter, Josie, graduate from the University of Kansas and not only achieve professional success as a regional manager in pharmaceutical sales but become a "very strong black woman" whom Marian feels justifiably proud of. Since Josie and her husband have two children, Marian is now a proud grandmother as well. "I'm especially blessed to have two grandchildren," she described. "Now I can relax a little more and ...have a chance to laugh more and enjoy them."

Life may be a little easier for Marian nowadays, but that doesn't mean she accepts uncritically some of the changes brought about by the huge growth of women's collegiate sports in the post Title IX era. Since college "athletics is a business now," with all the money involved in women's as well as men's sports, coaches can lose their focus on the "specialness of working with a young person ...and having such an incredible impact on them."

For herself, though, Marian Washington hasn't lost sight of what has always been a central part of her long coaching career—her relationships with her players. "I have been very fortunate," she expressed, "that I've had a lot of my athletes maintain an unbelievable relationship with me. They are truly a part of my life." Even when she's retired from coaching, Marian envisions, "I will have a family of former players that will remain in my life. And I think that's probably the most rewarding part of my experience as a coach."

———————

Judi Garman, another veteran coach, grew up on the plains of western Canada, a small town girl with big plans. She was going to live in a big city, become a physical education teacher, and last but not least, drive a sports car. As she envisioned her future, the three items were a package deal.

It all came true for Judi, in a bigger way than she had imagined. The small town girl who looked up to John Wooden, the famous UCLA men's basketball coach, became a well-known coach herself, coaching softball and other sports at several U.S. colleges, and ending her career as head softball coach at Cal State-Fullerton. In 1986, Judi's team won the NCAA Division I national championship. At the junior college level, starting in 1972 thru 1975, her teams won national championships four consecutive years. By the time Judi retired from her position as head coach, she had led her teams to the highest number of wins—1,124—of any U.S. collegiate softball coach.

Judi's official retirement date of March 27, 2000 was also her birthday, the day on which she turned 56. And although retiring at four years short of 60 left Judi still ineligible for most senior citizen discounts, she was old enough to have taken part in an important piece of history. Like Barb Viera, Marlene Piper and Marian Washington, Judi Garman began her coaching career at a time when equity for females in sports simply didn't happen. And like many other women coaches, Judi did far more than simply train her athletes. She fought long and hard for the levels of support that would help make athletic excellence possible.

Growing up in Canada probably helped prepare Judi for taking part in that change. Until she was a senior in high school, when her family moved to the city of Saskatoon, Judi was raised in or near Kindersley, a small town of about 1,500 people. During the late '40s and '50s, the years when Garman was growing up, she as well as Marlene Piper benefitted from the sports opportunites for Canadian girls. Both boys and girls played hockey in the winter, baseball in the summer. In junior high school Judi played on her school's softball team, and she played Little League baseball as well until someone decided that girls shouldn't participate and kicked her off the team. In spite of that setback to her sports aspirations, when she and her family visited their relatives in the states, she still was surprised to see how much girls in the U.S. were left out of sports opportunities.

Luckily, for Judi sports opportunities continued. As an undergraduate physical education major at the University of Saskatchewan, she competed on the university's tennis team, and away from the university played on a club team for basketball. For a number of summers, she played on a softball team, the Saskatoon Imperials, which won Canadian national championships two years in a row and represented Canada at the second world championships held in Osaka, Japan, where enthusiastic fans requested autographs from players and games were held in front of crowds of twenty or thirty thousand.

After those positive experiences, Judi's experiences as a graduate student at the University of California-Santa Barbara were a crash course in the bleak realities of the pre-Title IX era in the United States." I was just shocked by the negativity towards women athletes," Judi recalled. When she wore the athletic jacket she'd earned as an undergraduate, people advised her to take it off. "Don't tell people you're an athlete," they warned her, mentioning the "negative stereotypes" she'd encounter.

Why couldn't you tell people that you'd played on a national championship softball team, Judi wondered. Why shouldn't that be a source of pride rather than an embarrassing secret? Judi wrote her master's thesis on attitudes toward female athletes, and her research revealed discouraging results. Athletes in team sports, which for females had marginal social acceptance at the time, had especially negative attitudes about themselves. Softball players, for example, often bought into society's stereotypes, perceiving themselves as "less feminine" and "more aggressive" than other women.

For a woman who had loved sports all her life like Judi Garman, it was obvious that change was badly needed. And her early experiences as a college coach and physical education teacher only reinforced that perception. At Westmont College in Santa Barbara, where she coached volleyball, basketball and softball, in addition to teaching physical education classes, women's sports received only a minimal budget. And like numerous other women collegiate sports professionals at the time, Judi Garman had to fight for what she and her teams did get.

While the coaches of male teams at Westmont could hire assistants, Judi could not. When the men's teams went on the road, they had drivers to get them there while Judi had to personally drive her team to events. One of her early battles at Westmont was about team uniforms. "You don't need uniforms," the administration told her. "Yes, we do," Judi affirmed. The college supplied Judi with uniforms left over from men's basketball, hand-me-downs she adamantly refused to use. She finally did receive one set of uniforms to use for both girls' basketball and volleyball.

In 1973 Judi moved on to Golden West College, a community college that actually was a big improvement for her. Although she worked a marathon schedule—teaching 11 classes each semester in addition to coaching both basketball and softball—male coaches and physical education instructors had similar workloads. The athletic director at Golden West was supportive, the facilities relatively good, and the league Judi's teams played in was a strong one. At the time, in fact, community college softball programs in California were stronger than four-year college softball programs.

The first time Golden West hosted a softball game against UCLA, the differences in levels of support hit home to Judi. Lacking uniforms, the UCLA women took the field in an assortment of T-shirts and sweatpants. Their coach only held a part-time position. And the next year, when Golden West travelled to UCLA for a game, the game action came to a stop not once but three times. The reason why? Because the UCLA women lacked a field of their own, they had to compete on an intramural field. During the game between UCLA and Golden West, a male kite flier in central field simply refused to fly his kite elsewhere so the women could get on with their game!

"It's just the way things were at that time," Judi commented about the ludicrous situation. Sports opportunities for women, in many people's eyes, just weren't particularly important. But even though Judi was well aware of the glaringly unequal conditions that most female athletes experienced at the time, that didn't mean that she accepted those conditions as the way things should be. Instead, like many other women coaches at the time, she did what she could to create positive change.

One of her survival strategies was to raise money. Money alone didn't make for a good team, of course, but funding for scholarships, equipment, etc., could certainly help. Although Judi never held a bake sale, she did just about everything else. Over the years, she and her athletes washed cars, sold countless raffle tickets, held clinics for young players. Judi herself grew experienced at appealing for donations as well. "I figure I've raised over $750,000 in the years I've been coaching," she said. "I guess if there's any reputation I have it's that I can get money out of a rock."

In 1977, while Judi was coaching and teaching at Golden West, Billie Moore was hired as a full-time women's basketball coach at UCLA, making her, Judi described, the first woman in the country hired simply to coach full-time. "Do you ever think the day will come when a college will hire someone to coach only softball and not have to teach?" Judi and other softball

Judi Garman

coaches wondered. "Many of us felt it would never be in our life-time," Judi added. But the crystal ball she and other coaches gazed into didn't offer a vision extending far enough into the future for U.S. women's collegiate sport. Post-Title IX, that future was one of extraordinarily rapid growth, and Judi herself would help to make part of that fast-paced history. In 1979 she took a position at Cal State Fullerton as the first full-time softball coach in the entire country.

What now seems commonplace was most definitely not so at the time. To hold a position coaching only softball was "unbelievable," Judi recalled. It was a welcome change not to coach other sports as well and not to teach physical education classes in addition to coaching. Judi had even been willing to take a pay cut for the UCLA job, but was pleased to learn that she didn't have to do so.

At Fullerton, Judi still had to fight many more battles, however. As the section on Judi in *Celebrating Women Coaches* describes, Judi's search for a place on campus to build a softball field revealed "an old orange grove with trees so embedded in the ground that no one could figure how to get them out. Naturally, Judi Garman found a way. She contacted the Army Core of Engineers to dynamite them out."

Money was another concern. At Fullerton, while head softball and baseball coaches were paid comparable salaries, softball and baseball assistant coaches were not. For years the men's baseball coach received additional income from the athletic booster club, while the softball coach did not. For many years women's teams didn't receive the type of support with equipment and promotions that men's teams took as their due. It wasn't until sometime in the '90s when the women's softball team discovered that while they had been doing their own laundry on the road, when the men's teams travelled, their laundry was done for them. "Well, you never told us it was a hassle," was the laughably weak rationale Judi received.

The list of inequities went on and on. And always there were the negative comparisons made between softball and baseball. "You don't get the crowds," was a common criticism. But to get a higher level of fan support, Judi knew, softball players and coaches needed a higher level of athletic department support than they typically received. "It becomes such a big vicious circle," she commented. "You can't win because you don't have the help to do it."

A classic example of that lack of help came in the early '90s, when the college began a fundraising campaign to raise money for a sports complex. The plan was to finish the football stadium and track, build a new baseball stadium and improve the softball stadium. But when fundraising fell short and construction estimates came in higher than planned, something had to give. Judi sat on the university committee where a less-than-essential improvement to the football stadium was debated. For an extra $40,000, the already air conditioned press box there would also have removable windows. In order to make the press covering football games marginally more comfortable, most of the planned improvements to the softball field would no longer be funded. Even after several women on the committee strongly objected, the vote still went in favor of football.

Deeply angry, Judi threatened to take her story to the local papers. "You've got to be a team player," the university told her, the kind of coded message many other women coaches have also received. Get used to settling for less was the real message. In the end, softball was only able to improve their bleachers on the third base side, where home team fans sat. And once again there was a catch. The money finally allotted for softball improvements was $14,000. But the bill for the bleachers turned out to be $16,500. Judi went back to the athletic department, asking for the small amount of additional money. When her request was refused, she was left with only one option. "I had to personally write a check for $2,500," she recalled, "or they wouldn't allow us to order the bleachers." She was angry yet realistic. Paying for some of the softball improvements out of her own pocket was simply "the only way I knew to get it done."

The same story of inadequate support from her athletic department occurred again and again during Judi's coaching career. On another occasion, when she had a meeting with a corporate office to request a donation for softball, she saw the promotions and marketing manager for Cal State-Fullerton leaving the corporate offices just before her. The man Judi spoke with showed her the fund-raising plan the university had brought him, a plan that included only men's sports. "Why did he not have you included in this plan?" the man asked her. To Judi, the answer was obvious. "That's the way things have been for so many years," she summed up. "Those are the subtleties that undermine women's programs."

At Cal State-Fullerton, a Title IX lawsuit that a female volleyball coach successfully mounted in the mid-'90s brought much needed help for Judi and other women coaches there. In the wake of that lawsuit, the women's athletic budget at Fullerton increased significantly. Judi now had enough scholarship funds to cover all her players. By 1998, Judi was finally able to pay her top assistant coach a salary almost equivalent to the comparable assistant coach for baseball. In 1999, the salary package for Judi's third assistant coach finally included medical benefits. Although the baseball coach had long been given a car as part of his benefits package, Judi finally received a car five years before she retired. As if to provide one more illustration of the inequities older coaches have long experienced, while the man coaching baseball received a Honda Accord, Fullerton provided a lower-cost Hyundai for Judi.

Even in the wake of the lawsuit, Judi still had to fight for a first-class facility for her athletes. The softball stadium at Fullerton was far inferior to the baseball stadium. Because of the lawsuit, the university refused to fund improvements to the men's baseball stadium until improvements to the softball facility were funded, but the athletic department was slow to acknowledge the change in university priorities. "What would you settle for?" the associate athletic director asked Judi.

"Make our field look exactly like the baseball field," Judi responded.

"You won't settle for anything less?" the associate athletic director asked.

This time Judi held the winning hand. No, she wouldn't, she told him. Although the athletic department had claimed they couldn't raise enough money for the softball field, within a month the extra money was found. The Cal State-Fullerton softball program would at last have a stadium which was no longer inferior to the men's baseball facility.

Judi was tempted to coach a little longer so she could have the satisfaction of coaching her team in the improved softball stadium. But in the end she decided she'd coached long enough. "I think the battle just finally wears you down," she said, speaking not only for herself but for many other older women coaches.

It's not surprising that longtime coaches like Judi Garman and Barb Viera are ready to leave the coaching profession and move on to other things. Like so many veteran coaches, Judi Garman, Barb Viera, Marlene Piper and Marian Washington have all fought their share of battles and done a great deal to pave the way for a younger generation of women coaches and female athletes. In spite of the often difficult conditions they've worked under, older coaches retain a love for their profession and a clear sense of how much their involvement in the coaching profession has meant to them personally and to others as well.

"I think women need to have the opportunity to coach," Judi Garman stated. "Thank goodness my dreams could come true and I had the opportunity." And even in retirement, like many coaches Judi didn't lose sight of what a difference she'd made in the lives of her players. Years after they'd played for her, women would thank Judi for all she'd taught them and the positive effect she'd had on their lives. In the end, it was those personal victories, rather than her impressive number of victories on the softball field, that was the most priceless memory of Judi's coaching years. "Those," she described, "are the wins and losses that you remember."

Teachers, Role Models and Mentors

College coaches are important figures in their athletes' lives. Coaches, both male and female, spend large amounts of time with the young men and women on their teams—at practices and home games, on the road travelling to and from away games. The power coaches possess over their student athletes—the power to compel athletes to spend large amounts of time in team practices, for example, and in many cases the ability to give or withdraw college scholarships—can and has been abused. But the power college coaches possess also creates opportunities. Coaches can teach far more than just the techniques and strategies of a particular sport. College coaches can be powerful role models for their student athletes, as well as mentors for those athletes with an interest in the coaching profession.

There is no doubt that male coaches can do an excellent job of teaching female athletes both about sports and about the positive character traits sports often develop. Numerous women coaches, in fact, cite personal examples of positive lessons they learned from their male coaches in high school or college. However, when women coach female athletes, something qualitatively different is happening. By virtue of their gender, women coaches can provide direct life lessons about what it is possible for a woman to be and to do.

Anthropologist Joan Cassell reflected on this kind of teaching in her book on women surgeons, *The Woman in the Surgeon's Body*. She wrote about the concept of "embodied" knowledge, "not something that you think but ...something that you are...," the kind of knowing that is nonverbal, intuitive, often below the level of consciousness. Gender roles, Cassell explained, can be defined as "the embodied, wordless knowledge of what it means to be a woman or man in a particular social setting." According to this way of thinking, women and men teach what it is to be a man or a woman not just by what they communicate verbally but by the complete package of who they are.

As Cassell studied women surgeons, who like women coaches are working within a male-dominated field, she concluded that women learning to be surgeons from the mostly male chief surgeons were not in fact having an identical learning experience as to men learning from the same male surgeons. Just as female doctors, for example, express their gender in ways that "are so much a part of them that the women are unaware of it," the same is true of male doctors. Because of their gender, it would seem, the male chief surgeons simply didn't provide the same kind of role models for female surgeons in training as they did for male trainees.

In *Ground Zero: The Gender Wars in the Military*, author Linda Bird Francke described the need for women cadets and midshipmen at Annapolis and West Point, both heavily outnumbered by their male counterparts, to have female role models, especially women officers who had graduated from these institutions and were successfully making a career in the military. At Annapolis, as late at 1990, this need was not being met, since there were no female Annapolis graduates on staff in the positions of faculty members or company officers. "Many midshipmen have never met a female graduate," Francke quoted from a 1991 Annapolis document. At West Point, on the other hand, female cadets were helped by a group of "enlightened colonels" who "showcased the hundred plus female officers assigned to the academy, among them 35 graduates, as role models for both female and male cadets." Did those women officers make a difference? One female West Point graduate strongly agreed that they did. "It takes women with experience telling these young (female) cadets right now that we know what you're going through, and it's OK to be a woman," army Captain Laurie Barone, a West Point class of '83 graduate, told Francke.

In the sports world as well, female role models are essential.

Vivian Acosta, who formerly coached numerous sports, sees women coaches as important role models for both males and females. "If you see a woman in a position of leadership and you're a young woman, " Vivian explained, "you think, oh, I can do this, but if you don't see them there you start questioning."

The importance of having female coaches is supported by a 1998 study of male and female college basketball players. All the male athletes included in the study were coached by men, but 72 percent of the female athletes were coached by women. Among these young women, the researchers found, those who had women coaches were more interested in the coaching field than were the young women who had male coaches. The female basketball players with women coaches also believed any discrimination they might face in the coaching field to be less of a barrier than did the female players coached by men. "These results," the researchers concluded, "strongly support the call for hiring more female coaches."

Sports sociologist Mary Jo Kane, a professor at the University of Minneapolis and Director of the Tucker Center for Research on Girls and Women in Sport, definitely agrees that women coaches are needed as teachers and role models. The gender of coaches matters, Mary Jo explained. "When I look at (University of Connecticut coach) Geno Auriemma," Mary Jo stated, "no matter how great he is as a coach... he is not who I am. (University of Tennessee coach) Pat Summitt is female." Female coaches, Mary Jo affirmed, can teach lessons about what women can do which go beyond the world of athletics. "Women can be leaders," a girl or young woman could conclude. "Women can be ...competitive, women can be a major success, and therefore I can be a success in the classroom, or as a police officer, or a college professor... I can do that because women before me have done that."

Numerous women coaches have expressed similar thoughts. And whether or not they articulate such ideas, numerous women coaches do in fact provide examples for their athletes. On one occasion, while Brown University hockey coach Digit Murphy was riding in the team bus, she was also pumping breast milk which would be Fed Ex-ed back to her baby in Rhode Island while Digit travelled with her team. A male coach, of course, could not model the same behavior, while a savvy female coach like Digit could use the situation as an object lesson in how a woman can fulfill the dual roles of mother and career woman. "That is so gross that you do that," Digit recalled a player commenting about her expressing her breast milk.

"Gross," Digit countered, "Why do you say that?"

"I don't know," was all the player, no doubt taken aback, could come up with for an answer.

"This is the greatest thing in the world," Digit responded about caring for her baby. Reflecting on the incident, Digit thought about the lessons her players were likely learning from the fact that their coach was also a mother. "I know that they're going to gain strength from that at some point in their life," Digit commented. "They'll say, 'My coach did it, I can do it.'"

On another occasion Digit did some instant gender education with her team. Just before the first game of the season, the Brown women's hockey team was gathered in their locker room. Digit had long argued that the women's hockey games should be officiated by three referees, just as was done in men's games. Finally, this season, the university had agreed and Digit passed the good news on to her players. "Oh guys, by the way, we got our three refs," she told them.

The players were happy with the news, but one player expressed a reservation. "Do we have the woman ref?" she asked, making it clear from her tone of voice that in her mind a woman referee was not a good thing.

Digit didn't let the comment pass. "Whoa, hold it right there," she told her team. "Let's talk about some gender issues here." It was true, Digit admitted, that some relatively inexperienced women referees were being put onto the ice in order to give more women referees a chance. But her team shouldn't be putting those women down. "I don't want to hear anyone on my team talk poorly about female officials..." Digit lectured. "Don't give them a bad rap just because they're females."

A male coach, of course, could make the same point to female athletes. And yet it seems unlikely that the message communicated, in that case, would be wholly the same. In the case

Digit Murphy

of the women official, the lecture Digit gave to her team surely passed on another, nonverbal message about female solidarity when as a woman coach she defended a woman referee.

Although women coaches are quick to agree that men can make excellent coaches for female athletes, most women coaches also argue that there are many positives for women coaching female athetes. As Fresno State softball coach Margie Wright, a veteran of over 25 years of coaching, put it, "There are good coaches in both genders ... but I definitely believe that the (female) athletes who are coached by females ... have a definite advantage, and the opportunity to see what those women have gone through."

Female athletes, Margie explained, can "try to emulate" their female coaches and can benefit from the fact that their coaches, as females, have had many similar experiences to their female athletes. As a former softball pitcher, Margie said, she can easily identify, more so than a male coach would, with the young women who pitch for her team at Fresno State. "I have felt everything they feel when they're out there in the field and in practice," Margie commented. "All the emotions, all the mentals ups and downs in a game. I've lived those. And I've lived them for over 30 years as a (softball) pitcher."

In *Are We Winning Yet?* author Mariah Burton Nelson told a story about female basketball coach, Vivian Stringer, that serves to illustrate Margie Wright's point about female coaches understanding female athletes. Vivian watched a male coach working with a female post player, telling her to "get your big ass over here." Vivian, on the other hand, understood that for a female athlete that kind of language was "insulting." Rather than continuing in the same vein with the young woman, she told her to "make yourself wide and block out," language that didn't alienate the young woman. Vivian also believes strongly in women coaches as role models. "Who better than a woman can tell women not only how to play basketball but how to get along in a male-dominated society? Who better can show young women you can be a leader and also a mom?"

Consider, on the other hand, the impact on both male and female athletes of the sexist coaches observed by the author of a *Newsweek* article, Dorothea Stillman. The all male coaches of a basketball program for boys and girls "belittled the girls and humiliated the boys by saying they were 'playing like girls.'" After a game where an all-girls team of seven year olds won a game over an all-boys team, "A smirk came over the (male) coach's face," Stillman described. "'Are you going to let a bunch of girls beat you?' he roared at the boys." In this situation, it doesn't take a rocket scientist to conclude that very negative messages about sports and gender roles were being communicated.

Fortunately, many male and female coaches are far more aware of the messages they're sending. Many women coaches describe the impact they have on their athletes, and the lessons they believe coaches can teach. As Stanford University basketball coach Tara VanDerveer sees it, she teaches her athletes far more than the x's and o's of her sport. To be successful on the court, her athletes need to learn about "working with other people, developing pride in how you do things. Coming out and playing hard all the time. Challenging yourself all the time, not just when you feel like it or when it's convenient or for a big game."

By having a woman as their coach, Tara believes, female athletes can learn other lessons as well. "I think it's good for the young women to see older women in leadership positions, decision positions," Tara commented. Having such a female role model should assist these athletes in "being able to envision themselves doing that someday whether it's coaching or in whatever medium they want..."

———

Marianna Freeman, head women's basketball coach at Syracuse University, knows the importance of having a role model. Essentially raised by her grandmother, a strong personality who herself provided Marianna with a powerful female role model, Marianna had the opportunity to play college basketball at Cheyney State College, a historically black college located near Philadelphia, under head coach Vivian Stringer, who became an important role model and mentor for Marianna.

By 1975, when Marianna graduated from high school, athletic scholarships for girls were newly available, and Marianna was recruited by three universities. Although this was far fewer choices than many athletes nowadays receive, Marianna still found it hard to decide. It was her grandmother who influenced Marianna's decision to accept a scholarship from Cheyney State head coach Stringer, an African-American female coach. Marianna's grandmother "understood the importance of having a role model that looked like me," Marianna remembered. After Vivian Stringer visited with Marianna and her family, Marianna recalled, "my grandmother was impressed, and my grandmother was a very difficult person to impress."

"I feel like she will do the right thing for you," Marianna's grandmother told her granddaughter, and her grandmother's intuition proved to be correct. Vivian Stringer, Marianna recalled, "really took interest in all of the young women that she coached." Marianna learned a multitude of important lessons that went way beyond basketball, such as "how to do things on time, to do them well, to have great pride in what it is that you do, whether people recognize the significance or not."

Marianna's grandmother had raised her granddaughter to feel pride in herself, and Cheyney State, with its plentiful supply of African-American role models, encouraged self-confidence as well. "I was expected to achieve," Marianna commented. Vivian Stringer provided an example of a hardworking coach who encouraged her athletes to work hard as well. And Vivian taught Marianna another important lesson, encouraging her "to have a great deal of self-respect."

A good athlete, although not the most athletic player on her team, one of Marianna's strengths was her "ability to think the game." Vivian noticed that Marianna often wrote down and diagrammed the team's plays in order to help herself learn them. "You really would make a good coach one day," Vivian told Marianna, "because you analyze things and you learn them well, and you also help your teammates a lot." That moment of positive feedback helped inspire Marianna's choice of coaching as a career. "That's when it first crossed my mind," she recalled.

Her influential female coach began to mentor Marianna. After taking part in a sports symposium at Slippery Rock College, Vivian Stringer's alma mater, Marianna met Vivian's former coach and was offered a graduate assistant position in the affirmative action office and the chance to work with the women's basketball team. Soon afterward, Vivian's network of connections helped 21-year-old Marianna obtain her first head coaching position, at Delaware State. "Had it not been for Coach Stringer and her connections," Marianna commented, "pretty much I wouldn't be coaching today."

The Delaware State coaching job came at a difficult time in Marianna's life. With her grandmother seriously ill with cancer, Marianna combined her coaching duties with caring for her grandmother, who lived close by. In spite of those responsibilities and the nine straight winless seasons Delaware State had

had, the challenge of her new position excited Marianna. She managed to turn the program around, finishing in first place in the Mid-Eastern Atlantic Conference in 1982-83.

When Vivian Stringer moved to the University of Iowa, Marianna Freeman accepted a position as Vivian's top assistant coach there. It was a coaching move that inspired Marianna to work even harder to excel. "I felt I needed to be a better coach. I needed to be on the level with her (Vivian) as her peer," Marianna recalled.

While working on Vivian's coaching staff, Marianna learned a great deal from her former

Marianna Freeman

coach. How to break down a basketball skill so it could be taught to a beginner as well as an advanced player. How to make a break down of plays from game videotapes, to prepare a scouting report for each player, and in general numerous approaches to coaching. But the two women's student-teacher relationship wasn't one-sided. Marianna offered ideas about how to recruit, developing a system of recruiting that was broken down by regions and states, and establishing her own reputation as a coordinator of recruiting.

As a coaching peer rather than a player, Marianna gained new insight into her former coach. Vivian, Marianna found, was a coach who "practically lived, and breathed, and died basketball, all year round." But when Vivian's husband, Bill Stringer, died suddenly of a heart attack on Thanksgiving day, 1992, the two women's roles shifted. Vivian temporarily relinquished her head coaching duties, leaving Marianna as the acting head coach. It was a position that scared her, and one that Marianna wasn't sure she would be able to handle. "You can do it, you're gonna have to," Vivian told Marianna, teaching another important lesson even at that moment of grief.

The bond that Marianna felt for her former coach was a strong one. "I would do anything for her," Marianna recalled. Yet leading the team wasn't easy. Bill Stringer had been a friend of Marianna's, and Marianna as well as Vivian was grieving for Bill. It helped that Marianna could once more draw strength from another strong female. "What doesn't kill you, will make you stronger," Marianna recalled her grandmother saying. Following that advice, Marianna and the other coaches hung in there, encouraging the players to "take each game, one day at a time," and to "do the best that we can do each day." It was a draining and challenging time for Marianna, and an amazing season that culminated in the team going to the NCAA Final Four. "I learned a lot about me that year," she recalled, "that I was a little bit stronger than what I thought."

The exposure Marianna Freeman received as temporary head coach helped her to obtain a head coaching position at Syracuse University. And appropriately enough, in her position as head coach she both recognizes and accepts her position as teacher and role model for a new generation of female athletes. "I think it's important that I use basketball to teach young people about life," Marianna commented. In the process of numerous speaking engagements and other outreach activities in the larger Syracuse community, she acts as a role model there, as well. "Don't think you can't do it just because you're a girl," she advises girls. "Nothing wrong with being a nurse, but it's OK to dream about being a doctor too."

Just as Vivian Stringer was an important role model for Marianna Freeman, Marianna recognizes that she now has taken on that role modeling position herself. " I think it's real important," she commented, "that I'm out there as a woman and ... as an African-American woman."

Chris Shelton, formerly a tennis coach at several colleges, now supervises graduate students in training to be coaches at

Smith College. Chris has seen firsthand the realities of declining numbers of female coaches. Among the students in the Smith program, Chris described, are numerous women who "have never seen a woman coach" and who make comments such as "I've never been coached by a woman." It's a coaching phenomenon that deeply concerns Chris Shelton, since she perceives it as "extremely important" to have women coaches at all levels of sport.

Donna Lopiano, executive director of the Women's Sports Foundation, strongly agrees. In a Women's Sports Foundation paper entitled "Do Female Athletes Prefer Male Coaches?", Donna Lopiano summarized research revealing that "female athletes who have never had a female coach believe that male coaches are better than female coaches. Male and female athletes who have been taught to devalue the athletic abilities of females may really believe that females cannot coach as well as males."

Fortunately, in spite of the statistically low numbers of women college coaches, there are still numerous highly qualified women out there who disprove the stereotype that females can't be good coaches. These conscientious women coaches are fully aware of the role they play in teaching important life lessons to their athletes.

For Notre Dame head women's basketball coach Muffet McGraw, the thing she wants most to teach her players is to be "accountable, responsible." After a game for example, she and her team will talk about what players did well and what they need to work on. If shooting is a concern, Muffet encourages the player to come in on her own for extra shooting practice. "You need to take some responsibility for that yourself," Muffet will say to players. Muffet works hard to encourage a team atmosphere where rather than blaming teammates for poor performance, players will take responsibility for their own shortcomings. Instead of a player blaming a teammate by saying "Boy, if you would have done that better, we would have won the game," Muffet encourages her players to think, "Here's what I could have done to win."

Willamette University volleyball coach Marlene Piper takes a similar approach to coaching, encouraging her athletes to take both individual responsibility and personal ownership of the game. "This is your program," Marlene tells her players. "When you get on the court, don't you be looking at me and saying what'd I do wrong." Marlene feels the player should already have learned the lessons in practice. At times the young women on Marlene's team show her that their coach's lessons have taken hold. "They know that I want them to stay behind the ball and be hitting the ball in the power position," Marlene recounted humorously. "So when they start launching that ball out, instead of looking at me quizzically and saying, 'What am I doing wrong,' so Piper can yell for the ninth millionth time, 'Stay behind the ball,' they're saying to me, 'I'm staying behind the ball,' and I'm smiling."

University of Massachusetts education professor Pat Griffin, who coached swimming at the university for a number of years, used the rest intervals of swimming practice to educate her athletes about matters that went beyond swimming. Pat laughed at the memory: "They'd be gasping for breath, and I'd be doing values clarification exercises with them." What, for example, would a woman do if she had to choose between a social obligation and a team obligation? And Pat and her swimmers would often discuss a topic of special concern to female athletes: not diets or menstrual cramps but muscles!

Since Pat coached from 1971 to 1976, a time period when female athletes were far less accepted than they are today, it isn't surprising that many of the women on her team expressed negative attitudes about their bodies. They "didn't want to wear sleeveless shirts because they were too muscular," Pat's swimmers would say. In contrast, Pat encouraged her swimmers to admire both their own and other women's strong, athletic bodies. "You worked hard for these muscles," Pat would say, "What makes you think they're unattractive?" For athletes concerned that an overly muscular build would make them appear less feminine, Pat's response was to the point: "If you have muscles, they can't be manly. ...You're a woman, and if you have muscles, they're a woman's muscles."

Beyond lessons about body image and taking responsibility, what women coaches can teach is, simply, that women can be effective coaches. Former Pomona College tennis coach, Lisa Beckett, for example, who had both male and female tennis coaches when she herself was playing, found that her relationships were different with her women coaches. "I just think I connected to them in a different way," she described. "I think I was drawn to them because they were role models for me." Having women coaches herself helped give her the idea that women could be coaches.

As was true for Marianna Freeman, women coaches have often assisted female athletes in entering and continuing with the coaching profession. In Lisa Beckett's case, a number of women coaches became significant mentors for her. Lisa's Sonoma State tennis coach, Martha Yates, advised Lisa to look for teaching assistantships as a way to get into college coaching. At Washington State, another woman coach, Terry Coblentz, helped Lisa learn how to handle recruiting and other coaching situations. In 1984, when Lisa returned to her alma mater, Sonoma State, Lisa's former volleyball coach, Vivian Fritz, offered Lisa the position of assistant coach for volleyball and tennis, knowing it could soon lead to the position of head tennis coach for Lisa. Vivian also encouraged Lisa to apply to be the Pomona tennis coach. Vivian saw the job announcement in the *NCAA News* and handed Lisa the paper. "I always kid her," Lisa said, "well you're the one that got me this job." In general, Lisa is well aware of the debt she owes to the women coaches who mentored her. "That's a long span of being helped by someone in the profession," she described.

Other coaches agree about the importance of women coaches as mentors for them. For Mills College cross country coach Sharon Chiong, one of the reasons she entered the coaching profession was another woman coach, Judy George. Originally, Sharon was planning on becoming a corporate fitness instructor. "I had no clue that I ...would be a coach," Sharon commented. But that was before she met Judy George, a coach and visiting professor from Depauw University, appropriately enough in a women's sports history class Judy was teaching. After class one day, while the two women sat and talked, Judy told Sharon that increasing numbers of girls were playing sports but that the numbers of women coaches were decreasing. "Have you ever thought about coaching?" Judy asked. "She planted the seed for me," Sharon remembered. When Judy offered Sharon a job in the field hockey program at Depauw, Sharon accepted even though she "didn't even know a stick from a ball."

After Depauw, Sharon became the head cross country coach at Florida Atlantic University. In a situation strikingly similar to Lisa Beckett's experience, in Sharon's case, her mentor Judy George was the one who noticed the advertisement, also in the *NCAA News*, for the position of full time cross country coach at Mills College, and who let Sharon know about that position. Thanks in part to the information provided by Judy, Sharon got the job at Mills, a position she still holds today.

———

When University of Nebraska head softball coach Rhonda Revelle was in elementary school, she pictured herself as a school teacher with her summers off to play softball. But it wasn't until she was a college athlete, playing softball at the University of Nebraska for Coach Nancy Plantz, that Rhonda began to envision coaching as a serious career possibility. "I saw that she was coaching for a living, and she was a woman," Rhonda recalled. It was something of a new recognition, because growing up she'd had numerous male coaches. Since Nancy Plantz and other women coaches have made a difference for Rhonda, it makes perfect sense that Rhonda is well aware of how she herself is a role model and teacher for the young women she coaches.

Rhonda discussed the coaching field with Nancy Plantz, and Nancy offered Rhonda a position as an assistant coach. With a year of college left to complete, Rhonda didn't accept Nancy's job offer, but after college Rhonda took her first coaching job, a part-time position paying the grand sum of $900 a year, forcing her to sell life insurance on the side to make ends meet! In the fall of '88, when Rhonda accepted the position of first assistant coach at San Jose State, she began working for a head coach, Kathy Strahan, whom Rhonda described as a "wonderful mentor ...the most active mentor I've had to date in coaching."

The two women shared an office for four years, and Rhonda learned a great deal from Kathy—how to make a budget for the softball program, how to run a tournament, and all the other coaching minutae that head coaches need to know. The fact that the two women had played different positions as players—Kathy had been a middle infielder and Rhonda a pitcher—made for some mutually beneficial sharing. On a daily basis, the two women would talk softball. Together in their shared office, they would "get in all funky positions going through footwork and stuff" as Rhonda demonstrated pitching techniques and Kathy, approaches for fielding.

Just as numerous men in positions of authority have helped promising younger men, Kathy did the same for Rhonda. Rhonda can easily recall many of the lessons Kathy taught her. "It's important to delegate," Kathy would explain, and yet a head coach also needs to know that "the buck stops here." As if to illustrate both these points, after Rhonda had only been an assistant coach at San Jose for three months, Kathy, noting Rhonda's outgoing personality, put Rhonda in charge of recruiting. "She put my feet right in the fire..." Rhonda described. "I really took it as a challenge. That's probably the best thing she could have done for me personally." That confidence-building strategy of delegating significant responsibilities is one that Rhonda now uses herself with assistant coaches.

When Rhonda returned to the University of Nebraska in August, 1992, this time as a coach rather than a player, she took charge of a softball program that had been strong in the '80s but had hit bottom in the '90s. As a first-time head coach, Rhonda felt an "awesome sense of responsibility to restore a program to national prominence." But while wins on the field mattered to her—and her recognition as 1998 Big 12 Coach of the Year is one indicator of her coaching success—Rhonda also did and does define her success as a coach in other ways. Like many women coaches, she emphasizes her relationship with her players, and her own position as a teacher of lessons that transcend softball.

"We have a responsibility to our gifts, ...to do justice to them and show humility," Rhonda tells her players about their athletic abilities. She talks about and tries to show by example the

Rhonda Revelle

qualities of integrity and honesty: "the courage to say the hard things ...to confront things that make you fearful, the courage to do the right thing even when you sometimes don't want to," such as talking to the coach about another player doing something to hurt the team, even if that player is a close friend. She talks about discipline as well, such as keeping to training programs even over breaks from school. And for both her players and her assistant coaches, Rhonda tries hard to pass on a work ethic. "I'd never ask them to do more than I do," Rhonda said about her assistant coaches. But all coaches, Rhonda feels, have to set an example of hard work. "How can we expect our players to bust their chops day in and day out if the coaches don't do the same?" she asked rhetorically.

Many coaches speak eloquently about their profession, and Rhonda Revelle is no exception. The essence of coaching, she explained, is "trying to bring a group of people together to work for a common goal." It's about "what that feels like to work together, that group experience, and the ebb and flow of it, the ups and downs, the struggle, the adversity, the love, the frustration."

Her players, of course, go through all of those emotions as well, and as their coach Rhonda tries to help them with a variety of situations and feelings. She's had players raped, players with eating disorders, players cited for possessing alcohol as a minor. "I think there's a reason I'm called a head coach," Rhonda commented. During the school year, in the conferences she has with all her players, she asks about academics and then offers an opportunity for a player to talk about whatever is on her mind—playing time, the death of a family member, whatever. "It's amazing. Last year all but one player cried in this office," Rhonda described. Is that because she's such a mean person? "I think so. I've got this whip," Rhonda joked, quickly adding, "I think it's healthy" that the players can express their feelings so openly.

Those kinds of interactions with her players are the most rewarding part of coaching for Rhonda. "I didn't get into coaching to win trophies," she commented. "I hopefully have a positive impact." She mentioned men's basketball coach John Wooden's idea about the "relationships beyond the playing years."

Wooden wrote, "I often told the players that, next to my own flesh and blood they were the closest to me. They were my extended family..." Along the same lines, another men's basketball coach, Mike Krzyzewski, described how at their first team meeting each year, the coaches "emphasize... that the new guys are not just joining a basketball team, but a basketball family."

Like John Wooden, Mike Krzyzewski, and numerous women coaches, Rhonda Revelle also uses a family model of coaching, and many of her former players clearly still consider their coach part of their own extended family. By late July, 2000, as Rhonda headed for her ninth year as a head coach at Nebraska, she's had numerous players calling her to tell her about their new babies or other milestones in their lives. "That's really special,"

Rhonda commented about what she sees as lifelong relationships.

That summer Rhonda received a letter from a player who graduated from the Nebraska softball program five years ago, a woman who as a player "really butted heads" with Rhonda. In her letter, the former player told Rhonda that "she's very thankful for how I hung with her" and "how inspiring I was." The former player, now a coach herself, wrote Rhonda that her approach "has really influenced her passion" for the game. Rhonda's "never-give-up-attitude-on-people," the former player added, had shaped the approach to coaching she now uses herself.

Those heartfelt words meant a great deal to Rhonda. After reading the letter, she described, "I didn't even make it back into the house. I sat in my garage and cried like a baby."

Other women coaches tell similar stories. Retired softball coach Judi Garman has heard from many former players about just how much of an impact Judi had on their lives. "Thank you for what a difference you've made in my life," is the basic message numerous former athletes have given to Judi. She described the self-assessment one former player had shared with her: "There's no question she'd be in prison now if it wasn't for the fact that I was willing to take a chance on her and let her into the program." Whenever that woman sees Judi, she runs up to her former coach to hug her and to thank her.

Another of Judi's former players lives near Judi and keeps in touch with her ex-coach. The woman, who is in her late 30s and a homicide detective in the Los Angeles Police Department, told Judi how she helped her to become a success. "You helped drive me to be the best I could be," the woman told her former coach.

"I think girls should see qualified women as role models in athletics," Princeton University field hockey coach Beth Bozman argued, "and think that that's an acceptable profession." For a job opening on a women's team, Beth believes a female coach should be hired over an equally qualified male coach. If female coaches are not out there as role models for female athletes, Beth asserted, then female athletes are "learning that it's only OK for men to go into athletics, into coaching," which is, "a pretty sad message we're sending."

Numerous coaches and administrators agree that a different message is needed. The responses Vivian Acosta and Linda Carpenter received to a 1988 survey of male and female athletic administrators revealed a truth about coaching that hasn't changed. "We need role models for young women that say women can be #1, not just somebody's assistant," one person replied. "Women better understand the self-esteem problems that women athletes may have better than men," a second person replied. "[We] need role models for young women to aspire to, and for males to see competent females in these roles," another person wrote. Almost every respondent, in fact, mentioned the importance of female role models.

"Girls and women," Vivian Acosta and Linda Carpenter eloquently summed up, "in order to visualize the extent of their own capacities, must be able to see females in positions of leadership and decision-making as well as the more common nurturing and supporting roles. The benefits transcend sport and reach to all phases of life and development and accomplishment."

In the Limelight

Coach Jody Conradt walked onto the stage, her shoulders back, her posture straight, and her broad smile speaking volumes about how pleased and proud she felt. Obviously used to her position as a public figure, Jody looked both poised and stylish in a long black dress and sparkly earrings. The only woman among seven new inductees into the Naismith Memorial Basketball Hall of Fame in October, 1998, only the second woman to be so honored, and a trailblazer for women's college sports, Jody seemed comfortable in her role.

"Women's basketball has arrived," Jody announced. Always personable, she paused to smile again at the audience. Then she shared some personal history, describing her mother as "the best third baseman I'd ever seen," and describing the sports opportunities she herself had had growing up in a small town in Texas, opportunities she later learned many other girls had been denied. Jody Conradt was now a successful head coach at the University of Texas, and University of Texas women's athletic director as well. But as Jody explained, her path to success had been far from simple. "I didn't know I could coach because all my coaches had been men," she told the audience.

At the University of Texas, Jody Conradt built one of the top women's basketball programs in the country. In 1980, she reminded the audience, at a time when women's basketball hadn't reached anything like its current level of popularity, Texas women's games could draw 8,000 fans. Even so, Jody didn't trumpet her personal achievements. "I don't represent an individual," she said simply. "I represent women's basketball."

Jody Conradt's disclaimer may seem like false modesty. As the winningest coach ever in women's college basketball, with 746 wins to her credit after the 1999-2000 season, Jody Conradt is well-known among women's basketball fans for her stellar coaching career and the outstanding teams she's coached. In addition to her induction in the Basketball Hall of Fame, she has received numerous other personal honors, including recognition in the International Women's Sports Hall of Fame, and the Texas Sports Hall of Fame. In 1987, the Women's Basketball Coaches Association, recognized Jody with their highest honor, naming her the recipient of the Carol Eckman Award. Yet career advancement was never Jody's main goal. Instead, like many other women coaches, she was focused on a broader objective: growing both her own sport and women's sports overall.

Women college coaches like Jody Conradt have worked long hours to build fan support, improve their facilities, raise their budgets, and increase media coverage of female athletes. As individual coaches have worked to improve their teams and to promote their programs, they've also played crucial roles in raising both the level of play in particular sports and the level of public awareness of women's sports overall. As a result, coaches like Jody Conradt have become public figures themselves, women used to the bright lights of media scrutiny.

In Jody Conradt's case, she advanced her sport as a technical innovator, as women's basketball moved from the old, restricted, half-court game to a more free-flowing, faster, full-court style. But perhaps more importantly, Jody led a kind of women's sports movement, actively promoting interest in women's basketball and using basketball as a flagship sport to increase support for all women's sports at the University of Texas.

Jody's involvement in sports started in her hometown of Goldthwaite, Texas, a small town about 100 miles northwest of Austin. Growing up in the '40s and '50s, she was fortunate to receive the opportunity to participate in a variety of sports, minus the negative attitudes about females in sports that many

Jody Conradt

girls encountered at the time. Sports were her "passion," Jody remembered. She starred at high school basketball, scoring an average of 40 points per game for her team!

In spite of Jody's athletic achievements, with no role models of women in coaching, she was planning on a career in teaching when a male superintendent of schools outside of Waco, Texas, who was also the girls' basketball coach, asked Jody to be an assistant coach. "That was the first time that it ever occurred to me that I could coach," she recalled, "and it was the first time that I'd ever thought that it might be something I would want to do."

Her first college coaching job, which she accepted in the fall of 1969, was at Sam Houston State University in Huntsville, Texas. She coached three sports—basketball, volleyball, and track—taught classes as well, and considered her position "the best job in the world." In 1973, she took a coaching position at the University of Texas, Arlington, once again coaching three sports, which was typical for women's sports at the time. Then in 1976, Jody was hired by a new, forward-thinking women's athletic director, Donna Lopiano, to coach at the University of Texas. The two strongminded, competitive women would work together to build a first-rate women's sports program at Austin.

"It was probably too radical to think that I would be hired here to coach one sport," Jody recalled. So at first she took on the dual job of coaching women's basketball and volleyball. Even so, her hiring was controversial. "Woman Takes Texas Job at

Man-Sized Salary" read the headline in a local paper. Jody's initial salary was all of $19,000.

There was nowhere to go but up when Jody Conradt and Donna Lopiano began building the women's basketball program at the University of Texas. "There was no fan base, there was no media coverage. It was basically starting from ground zero," Jody remembered. When she began her coaching career at Austin, women's basketball games were scheduled at 5:00 p.m., before the men's games, and drew few spectators beyond the maintenance crew and family members.

"Why has women's basketball become the flagship for women's athletics?" author David Salter questioned in *Crashing the Old Boys' Network*. "Why has women's basketball achieved such high interest and earned the commitment of television contracts? ...The foundation began with a handful of coaches who have not only championed the cause of their own team, but have promoted women's basketball and women's athletics as well."

Jody Conradt was one of those pioneering coaches. Together with Donna Lopiano, she was willing to take the risks necessary to bring about change. One of the first steps the Conradt-Lopiano team took was to separate women's basketball from its Siamese-twin embrace with men's basketball, a pairing in which the women's game was by far the weaker twin of the two programs. Women's basketball games would now be scheduled on different nights from the men's games, a calculated risk that meant women's basketball had to pay separate rent for their arena and hire arena staff as well. It was a move that flew in the face of prevailing ideas about women's basketball, that the same people who came out for the men's game would support the women's as well. But Jody believed that women's basketball would find its own supporters.

Few fans would be interested in a mediocre basketball team, of course. Although Donna Lopiano was from the east, when she took over at Austin, she knew that she needed a coach with Texas roots to recruit from the strong pool of talented basketball players coming from Texas high schools. "I was out to hire the best coach in Texas," Donna Lopiano recalled. After she watched Jody coach a game, Donna came away with a very positive impression. "She was a class act," Donna Lopiano described. "She knew what she was doing, she had a disciplined team that gave 100 percent, and she treated her players with respect."

Fairly soon Jody's teams of talented athletes began to pile up the wins. In only her second year, her team was ranked number 15th in the nation, and it was fifth in the nation by Jody's third year. Jody "put together a great coaching staff and a very strong schedule that indicated she was out for a top 10 ranking," Donna Lopiano described. But the two-woman team of Jody Conradt and Donna Lopiano still had to get people to pay attention, to notice what was happening with women's basketball at Texas. "When you run something up the flagpole," Jody described, "you have to run it up with winds, and we had winds." What Jody was perhaps too modest to say was that she and Donna did a great deal to create those favorable winds.

In spite of their on-court success, getting media interested had been tough. "We were struggling with media coverage," Jody remembered. "We heard the chicken-and-egg story a thousand times. We're not going to write about it because (nobody) cares. Well, how can anybody care if they don't know," was Jody's slightly-exasperated, exactly-on-target response.

For Jody and Donna, almost nothing was too hokey to draw fan and media attention. "We almost plastered the grade point average on each athlete's chest," Jody described humorously. Although she and Donna didn't literally use their players as walking sign boards, they did everything but, telling anyone who would listen about what fine role models, excellent students and good athletes the players were.

A media-and-fan-friendly event the two women created was what they called the "Fastbreak Club." After each home game, Texas coaches and players would head for the arena ballroom with the picturesque title of the Burnt Orange Room. There interested fans could meet the players, shake their hands and talk with the Texas coaches as well. Texas women's basketball was establishing itself as a team with the kind of down-home personality fans could easily connect with. Creating the Fastbreak Club, Jody assessed, "was probably the single most important thing that we did to try to build a fan base."

Jody's outgoing personality was a key factor as well. "Jody had everything a public relations person would want," Donna described. "She was a talented speaker with a great sense of humor. She said yes to every invitation to speak about her program or do anything in the community. ...She was very popular with the media and spent whatever time necessary with them. She related to every group–donors, the press, the faculty, fans, coaches–in the most perfect way you could imagine. She was a PR director's dream."

All that PR of various sorts had an impact. More and more people turned out for Texas women's basketball games. And Jody and Donna continued to beat the bushes for still more fans who could be shown just how exciting the women's game had become. "We did a grass roots campaign," Jody told David Salter. "We believed if you get them to the game once, they would come back." Jody and Donna telephoned friends and acquaintances and invited them to games, then asked those new fans to bring in still more people to upcoming games. "It was a lot like a pyramid scheme," Donna Lopiano told a reporter. The two women also reached out to prominent women in the Texas community, with former governor Ann Richards and former U.S. Representative Barbara Jordan becoming strong supporters. "Not necessarily," Jody commented, "because they loved basketball, but because they saw this as a breakthrough. Women performing in nontraditional roles and people supporting that."

"Nontraditional" was a good label for some of the strategies Jody and Donna employed. When they began to build up their program, they lacked the clout to get the University of Texas band to play at women's basketball games. As a low-budget alternative, Donna ordered kazoos and had them distributed to student supporters at games. Native-Texan Jody was far from thrilled by the idea she described as a "runaway Lopiano train," but the kazoo "band" actually did play "The Eyes of Texas," the school fight song, at a few games before the musical experiment was abandoned, consigned to a less-than-glorious place in University of Texas women's athletic history.

As girls' and women's basketball outgrew the era of restrictive rules, changing into a much more wide open, running and

Jody Conradt

passing game, Jody changed her coaching style. As she recruited increasingly talented players, as her players streaked downcourt towards the basket, the wins mounted up as did the numbers of enthusiastic fans. By the early '80s, they had a breakthrough game against in-state rival Stephen F. Austin where 8000 fans showed up to watch the home-team win. "We felt exhilarated," Jody remembered. Yet she couldn't escape a feeling of doubt about what she and Donna Lopiano and the players had built. "Wow, is this really happening?" Jody wondered.

As if to answer that question, in 1986, the Texas women's basketball team climaxed a storybook, undefeated season by winning a national championship in Lexington, Kentucky. The first women's basketball team to add a NCAA Division I national title to a perfect record, their achievement did not go unrecognized. Later that evening, when a charter flight brought coaches and players back to Austin, large crowds of excited fans were there to greet the returning champions.

Soon afterward, the University of Texas women's basketball

program, and women's college basketball overall, reached another milestone. Nowadays the women's Division I basketball Final Four sells out a year ahead of time, but in 1987, when the University of Texas hosted the women's Final Four at Austin, that championship tournament was the first ever sold-out women's Final Four! To commemorate the event, Jody and Donna had their pictures taken together, standing out on the street under the marquee, under the sign reading "sold out." Before the second semi-final game, Donna Lopiano described, she and Jody stood against the metal railings in the Erwin Center, near where the teams would walk onto the basketball court, and just looked out at the crowd of spectators. The feeling of accomplishment was "exhilarating," Jody remembered.

For Jody Conradt and for the Texas women's sports program she and Donna built, both accomplishments and challenges have continued. In 1992, after Donna Lopiano left the University of Texas, Jody added the position of women's athletic director to her already full schedule. Why was she willing to take on still another challenge? "We built something and it was my obligation to try to help us maintain it," she said simply. During her tenure as athletic director, Jody hired some outstanding coaches, including Beverly Kearney, Susan Watkins and Jill Sterkel.

Although hiring top coaches was satisfying, serving as the administrative point person for the women's program was far from easy. In a turn of events that Jody described simply as "ironic," in 1992, the University of Texas was sued by a group of athletes for not providing sufficient opportunities for women's sports compared to men's sports at Texas. Texas had, in fact, built a strong women's sports program by then, and yet the equity mandates of Title IX meant that the university needed to do even more. No doubt in part because of Jody's input, Texas agreed to a settlement, adding three women's sports: soccer, softball and rowing.

It was a painful chain of events for Jody, who as women's athletic director was right in the center of the Title IX storm. "It was very difficult," she recalled. "This was probably the most difficult thing professionally: to know that... on the one hand that the administration at the University of Texas had made a huge commitment (to women's sports) but on the other hand that I was a part of a system that was denying opportunities." It was an odd position for someone who had spent years working to increase opportunities for women in sports.

As women's basketball coach, Jody has also had to adjust to the fact that the Texas women's basketball team, although always strong competitors, haven't been as dominant recently as they were in the mid to late '80s. Other women's basketball programs, such as those at Tennessee and Stanford, have become basketball powerhouses and won national championships. "The ultimate for the sport," Jody and her assistant coaches had discussed in years past, "would be that there would be parity. That there would be a lot of programs that would be competitive. ...It wasn't going to be as good for Texas when it happened," Jody predicted, "but it was going to be better for the sport. And that proved to be true."

In April, 2001, Jody resigned as women's athletic director so she could concentrate on coaching, which she told reporters was "my heart and my passion." But although Jody Conradt remains fiercely competitive as a coach, her vision isn't limited by the borders of the Lone Star state. "Texas pushing the envelope," Jody knows, has helped to grow women's basketball across the country.

———◆———

Prominent women coaches like Jody Conradt are often surprisingly modest. "I just happened to be in the right place at the right time," was one way Jody assessed her career. And yet the women who coach top programs recognize and accept their roles as spokeswomen for their teams. And because those teams have accumulated so many wins, the coaches themselves have become accustomed to their positions in the limelight.

It's tough to have a bad hair day when you're the head coach of a nationally-ranked team in a program with good fan support. "I don't dare go to the grocery store without makeup," Jody Conradt commented. There's the potential for someone to

recognize her almost any-
where.

Tara VanDerveer, another
nationally prominent figure in
women's sports, is head
women's basketball coach at
Stanford University. The fact
that the Stanford women won
national championships in
1990 and 1992 would alone
guarantee some media recognition. But Tara was also the
head coach for the U.S. national team that toured the
U.S. and internationally for
about a year, then climaxed
their undefeated record by

Tara VanDerveer

winning gold at the 1996 Olympics.

Tara's very public position can lead to odd situations. "I could
be driving across the country," she described, "and in the middle
of the night, three in the morning, I'm driving all night and
haven't combed my hair and I'm not wearing anything that says
Stanford or USA on it. And I'll go into some tiny little roadside
Seven-Eleven or something and somebody in line will say, 'oh,
you know you look really familiar. I recognize you.'" At moments like those, Tara sometimes tries to step away from her
public position. "Aren't you a basketball coach?" someone in
the store will ask. "Oh, no," she'll respond. "People say that all
the time."

And yet Tara VanDerveer can't move very far from her public
identity. At Stanford University, she built the women's basketball
program into a nationally-ranked contender. As head coach for the
1996 Olympic team, she helped bring women's basketball to the
level of popularity the sport enjoys today. "If I was listing the top
five coaches in the history of women's basketball," prominent sportswriter Mel Greenberg was quoted as saying, "one of the first names
out of my mouth would be Tara's."

Tara's achievements as a coach have inspired letters and calls from younger coaches and fan letters from a wide variety of people. "It could be a housewife with three kids," Tara described, "who says, 'You know it's great to see someone like me doing what you're doing.' They're some really touching letters I've gotten."

To reach the position she holds today, like Jody conradt, Tara VanDerveer made quite a journey. "I grew up among the last wave of girls who had to fend entirely for themselves, for whom few (sports) opportunities were available, much less supported by law," Tara wrote in the book about her experiences, *Shooting from the Outside*. When I was a kid, girls aspired to be head cheerleaders, not head coaches. How could I imagine that I would end up in charge of a $3 million Olympic program that was expected to win the gold medal?"

The adults in her life lacked that kind of vision as well. "Basketball won't take you anywhere," Tara's father would say as he watched her playing pick-up games as a girl. "Come in and do your algebra." In retrospect, the childhood story seems ironic and Tara's father's advice shortsighted, to say the least. Yet in terms of the extremely limited sports opportunities for girls and women at the time, his advice made sense. Tara graduated from high school in 1971, a year before Title IX even became law. Although she did play basketball on college teams, including at the Indiana University's relatively high-level women's team, at the time the playing opportunities in women's college basketball were far more limited than what athletes like those on Tara's Stanford teams enjoy today.

Early in Tara's coaching career, when she attended a Bobby Knight-led coaching clinic at Indiana, she was treated as an interloper. "What do we have here?", a male coach asked her. "Honey, did you get lost?" But Tara's coaching record indicated differently. At Ohio State University, where Tara became head coach in 1980, her team was ranked seventh nationally in 1985. Her overall win-loss record at Ohio State was an impressive 110-37.

After all that success, in May, 1985, Tara made a radical career move—leaving the Ohio State team she'd been so successful with and taking the position of head women's basketball coach at Stanford University, a program with a worse than mediocre record and little fan support. For Stanford athletic director Andy Geiger, recruiting Tara VanDerveer for Stanford seemed like a smart decision. "She was a bulldog," Andy recollected to a reporter. "She was relentless and determined beyond just about anybody I have ever known." Tara herself faced the challenge of building her Stanford team from the ground up.

Katy Steding was one of Tara's first two recruits for Stanford, a talented player who along with fellow recruit, Jennifer Azzi, would help to turn around Stanford's basketball fortunes. Her goal was to win a national championship at Stanford, Tara told Katy when she recruited her. "Even though it sounded good, I was skeptical," Katy recalled, "but she made me a believer in her and myself."

In subsequent years, Tara and her assistant coaches recruited other top players for the Stanford program. But recruiting was only one part of what made Tara so successful at Stanford. There was also Tara's sharp grasp of basketball strategy, her vision of success and her ability to inspire the young women on her team to believe in that vision. "She has those high expectations for you as players and for the program in general, and she does what it takes to make you perform at your best," Katy Steding described.

The high goals Tara communicated to her recruits began to become reality. During Jennifer Azzi and Katy Steding's sophomore year, the team reached the NCAA Sweet 16, and in their junior year, the NCAA Elite Eight. The next season Tara hung a sign in the Stanford locker room: "Stanford University, 1990 NCAA Champions, Get Comfortable with It." The sign hung on the locker room wall all season, Tara's way of inspiring her players to reach for the highest possible goal. "It made us think like champions and expect to be champions," Katy Steding recalled.

In Knoxville, Tennessee, on April 1, 1990, Tara and her players won their national championship, beating Auburn 88-81 in front of over 16,000 fans in a game that was nationally televised. The accolades were quick in coming. Post-game, University of Tennessee head women's basketball coach, Pat Summitt, whose own team had won the championship last year, complimented Tara for coming so far, so quickly at Stanford. "This is one of the greatest success stories in the history of the game," Pat applauded.

In a post-game media conference, Tara showed off her national championship ring. "We worked so hard to get this. It just feels great," Tara told the assembled reporters. Members of the press added high praise. "Stanford showed the country just how good women's basketball can be," wrote *San Francisco Chronicle* sports writer Gary Swan. According to a sports writer for *USA Today*, the NCAA championship was the culmination of "Tara VanDerveer's five-year resurrection" of the Stanford program.

Winning the national championship led to a new level of recognition for Stanford women's basketball. The team and their coach were honored with a trip to the White House and a special meeting with President George Bush. The women's basketball office at Stanford was deluged by phone messages from media and numerous others and congratulatory gifts. "We had so many floral arrangements that people made jokes that the office looked like a funeral parlor," DeeDee Johnson, the women's basketball secretary, told a reporter.

Even after winning a second national championship in 1992, Tara VanDerveer wasn't the kind of coach to rest on her laurels, or to allow her athletes to do so either. Throughout her career, in fact, Tara has helped raise the level of competition in women's basketball by both pushing and inspiring her athletes into ever higher levels of achievement. "Developing pride in how you do things" is one of Tara's goals for her athletes, as is "coming out and playing hard all the time. Challenging yourself all the time, not just when you feel like it or when it's convenient or for a big game."

One of Tara's former players, Kate Paye, described the advice Tara gave her one momentous day in October, 1991. After a practice, coach and player sat down together outside the locker room, near Maples Pavilion where the team would play. "'You made the team,'" Tara told Kate. But instead of congratulating her, Tara advised Kate to push herself for even more achievement. "You need to improve your conditioning, your skills," Tara instructed Kate. "Keep working harder and don't be satisfied." That was, Kate Paye recalled, a "typical Tara" moment. Tara's approach, Kate described, was "If you did one thing, go ahead and shoot for something higher."

In 1995, Tara accepted another level of challenge, taking a leave of absence from Stanford to coach the U.S. national team which would become the 1996 Olympic team. The coach with a strong perfectionist streak who was used to working herself and her athletes as hard as they could so that they could put their best game of basketball out on the floor, now had to win games but also promote women's basketball, to show America just how high level the women's game had become. "Winning the gold was the top priority," Tara wrote, "but riding on that success, just below the surface, was the future of women's basketball itself."

The team Tara was given to coach was a group of elite players including Dawn Staley, Teresa Edwards, and former Stanford teammates Jennifer Azzi and Katy Steding, most of whom had played in pro leagues around the world. As coaches in the NBA experience every day, molding a group of superstar athletes into a team is far from easy, but Tara had the right stuff to do so. "She's a great teacher," Dawn Staley told a reporter. "When we saw what and how she taught in practice and games, players automatically gave her respect. ...She took a dozen of the best talents in the country and taught us to play together."

The U.S. national team crisscrossed the country, winning big against college teams and remaining undefeated against international opponents as well. Wherever they went, they attracted a high level of both fan and media attention. Essentially, both Tara and her players were living their lives within a media spotlight with a mental Olympic "clock" that continued to tick, marking time especially loudly for Tara as head coach. "We knew that every day, whether we were practicing, playing a game or even on a rest day..." Katy Steding described, "Tara felt like each day was one step closer or farther away from the gold medal..."

"The expectations were high," assistant Olympic coach Marian Washington commented. "The promotions and marketing of that team was like the greatest in the history of any women's sport ever." For Tara as head coach, Marian realized, "there was enormous pressure." As she watched Tara cope with that pressure on a daily basis, Marian felt "a lot of respect for the fact that she was able to handle it as well as she did."

Finally, the long, arduous journey reached a successful conclusion. Playing Brazil in their final Olympic game, the elite athletes Tara coached won Olympic gold in Atlanta. As the players received their medals, Tara's own emotions were mixed. She thought about all the women on her team who had worked so hard to reach this point: Teresa Edwards, Katy Steding, and all the athletes who "paid the price to make it happen." For herself, Tara knew that she'd reached a high point of achievement as a coach, and that she'd reached an ending as well. "There was a little bit of relief," she remembered, "in that you have this goal and there's the pressure to win. And I think it was kind of sad because I knew that something really special was over. And there was tremendous joy in that we'd taken on and beaten the world."

It wasn't easy to come back to life at Stanford afterward. Like her players on the Olympic team, Tara was very tired after all the travel, the publicity, the succession of games, and the unending pressure to win Olympic gold that fell most heavily on the head coach's shouders. The whole experience had taken its toll. "I didn't realize how emotionally drained I was," Tara recalled, adding that she was "physically exhausted" as well.

Even so, Tara was glad to be head coach at Stanford once again. And her Stanford teams continued to present her with new challenges. In the 1996-97 season, a talented Stanford women's team lost to Old Dominion in the NCAA semi-finals. "That's the worst feeling," Tara described, "knowing that you have a shot at winning the whole thing." Then in 1998, 1999 and 2000, the Stanford women went to the NCAA tournament, only to be eliminated in the first round twice and the second round in 2000. To reach the tournament alone, Tara explained, would mark a successful season for many programs. But at Stanford the expectations were and are higher.

Coaches, like athletes, have to live with those raised expectations. "Whatever you do is never going to be good enough," Tara summed up. The fact that basketball is now the flagship women's sport at most colleges, typically receiving the largest amount of funding, including the highest salaries for coaches, the greatest amount of media attention and fan support, creates a pressure to win that affects even already successful coaches. "Three seasons that aren't in the Final Four for (Tara)," commented Chris Shelton of Smith College, "she's going to be starting to ask herself, should she move on."

In the spring of 2000, after a disappointing early exit from the NCAA tournament, Tara spoke positively about the upcoming season. "I'm very optimistic about next year," she said, "because we have so many really talented kids coming back. And people are working really hard. And we signed a great freshman class." But Tara remained aware of the expectations she faced. "I think that we've almost created a little bit of a monster," she commented. After such a high degree of success at Stanford, "sometimes it's hard to enjoy simple successes, you know, winning a certain game."

Tara's own assessment was amply supported by the coverage both her program and she herself as a public figure received during the 2000-2001 basketball season. "Will VanDerveer, Stanford shake Olympic blues?" questioned a *Real Sports* article. "Expectations put heat on Stanford" was the title of an *Oregonian* article that described injuries, dwindling attendance for Stanford women's basketball home games, and included the reporter's comment that both "the injuries and past success" are "casting a long shadow..."

Tara VanDerveer herself is hardly in the shadows, though. And it seems unlikely she and her teams will escape the media spotlight Tara has helped to generate by her own coaching success. Yet as well as acknowledging the pressure cooker coaching in an elite program can become, just like Jody Conradt, Tara clearly sees the larger picture and recognizes what she has helped to build. "Women's basketball is becoming mainstream," she commented. "People are watching it. People care about it."

While basketball is the most prominent collegiate sport for women, women's ice hockey is a relative newcomer to the women's college sports scene. The number of Division I colleges offering women's ice hockey as a varsity sport—only 6.6 percent in the year 2000—was dwarfed by the 98.1 percent of Division I schools offering women's basketball. But ice hockey for women is also a sport whose time appears to have come, with the number of Division I women's hockey programs doubling from 1996 to 2000.

As Tara VanDerveer experienced, Olympic competition can provide a spotlight for a sport, and winning Olympic gold, as the women's basketball team did in 1996, further heightens public interest. At the 1998 winter Olympics, held in Nagano, Japan, women's ice hockey was included as an Olympic sport for the first time. In the championship game the U.S. team won gold medals, an event that both recognized and seemed likely to encourage the growth of the sport in the United States. At the end of that hard-fought hockey match, Shannon Miller, head coach of the silver-medal winning Canadian women's team, could have been nominated for a special medal of her own. At 35 years old, she was the only female head coach of a women's Olympic ice hockey team.

The ice is thin for pioneers of any sort. For Shannon Miller, it wasn't easy to be an "only," with some of the media attention she received far from friendly. A little over two years after the Nagano Olympics, Shannon still vividly recollected exactly what that position had been like. On April 11, 2000, when she spoke at the Tucker Center for Research on Girls and Women in Sport, at the Minneapolis campus of the University of Minnesota, Shannon didn't mince words: "So what was it like to be the first ever and only female head coach of an Olympic team anywhere in the world? If you really want to know what it was like ... during hunting season, you should run through the forest with antlers on your head. You'll get a very good understanding of what it was like coaching, being the only female at that level."

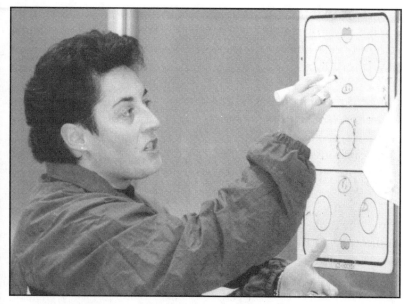

Shannon Miller

After the Olympics, Shannon made a major life change: accepting a job as head coach for the new women's ice hockey program at the University of Minnesota-Duluth. As she stood before a full house at the Tucker Center, Shannon came across as someone with an open, engaging personality. Dressed simply in a black blazer and white blouse, with her short dark hair slicked back, she smiled easily and frequently used humor in her talk. But she was dead serious about what it had been like to be the only female head coach for women's international ice hockey competition. "After two years of coaching on the world stage, under a tremendous amount of scrutiny, under a microscope really," Shannon recalled. "I can tell you that I know what it's like to walk through landmines and lose a limb. I know what it's like to be a walking, living target."

To illustrate her point and perhaps to show that she was not simply overdramatizing her situation, Shannon told the Tucker Center audience a revealing story. After the 2000 world championships in Toronto, where Canada won in overtime over the United States, a former sports reporter for the *Toronto Star* approached Shannon. At the Nagano Olympics, he told Shannon, he shared a taxi ride with two other male reporters who usually covered NHL hockey for the *Star*. Those men had talked about how angry they were that Canada's women's ice hockey team was led by a woman coach. In the course of that taxi ride, "they plotted and planned about how they would pick a fight with [Shannon Miller] after our first game, how they would attack women's hockey and [Shannon] personally on the world stage, and continue it through day after day at the Olympic games, and then maybe just maybe we would get the point that we don't belong ... at the Olympic level."

Although ice hockey is essentially the Canadian national sport, the male reporters' negative attitude illustrates the scorn, indifference, or worse with which female ice hockey has often been received. Canadian women's ice hockey flourished in the early years of the 20th century, Elizabeth Etue and Megan Williams described in *On the Edge: Women Making Hockey History*, but over time female hockey players lost both access to skating facilities and public acceptance. Even as recently as the mid-'90s, according to Etue and Williams, "women's hockey in Canada remains a second-class citizen" and "female players are still largely looked upon as the little sisters who don't really belong in hockey."

In spite of such attitudes, Shannon grew up playing hockey. A Canadian native from Melfort, Saskatchewan, Shannon had competed on the club team at the University of Saskatchewan and in four Canadian National Championships before she ended her playing career in 1989. Because Canadian universities don't offer paid coaching positions or athletic scholarships, the best hockey teams are typically club teams and coaches are typically volunteers. "You don't get paid to coach women's hockey in Canada," Shannon told a *Boston Globe* reporter. Instead, while Shannon coached hockey at the club and eventually at the national team level, she also worked off the ice as a police officer in Calgary, a job she enjoyed because it offered the chance to help people, catch criminals, and sufficient amounts of "action and excitement."

Shannon's hockey coaching résumé is impressive. She started an international ice hockey program located at the University of

Calgary, the first for female hockey players. Both at the assistant and the head coach level, she coached the Canadian national team, and in 1995, 1996 and 1997, she led her team to gold medals at major international competitions including the Women's World Ice Hockey Championships in 1997. Yet one of her most memorable coaching experiences was in a much more down-home situation.

In the 1988-89 hockey season, Shannon coached a hockey team for 13- to 15-year-old girls in their first-ever game, which they lost by the lopsided score of 19 to nothing. Despite the score, Shannon understood exactly what that first game had meant. "It was a hell of a battle to get a girls' team going," Shannon recalled. "They didn't want us to play in the league." Shannon and another woman met with resistance from the Calgary Minor Hockey Association and had to fight for their girls' team to be included in an otherwise all boys minor hockey league. So when that first game was finally played, the fact that Shannon's team had lost the game by a wide margin didn't matter. Instead, the game was a cause for celebration. "It was like wow," Shannon enthused, "we just put together the first ever girls team and we just had our first game."

The 1998 women's Olympic ice hockey competition was also a first. As Nancy Theberge described in *Higher Goals: Women's Ice Hockey and the Politics of Gender*, it "marked a new stage in women's struggle to claim a place in the sport," providing "a measure of the recognition and legitimacy that supporters have been seeking" and bringing "women's hockey more squarely into the arena of commercial spectator sport." Shannon herself as head coach was right in the center of that increased publicity, with the media coverage of her often far from favorable.

In a *San Francisco Chronicle* article written from Nagano after the U.S. women's hockey team won gold, sportswriter C.W. Nevius characterized Shannon as "the snarling Canadian hockey coach," although he did go on to describe how he had been moved by the fact that a woman hockey player had received an Olympic medal. In an interview for the *Boston Globe*, Shannon mentioned media descriptions of her as "feisty, arrogant, overdemanding," as a Hitler-type coach, and as someone who made another coach known for his nastiness "look warm and fuzzy." Her past experience as a police officer helped make her a target as well. "They said I had the cop walk," Shannon described at the Tucker Center. "I was portrayed in the media like I was this big mean cop coach."

Fortunately, some of the media attention Shannon received as an Olympic coach was more favorable. Women sportswriters interviewing her, Shannon remembered, would "take the time to get to know you as a person," and would describe positively the fact that she was not the only female hockey coach but quite youthful as well. The large amount of positive fan mail Shannon received also helped cheer her on. "We're so proud of you and we're so much behind you," women and men would write. "Maybe you don't get a lot of fan mail from guys," one man wrote Shannon, "but I think you're an awesome role model for my son."

The pressures on Shannon and her team were enormous. Canada and the United States were perennial hockey rivals, but the nationalism the Olympics can evoke went well beyond the competition of two neighboring countries. Shannon and her players tried to stay focused and relaxed in spite of the pressure. The night before the gold-medal game, Shannon played a song about "believing in yourself" to her team and showed a video that included pictures of the players as babies, as older girls and young women, and of people the players loved. Previously, Shannon had used the image of "a giant snowball, rolling down the mountain, gathering more and more momentum, growing bigger, stronger, faster" as a psychological tool for her team. The day of the gold-medal game, Shannon bought some tiny crystal snowballs. After the first two periods, during which she didn't feel her team had played as well as they could, she handed out the crystal snowballs to her players. "Toss this around," she told her players. "Think back to last year, the confidence we had, how strong we were, how much momentum we had."

Shannon's snowball reminders had the desired effect on her team. During the third period, she felt her team was "awesome," playing as if they had "nothing to lose." When the team did lose, however, by a score of 3-1, the Canadian players wept, and

Shannon cried also as she and her players walked back from the rink to their dressing room. And yet she didn't feel that either she or her team had failed at what they'd set out to do. "If you can look in the mirror and say I did everything I could," Shannon commented, "I didn't cheat, I carried my own weight, then you can accept the results."

But after Canada's second-place finish, the weight of media criticism continued to fall on Shannon's shoulders. "Shannon Miller didn't lose the women's hockey gold medal for Team Canada—no coach ever does—" wrote sportswriter Steve Simmons, "but she didn't provide her team with every opportunity to win." Simmons described the support Shannon received from her players as "almost in a cult-like manner," an oddly backhanded compliment. He then went on to describe Shannon's "arrogance," her "swagger," and her inability to "make an easy decision."

After the Olympics, the Canadian Hockey Association didn't renew Shannon's contract. Not long after that disappointment, in April, 1998, Shannon made her own personal border crossing. Through the internet, a friend had found out about the job opening for a head hockey coach with a new women's hockey program at the University of Minnesota-Duluth and Shannon had sent in her résumé. Bob Corran, the new UMD athletic director contacted Shannon. "Are you serious? You would seriously consider coming down here?" he asked her.

"Yeah, I would," Shannon replied simply. "I want to coach hockey full time." For years the Canadian-United States hockey rivalry had been a significant part of Shannon's life, with Shannon's allegiances, of course, solidly on her side of the border. Yet Canadian universities didn't offer full time, paid positions to coach women's hockey and thanks to Title IX, United States universities did.

Ironically, Shannon arrived in Duluth on July 1, Canada Day in her native country. As she drove down the road she listened to a radio host's attempt at humor about the Canadian national holiday. "What do you think they do on Canada Day?" Shannon recalled the radio host asking. "Well, I think they probably just stand around ... and sing 'Oh, Canada' over and over," was the on-the-air response. Later, Shannon was able to laugh at the moment, but at the time it felt like an inauspicious beginning to the new phase of her life.

After years of juggling various jobs, after her hard work as national team and Olympic team coach, after dealing not only with hockey concerns but with the storm of publicity her job had entailed, Shannon came to Duluth extremely tired. But she still brought the kind of inner drive she had encouraged in her athletes, in this case the drive to build "a foundation of excellence" for the new program. Her former position as Canadian Olympic coach was more of a deterrent than an asset when recruiting American players, so she recruited internationally, signing outstanding athletes from Canada, Finland and Sweden, and then adding former U.S. Olympic player, Jenny Schmidgall, to her Duluth team.

Aside from the challenge of recruiting, there were other difficulties to overcome, such as learning to negotiate the potential minefield of numerous NCAA rules, all new to Shannon. On the plus side, Shannon enjoyed the close relationships she developed with players on her team. "I'm one of those coaches that spends a lot of time with my athletes off the ice, " she described, "and gets to know them as people... I become a part of their life, they become a part of my life."

Coaching at the college rather than the international level, Shannon hasn't lost her fire as a motivational coach. Think about being "disciplined and dangerous," strong like five fingers compacted into a fist, Shannon tells her UMD players. And even though Duluth is a smaller city of about 85,000, it's still not a place where she can escape the limelight of publicity and public reaction generated by her background, her current position, her outspoken personality, and the fact that hockey is still a relatively new sport for girls and women.

"I've had some women say to me, 'you should hear what my husband says about you.'" A husband might say, for example, "I'm not gonna go support a bunch of dykes that play hockey." The wives, on the other hand, Shannon said, support the Duluth women's hockey team, are friendly to Shannon, and often laugh about their husbands' attitudes.

"She's gutsy, and she's a great coach," the University of Minnesota's Mary Jo Kane said about Shannon, adding that Shannon is "an extraordinarily hard worker" who is "really dedicated and committed to women's hockey." As head women's hockey coach in Duluth, Shannon now receives her share of positive media coverage. In July, 2000, when Shannon received a new contract as coach at UMD, the *Duluth News Tribune* reported the event as "good news for Minnesota-Duluth women's hockey fans." The same article quoted athletic director Jim Corran's verdict on Shannon: "She had some very high goals right from the start. ...She did everything we asked and more."

When Shannon first took the position as hockey coach at the University of Minnesota-Duluth, she was criticized by some members of the Canadian media for letting down her country's side, so to speak. But Shannon has another perspective. "I'm a very international person," she said emphatically about her decision to take the coaching job at UMD. "As far as I'm concerned, I'm doing something for women, and then secondly, for women's hockey."

As if to confirm the truth of Shannon's words, when the inaugural women's NCAA ice hockey championships were held in late March, 2001, the UMD women were one of the four elite teams competing in the Women's Frozen Four. And on March 25, in front of 3,079 fans at Mariucci Arena in Minneapolis, the Minnesota-Duluth Bulldogs won the championship game 4-2 over St. Lawrence. In only her second year of coaching at Duluth and only the second year of her program, Shannon's ability to recruit top players from all over the world and foster their ability to work as a team had paid very public dividends.

Shannon's players acknowledged their coach's part in their victory by drenching her with the traditional bucket of water. Two of her players carried their coach on their shoulders around the ice in a kind of victory lap. "Obviously, I'm very proud of what we accomplished," a happy Shannon told a reporter. Clearly, her accomplishment had gone far beyond winning a hockey game. As the coach of the first-ever women's ice hockey NCAA championship team, she had done her part to bring a fairly new women's sport into the media and public spotlight.

"It's been a long journey," Shannon told a female sports-writer after the championship game. Other prominent women coaches might well have said the same. Across the country, women coaches like Shannon Miller, Jody Conradt and Tara VanDerveer will continue to work for excellence in their sports, and continue to live with the media and public attention created by their coaching successes.

Fighting for Equity

Just before 8 a.m., University of Minnesota head volleyball coach Stephanie Schleuder waited in her office. She had a knot in her gut, a bad feeling about what might happen on this chilly December morning in 1994. Yesterday she and the women's basketball coach, Linda Hill-MacDonald, had received phone messages from the secretary for the women's athletic director. The coaches were to be in their offices for meetings with the women's AD at 8:00 and 8:30 respectively.

Stephanie had called her attorney, Tim Stoner, after she received the message. "I think I'm gonna get fired," she told him.

"There's no way they can fire you, Steph," he reassured her. Perhaps he was thinking of her many years at the university and her many winning seasons.

Stephanie wasn't so sure. "I don't know," she told Tim. "I don't feel good about this."

There were solid reasons for Stephanie's uneasiness. The contract proposal she had submitted back in June, along with a similar proposal by the women's basketball coach, asked for equity in terms of her pay and other areas. Essentially what she was asking for was that her compensation be similar to that of coaches of comparable men's sports. It was a contract proposal supported both by Title IX and by the Minnesota Pay Equity Act, but that had received a far from positive response within the athletic department.

Stephanie Schleuder wouldn't forget what happened next on that December morning. At the scheduled time, Chris Voelz, women's athletic director, arrived along with another adminis-

Stephanie Schleuder

trator, the Vice President for Human Resources. The two administrators sat down on a couch and Stephanie sat facing them on the chair she pulled out from behind her desk. But there was no need for anyone to get too comfortable. The meeting was short although not very sweet.

"We've decided not to renew your contract," Chris bluntly told Stephanie. Chris handed Stephanie an official letter, which she was told had the approval of the university president. Stephanie opened the letter, scanned a line or two. "Do you have any questions?" Chris asked her.

No, she didn't, Stephanie replied. She was too much in shock to say anything more at the moment. "Devastated" was the main thing she felt.

After the two administrators left, Stephanie walked quickly over to the office of her colleague, head women's basketball coach, Linda Hill-MacDonald. "I just got fired," Steph told Linda.

"The same thing's gonna happen to me, I bet," Linda replied. A while later though, Linda called Stephanie at home. As it turned out, instead of being fired, Linda had been taken to the president's office and offered a contract with a substantial salary increase. It was the kind of olive branch that was never extended to Stephanie Schleuder. For her, the battle for equity would continue.

The personal price for that battle would be high. A nationally known and highly successful coach for 13 years at the University of Minnesota and the recipient of numerous coaching honors, Stephanie Schleuder wouldn't coach again for two and a half years.

———

By waging her personal battle with the University of Minnesota, Stephanie Schleuder had joined a group of women coaches so far unrecognized by any sports hall of fame—the many women coaches who have fought for equitable treatment for themselves and for their athletes. In Stephanie's case, the roots of what motivated her personal fight for equity began years before that December morning when she lost her job.

Perhaps fittingly enough, she graduated from college in 1972, the same year Title IX became law. As a pre-Title IX female athlete at the University of Minnesota-Duluth, although she competed in five sports, including volleyball, she and other young women, like many other female athletes at the time, received anything but equitable treatment. They had coaches who were either unpaid or paid very little. Athletes drove their own cars to games, received no meal money, often bought their own uniforms. Coaches fought as best they could to improve conditions. For Stephanie, the women coaches she had, and their vision about the future for women's sports, helped inspire her own decision to go into coaching.

After brief coaching stints at Bemidji State University and the University of Minnesota-Duluth, Stephanie was hired by the University of Alabama as their head women's volleyball coach. At the end of nine seasons there, during which she received various coach of the year awards, in January, 1981, Stephanie accepted the position as head volleyball coach at the

University of Minnesota, a job that offered an opportunity to return home for the Twin Cities native.

There was one catch, however. Just after Stephanie accepted the job, she heard the rumor that a woman's sport was going to be cut at the University of Alabama. This was during the Bear Bryant era at Alabama when football was king, but a women's sport was to go on the chopping block in the interest of saving money. "If there is any chance they're going to cut volleyball if I leave," Stephanie told the women's athletic director, "I'm not leaving." Not to worry was the basic reply. Volleyball after all had been the most successful of the women's sports there, competing in three national championships. Then on March 1st, the signing date for recruits, the women's athletic director called Stephanie into her office. "Steph, we're cutting volleyball," the athletic director told her.

Stephanie was first incredulous, then outraged. "I can't believe this! How can you do this?" she asked. She was deeply angry about the promises broken to young women recruited for the volleyball program, and to her current players who were attending the university on athletic scholarships.

Anger moved Stephanie to action. "I went on a rampage," she recalled, "and I wrote a letter and sent it to every large school in the country saying what they had done and how disgusting it was and all the promises they'd broken." She tried to talk with the university president, but he refused to see her. When she was told she couldn't mail out letters without prior approval, she used the telephone instead, calling lawyers for her players and numerous others, until she was asked to leave her office. It was a good thing she had a job, the associate athletic director told her bluntly, because if she didn't she would never get another one.

"I left there very bitter about what had happened," Stephanie commented. Her efforts had resulted in the university agreeing to extend athletic scholarships for her current players for one additional year only, not even until all the young women had graduated. But nothing could save the women's volleyball program Steph had worked so hard to build.

During Stephanie Schleuder's 13 seasons at the University of Minnesota, she once more built a top-flight women's volleyball program. Her 561 wins at both Minnesota and Alabama made her the eighth most successful Division I volleyball coach nationwide. At Minnesota, she brought her team to its first-ever NCAA tournament in 1989 and took her team to the NCAA Sweet Sixteen in 1993. Along with wins on court, her Minnesota athletes won academically as well, graduating at a 95 percent rate. Stephanie wrote articles, held leadership positions in the NCAA and in volleyball organizations, received awards for her coaching, and was well known as a successful coach among volleyball professionals across the country.

Asked once by a reporter about the secret of her coaching success, Steph offered a humorous response: "I've been around a long time." But during that time, she put in long hours as a coach who cared tremendously about her athletes' success, on and off the court. "It's important that people are your first priority," she told the same reporter. A key part of her coaching philosophy, she wrote in a handout for the USA Volleyball coaches program, is to "assist student-athletes in their personal growth and development toward mature, self-sufficient, independent thinking adults."

Stephanie cared about justice for women in sports as well. And that concern for basic fairness extended to the treatment received by women college coaches such as herself. At the University of Minnesota, she discovered, she had more experience than any other head coach, yet she was paid less than most of the male assistant coaches, regardless of their experience. Over the past ten years while Steph's salary had increased by about 70 percent, coaches of major men's sports at the University of Minnesota had received salary increases of from 150 to 200 percent. After 11 years at Minnesota as the head volleyball coach, Stephanie's annual salary of $42,000 contrasted sharply to the football coach's annual base salary of $250,000.

The inequities didn't end with salaries. Male coaches kept the money they received for shoe company contracts for their athletes, but coaches of women's sports had to put that money back into the general athletic budget. The amount of money women's coaches could earn for working in summer camps was strictly limited, while male coaches could make about $30,000–

$50,000 over a summer. While Stephanie had been hired on a series of three-year contracts, coaches of men's major sports received five-year contracts, an extra measure of job security that could also help with recruiting.

In response to those kind of glaring inequities, Stephanie Schleuder and Linda Hill-MacDonald, the women's basketball coach, decided to take some action. At the time, Linda was earning a far lower salary than the men's basketball coach. The two women "tried, at great length," to have a discussion about their compensation with the women's athletic director, Chris Voelz. Finally, when it was clear that the athletic department would not respond to their concerns, Steph and Linda filed a formal complaint with the university's equal opportunity office. Six months later, the EEO recommended that both Stephanie and Linda receive substantial raises. However, the University of Minnesota did not follow that recommendation, and neither of the two women's salaries were increased.

In fact, money was never all of what Stephanie's fight was about. Her strong personal belief in the gender equity mandate of Title IX is evident in the clearly written and solidly researched contract proposal she presented to the university in June, 1993. Her proposal, she wrote, sought "to remedy the gender inequity of her salary in the same way that female athletes have sought equity in participation opportunities."

In support, she explained why volleyball should be considered a major sport for women; provided a comparison of men's and women's coaching salaries at the university; and explained how Title IX, The Federal Pay Equity Act, and the Minnesota Pay Equity Act gave a legal foundation for her claim. "Presently, the University of Minnesota discriminates against people who coach women's sports," Stephanie argued. She offered a plan for her salary and benefits to be increased over a five-year period. "This is a proposal of entitlement, not merit," she stated.

Faced with athletic department inaction, Stephanie and Linda changed their strategy. They decided to approach the Minnesota state legislature, since the legislature was a major source of funding for the university. A friend with connections there lined up some appointments, and one of Stephanie's former players at Bemidji State

University, now a state legislator, helped the two women as well. The result of all that lobbying was an amendment added to the Higher Education Finance Bill, directing the University of Minnesota to report to the legislature on pay equity for women coaches.

The apparent victory of that legislative directive didn't last long. "The battle over pay equity for coaches of women's sports teams escalated," the *Saint Paul Pioneer Press* reported in August, 1994, " when University of Minnesota women's athletic director Chris Voelz announced that the university has suspended contract negotiations with basketball coach Linda Hill-MacDonald and volleyball coach Stephanie Schleuder." On the university's part, the logical next step was not long in coming. In December, 1994, only two days after her volleyball season ended, Stephanie had her fateful meeting with Chris Voelz, the women's athletic director. The official version of what happened there was that Stephanie Schleuder's contract was not renewed. But clearly that was an institutional euphemism for an obvious fact. Stephanie Schleuder had just been fired.

Not surprisingly, the event didn't escape the attention of the local media. "It was very public," Stephanie recalled. "I woke up the morning after I got fired and the headline's about two inches high over the sports page. Schleuder fired."

The local media were well aware of Stephanie's coaching successes. In the previous year, her team had reached the Sweet 16 of the NCAA tournament, and in the current year, they had gone to the NIT tournament. With that kind of success behind her, combined with her friendly, easy-to-talk-with personality, it was also not surprising that the media coverage was overwhelmingly supportive of Stephanie.

"Voelz denied any connections to Schleuder's two-year push for pay equity," reported the Twin Cities' *Star Tribune* on December 10. The article included Stephanie's own statement: "I feel it's a fairly clear case of retaliation for the pay-equity battle."

"Is this what they call gender equity?" questioned Jim Caple from the Saint Paul *Pioneer Press*. Caple reported Chris Voelz's denial that the pay equity dispute was involved in Stephanie Schleuder's firing, but questioned why such a successful coach was let go.

"Voelz's firing of 'U' volleyball coach is vicious, uncalled for" read a *Star Tribune* headline on December 11. The media fallout continued. A December 14 *Star Tribune* article reported another public figure weighing in on the case. According to Minnesota Governor Arne Carlson, "I think it's a tragedy to lose a good volleyball coach. I hope the university would rethink its position." The *Pioneer Press* printed a letter from 22 of Stephanie's current and former players, who expressed their anger and concern. The American Volleyball Coaches Association, the *Star Tribune* reported, had asked for a "full investigation" and "immediate reconsideration" of Stephanie's firing.

Stephanie appreciated all the support—from the media, from her players, from other coaches, and from her network of friends. But losing her job still hurt. "My whole identity was tied up with who I was," she described. "I was the coach at the University of Minnesota." And now suddenly she wasn't.

As the shock wore off and anger took over instead, Steph was ready to fight for her job. She would file a lawsuit against the university, she decided, a legal battle she undertook and persevered with, in spite of the discouraging advice given her by a number of people. "Everyone kept saying, 'Title IX does not address coaches' compensation,'" Steph recalled. "Yes, I believe it does," was her own feeling.

At the time, however, there was good reason for many people's skepticism. They may have been thinking of the lawsuit filed by prominent basketball coach Marianne Stanley, formerly the head coach at the University of Southern California. In 1992, when her new contract was being negotiated, Marianne requested that the school increase her pay, which was far lower than that of the men's basketball coach, George Raveling. Since her job and the men's basketball coach's job, she argued, were essentially the same, he and she should be paid the same. But USC, her employer, did not agree, and Marianne refused to sign the contract they offered. Instead, on August 5, 1993, she filed a lawsuit against the University of Southern California, claiming "sex discrimination and retaliatory discharge." Unfortunately, the courts did not find in Marianne's favor, ruling that the unequal pay did not prove that Marianne Stanley was the victim of gender-based discrimination. Instead, the courts accepted the university's argument that the men's and women's basketball coaches' jobs were dissimilar enough to justify unequal salaries.

Neither the discouraging legal outlook nor the advice she received that she give up on a seemingly hopeless fight, however, were enough to deter Stephanie Schleuder. Instead, in the first round of what would prove to be a protracted battle, she and her lawyers went to court to get an injunction to prevent the University of Minnesota from hiring another volleyball coach until the discrimination claim had been settled. When the judge granted a temporary injunction, the stage was set for a hearing in January, 1995.

The Minneapolis courtroom was full for the hearing, with numerous reporters present. By then stories about the court battle were appearing on the front page of Twin Cities newspapers almost every day. The American Volleyball Coaching Association was involved in the fight as well, with Sandy Vivas, then Executive Director of the organization, testifying on behalf of Stephanie. In her view, Sandy explained later, Stephanie was "one of the well respected coaches in the country. "

After a weeklong hearing, the judge ordered mediation. By then, Stephanie's legal fees approached two hundred thousand dollars—a significant sum for someone who wasn't earning the large salary of the University of Minnesota football coach—and the university, with its large amount of financial resources, seemed determined to continue the legal battle. Facing that dauntingly high hurdle, Stephanie at first agreed to settle with the university. But at home that night, she lay awake thinking and rethinking her course of action. In the end, she couldn't take the easiest course and settle. She had fought so hard already that she couldn't give up. She would at least wait to receive the judge's verdict.

In February, 1995, when District Court Judge Robert Schiefelbein's decision was announced, it was a clear victory for Stephanie and her lawyers. The judge granted a permanent injunction, preventing the university from hiring a replacement coach for Stephanie. The judge ruled that although he could not definitely conclude that Stephanie Schleuder had been the victim of sexual discrimination, he did believe that she had been the victim of reprisal for her gender equity battle. The University of Minnesota, the judge also ruled, couldn't hire a replacement for Stephanie until the Minnesota Human Rights Department had investigated her claims of discrimination and reprisal.

"I'm so thrilled. I feel like justice has been done," Stephanie told reporters. Victory was sweet but the battle had been far from easy. "There's been a lot of pressure. There's been a lot of doubts in my mind whether I was doing the right thing," Steph added. "Everyone told me I didn't have a chance."

But her fight was still far from over. The University of Minnesota chose to appeal, and in late March and early April, Stephanie and her lawyers once more went into mediation to try to resolve issues with the university. By then it seemed clear that this was a legal battle that could potentially go on for years. Emotionally drained by the long struggle, Steph finally agreed to settle. As the *Star Tribune* reported on April 7, 1995, the University of Minnesota would "not admit to any wrongdoing," and would be free to hire a new coach. Stephanie would receive $300,000 and give up all claims against the university. But Stephanie had most definitely not, the *Star Tribune* article made clear, given up on her strong personal belief in gender equity, the belief that had motivated her long personal battle. "I think the principles were worth the fight," she told reporters. "I still believe in the principles of pay equity, and that will never change. Somebody else will carry on things from here."

Under the terms of the settlement, Stephanie herself couldn't speak about the rights and wrongs of her case. But her supporters were not similarly compelled to silence. "Stephanie Schleuder was right all along. There is a big-time double standard at the University of Minnesota," *Star Tribune* columnist Doug Grow wrote in support of Stephanie, referring to the significant pay differential for coaches of men's and women's teams.

"It is truly a disappointing day if a successful, long-standing member of the volleyball community is relieved of coaching duties for bringing attention to a decided lack of pay equity," stated the American Volleyball Coaching Association during Stephanie Schleuder's legal battle. "Though the University of

Minnesota administration claims that Schleuder's termination was the result of poor performance and not in retaliation for her position on equal pay, to the AVCA Board it appears there is contrary evidence."

In December, 1995, the University of Minnesota finally hired a new volleyball coach, Mike Hebert, from the University of Illinois. The salary he received, over $86,000, was more than the salary increase Stephanie had requested, and substantially more than the $50,000 she had received in her last season at the university. "We always pay for quality," Chris Voelz, the women's athletic director who fired Stephanie, was quoted as saying. The irony of that statement wasn't lost on Stephanie, nor was the fact that the new coach who ended up benefitting from her gender equity fight was a man rather than a woman. Although Stephanie knew that Mike Hebert was a well-qualified coach, she still found his hiring very disappointing. "You like to think," she commented, "that a battle like that will end up helping another woman."

After her busy years as a head coach, and after her long legal battle and the storm of publicity, Stephanie Schleuder was left facing an unaccustomed life situation. Like Marianne Stanley, who couldn't obtain another coaching position for several years after her unsuccessful lawsuit, Stephanie was now an unemployed coach with plenty of time on her hands. Enough time to think back on her personal battle for what she felt was right. Time to ponder where her personal future might lie, a future clouded by uncertainty. She briefly considered a new career in business, but found it hard to picture herself sitting in an office. Working mostly out of her home, she wrote a book on volleyball statistics. Even with her network of supportive friends, she felt isolated in a way she'd never experienced during her busy life as a coach. She missed the daily contact with her players, her colleagues, the college atmosphere.

In 1996, she applied for a coaching job at Carlton College, which competed in Division III. "Why wouldn't they hire me?" she thought when applying. She had been, after all, a quite successful Division I coach. But although she was one of the finalists, and very likely the most experienced candidate, she didn't get the job. "I may never coach again," she thought at the time.

She didn't apply for any other coaching jobs for another year. Then in 1998, she interviewed for a job at Macalester College, a small, private college that like Carlton competed in Division III. At her interview for the Macalester position, she was open with the hiring committee, offering to answer any questions they might have about what had happened between her and the University of Minnesota. " I understand that you might be concerned about somebody that would sue their university," she told them.

Steph was warmed by the committee's response. "We agree with everything that you did," the Macalester people told her. Although Stephanie wasn't sure what coaching at a Division III college would be like, she definitely wanted to coach again. When Macalester offered her the job, it was a no brainer for her to accept it.

It seems like a kind of justice that Stephanie Schleuder's story ended happily. At Macalester College, Stephanie has found that although she is no longer working with elite athletes, her players are bright, enthusiastic young women who are curious about the struggle she went through and who compete in college volleyball not for athletic scholarships but simply because they want to play. She appreciates the diversity of students on campus and on her team, as well as the liberal and politically involved atmosphere on campus, where "students protest anything and everything" and college employees are free to voice opinions as well. And although salaries for coaches are not high at Macalester, they are equitable. "None of us are paid a lot," was how Steph put it, "but we're all in the same boat."

Stephanie maintains her strong personal concern for equity. Her recent commentary, published in the *Star Tribune*, was titled "Beware the latest attempt to subvert Title IX." The article described attacks on Title IX from coaches of men's collegiate non-revenue sports such as wrestling, who claim that money given to women's sports is damaging some men's sports. In her article, Steph pointed out the weakness of such thinking, explaining how hugely expensive men's sports like football take a disproportionate share of revenue. "I urge individuals to look carefully at this issue," Stephanie concluded, "rather than respond to the false and misleading rhetoric of groups looking to dismantle Title IX."

Stephanie's professional peers know that she worked towards turning the principles of Title IX into reality, and numerous coaches have called her to ask for her advice with their own equity battles. "I think Steph stepped up and took it for a lot people who followed her," said Sandy Vivas. "She has certainly been a resource for everybody else."

Although her battle for equity was long and personally taxing, Stephanie doesn't regret her decision to fight. It's now a standard legal concept that Title IX covers not only athletes but coaches' compensation as well, Steph explained. Her own personal fight, Stephanie Schleuder knows, helped make that progress possible.

In theory, inequities between male and female sports at educational institutions should no longer exist. Within the realm of intercollegiate athletics, Title IX requires colleges to offer equal levels of financial assistance to male and female athletes, and to offer sports opportunities that reflect the numbers of male vs. female students. Additionally, colleges must offer equivalent amounts of financial support for their athletic programs, including money for equipment, publicity, and recruiting, and for levels of pay that provide student-athletes with a sufficient number and quality of coaches.

In fact, at universities such as Stanford, the University of Texas and Tennessee, women's sports programs receive generous funding and women coaches are well paid. In some other academic institutions, although sports budgets are well below the level of top programs, the money available for male and female sports programs and male and female coaches is in general equitable. In numerous other colleges and universities, however, the picture looks less bright. And across the board, women college coaches, as well as male coaches of women's teams, have still not achieved parity with the almost exclusively male coaches who coach men's teams.

Even though women's basketball coaches tend to be the highest paid coaches in women's sports, according to the 1999 survey done by the Women's Basketball Coaches Association, a difference of approximately $30,000 exists between the salaries of coaches of men's teams vs. women's teams, a salary difference that has remained essentially constant since 1994, and other benefits remain higher for men's team coaches as well, as does financial support for men's teams. This type of situation is not limited to women's basketball. As a winter, 2000 article in the *American Business Law Journal* described, "when gender-based wage discrimination in the United States intersects with discrimination in sport, the consequence is a stubborn and significant wage gap for females who coach women's teams." The author cited the NCAA's Gender Equity Study, which revealed that at Division I Colleges, "men's sports receive 60 percent of the head coaches' salaries and 76 percent of the assistant coaches' salaries." In general, the author reported, coaches of women's teams receive only 59 percent of the salary and 25 percent of other benefits as compared to coaches of men's teams. Similarly, the *Chronicle of Higher Education*, stated that nationwide at the Division I level, "universities continue to spend nearly twice as much on salaries for coaches of men's teams as on salaries of women's coaches."

Stephanie Schleuder's story is far from unique. Women coaches across the country have fought for more equitable salaries, budgets, practice times and facilities, and for the myriad other areas which legally should be equal for male and female collegiate athletes. In courts of law, numerous women coaches from colleges across the country have filed and often won lawsuits regarding equal pay and cases of unlawful termination or retaliation. Yet more than a quarter of a century since the passage of Title IX, the battles for equity continue. Advocates of women's collegiate sport must deal with mostly male-controlled athletic departments—in 2000 only 27 women were head athletic directors in Division I—that are not always sympathetic to women's sports and that have a poorer record of hiring women coaches than athletic departments headed by a woman athletic director. Storms of controversy still rage about whether money for women's sports will threaten men's college sports. In these ongoing struggles within collegiate sports, women coaches are at the center of the storm.

———◆———

Soccer coach Joann Wolf has survived her share of difficult weather. With the numbers of college women's soccer programs expanding at a rapid rate, coaching opportunities have opened up for women as well as men in the field. But the pay for coaches of women's soccer teams is typically low, and the support for women's soccer programs can be much less than for football, men's basketball, or even women's basketball. Joann's personal story, and the battles she's fought, reflect those realities.

A St. Louis native, 36-year-old Joann Wolf began playing soccer in seventh grade. After competing in soccer at St. Louis Junior College and Tarkio College, and graduating from Tarkio in 1987, she was taking the slow track to career success by becoming, as she put it, "a ski bum" in Colorado when she was offered a position in coaching at Tarkio. The first coaching clinic Joann attended, in Oshkosh, Wisconsin, during the summer of 1988, opened her eyes to one aspect of soccer coaching: the field is dominated by male coaches. Out of 150 coaches at the clinic, she was one of a grand total of three women there, a lopsided ratio that at times Joann found "very intimidating." Out on the soccer field, with the sun blazing down and the humidity high, wearing her trademark towel turban as a makeshift hat, Joann had to cope with nonmeteorological difficulties as well. The male coaches didn't verbally express their skepticism that a woman could play, but Joann could feel those vibes coming from many of the men. Often they wouldn't pass the soccer ball to her, effectively shutting her out of play.

Joann refused to stay in a soccer wallflower role. "I'm wide open all the time. Why aren't you passing the ball?" Joann asked one well-muscled man she described humorously as a "typical soccer stud dude." The dude mumbled excuses but Joann wasn't having any. "Just pass me the ball," she told him firmly. By the

Joann Wolf

end of the clinic, Joann's stock had climbed with her mostly male fellow coaches, who respected her for her soccer abilities.

At Joann's second coaching position, at Drury College in Springfield, Missouri, she started out part time but soon became a full-time coach, very full time in fact. Her job included coaching men's and women's tennis, a sport she had little experience with, as well as women's soccer. Since she only made $18,000 a year, she later added the job of concessions manager to bring in a little extra money. She juggled all those work demands, in addition to taking graduate courses, until in the spring of '94 she was told her contract was not being renewed.

"What's the problem?" she asked the athletic director. "Why am I not being renewed?"

"It's just not the direction we want to go," was the inadequate explanation he offered. Looking back on the situation, Joann could see another more telling reason. Around the time when she was let go, she was, "starting to be a little more vocal," telling the athletic director, for example, that the "tennis players need a real tennis coach," and encouraging the players to protest as well. So it was probably not accidental that Joann got her personal lesson number one about the way lack of job security can affect a coach. Many women in college coaching, Vivian Acosta explained, only receive one-year contracts, and with such minimal protection, "if you make any kind of waves or if you just don't get along with the athletic director, ...you can just kiss your job goodbye."

"I felt very used. I was angry. I was blown away, because I put my life and everything into that program," Joann remembered feeling. These were emotions she would experience again in the not very distant future.

In the spring of '95, Joann was offered a job at New Mexico Highlands University. As at both Tarkio and Drury, she would be starting up a women's soccer program. And once more, there was a catch. In addition to coaching soccer, she would also be expected to serve as an assistant basketball coach. Joann decided to take the job at New Mexico Highlands anyway, in part because she liked Rob Evers, the athletic director there. He was a "forward thinking" man, she described, who was adding women's soccer because he believed in adhering to the gender equity requirements of Title IX.

Joann made the move from her hometown of St. Louis to Las Vegas, New Mexico, and immersed herself in recruiting. For a while things went well. Joann was pleased and relieved when Rob Evers, the supportive athletic director, agreed that she could give up her secondary position as assistant basketball coach. She had an adequate budget for travel and recruiting, and the school had promised that a soccer field would soon be made ready for her team.

But at the end of June, 1996, after she'd been working at New Mexico Highlands for a little over a year, Joann learned that Rob Evers had been forced to resign. At a school where football was king, he'd committed the cardinal sin of forcing the football program to stay within its budget. Then in mid July, while she was away doing a soccer camp, Joann received a call from the senior women's administrator. Joann should return to campus right away. She needed to check out what was happening with her new soccer field.

Two days later, Joann was back on campus, eyeballing her field and in the process receiving a personal lesson about inequity in college sports. After the field was leveled, new topsoil and then grass should have covered the leveled area. Instead, the area had been covered with the cheapest material available, red New Mexico clay, that had killed the grass and left a surface which could become dangerously slick. "This is not acceptable. I am not putting my players on this," Joann protested. The assistant athletic director finally agreed to make changes on her field. In the meantime, Joann's players were forced to practice in a park area between buildings, a "very embarrassing" turn of events that Joann knew could undermine her credibility as a coach.

But women's soccer was far from a priority at the university. Joe Singleton, the new athletic director, was a New Mexico Highlands graduate, a former football player at the college who had also coached football in Las Vegas. "They wanted him to get football back to its prominency," at the college, Joann recalled. What that meant, Joann would shortly find out, was that other sports, particularly low-status women's sports like soccer, would have to give up any claims to equal treatment.

Joann and her players were finally using their new soccer field. But the football program, which didn't want to damage their own field during practices, wanted the soccer field for use as a football practice field. When the athletic department asked Joann to give up her new field, and even to play her home games off campus. Joann refused to back down. "I'm not moving off campus," she said emphatically. "We put a lot of work into this field."

"Why don't you practice on the outfield of the baseball field?" the athletic director suggested. Joann continued to stand up for her program. "That is not acceptable," she said.

The negative fallout wasn't long in coming. "Your coach is just a bitch," Joann's soccer players heard from football players, who echoed the sentiments of their coach. It was the women's soccer coach that was the problem, not the demands of the football program.

In still another reflection of soccer's low status, the new scoreboard for soccer and softball sat in the hallway of Joann's office for months, a situation that Joann found extremely frustrating. But when she spoke about the scoreboard to the director of alumni, the negative repercussions weren't long in coming. Instead of putting up the scoreboard, the athletic director came to a practice and chewed Joann out right in front of her players. He would "put it up when he's damn well ready," he yelled at her.

In fact, the scoreboard was never put up. Instead, the overall situation went from bad to worse. For daring to defend her players and her program, Joann was accused of not being a team player, which often has meant someone who doesn't want to go along with the status quo of low support for women's sports. Joann was faulted for spending too much money on recruiting at the same time the football program was recruiting large numbers of more expensive out-of-state players.

On December 11, 1996, Joann had an unforgettable meeting with the athletic director. "You've been on my mind," he told Joann with a scowl. He held up her contract. "We're just having a problem here with the field thing. And you seem to just keep bucking me." Joann tried to get her breath, tried to get a word in edgewise. But the athletic director continued lecturing her. "When I was brought in here, I was given the power," he told her, speaking slowly and spitting out each word. "The power to murder a career."

Looking at the athletic director, Joann felt afraid. "I'm going to get fired now, and I'll never coach again," Joann thought. If she didn't want that to happen, she needed to give a little ground. "Well I think we can work things out," she told the athletic director. Afterward Joann felt unsure what her next course of action should be. She should speak with a lawyer or with the Office of Civil Rights, the baseball coach advised her. Joann felt torn, wanting both to fight and to keep her job.

The inequities continued, such as the embarrassingly bad media guides the women's soccer program finally received. Whereas the football media guide was about 60 pages long and printed on high gloss paper, the women's soccer media guide, Joann recalled, had "like construction paper on the outside," and photocopied pages within. Since such an unprofessional looking guide would undermine her efforts to get media coverage and recruits for her team, Joann went to the athletic director to protest, bringing along an article from the *NCAA News* which pointed out that under Title IX, media guides for men's and women's teams needed to be of equivalent quality. The athletic director threw the article back at her, describing it as "written by a bunch of wild feminists."

In meeting after meeting with the athletic director, Joann continued to stand up for her program. She also met with two men who coached women's softball and volleyball respectively, Galen Paton and Peter Cosmiano, both of whom were supportive of her and who also had difficulties with the athletic director. In the spring of 1997, the three coaches wrote out their concerns and met with the senior women's administrator. Shortly afterward, on April 15, 1997, both Joann and Galen were sent the coaching equivalent of Dear John letters. "We are not renewing your contract," Galen's letter read simply. No reasons were given. The letter Joann received delivered much the same news in an unintentionally humorous fashion. Her contract would be extended seven months only, until November 31, a nonexistent date in which Joann could find a little badly needed comedy. "Oh, so it's an infinity," she said about the date when her job would end.

A week later, when Joann met one-on-one with the athletic director, she had to argue with him about his low ratings of her coaching performance. While before she'd never been rated lower than 4 on a scale of 1 to 5, the New Mexico Highlands athletic director was giving her 2's and 3's, scores that would go onto her permanent employment record. After he finally did raise her scores a little, she signed the evaluation, but only under protest. "It's a shame that these scores reflect the out-of-office problems that we are having," she wrote.

By now Joann, Galen and Peter Cosmiano, who was fired in August, had hired a lawyer who specialized in equity litigation based on Title IX. Joann had also received a coaching job offer from another university, but although the new job tempted her, she didn't want to leave the players she had recruited or run away from a situation she knew was unjust. "Part of me wanted to get the heck out of there," Joann remembered, "but part of me wanted to fight."

On October 21, the three coaches' lawsuit was filed. Then in early November, Joann received a phone call from a man in personnel, asking to see her ASAP. Before the meeting, Joann called her lawyer, Kristen Galles, warning the lawyer that she thought she was going to be fired. "They wouldn't do that. They wouldn't be so stupid," Kristen told Joann. But that in fact was what had happened, Joann told her lawyer after the meeting. "You've got to be kidding me," Kristen Galles replied. The firing simply meant more legal ammunition, and the lawsuit would now include a claim of retaliation.

Even with the support of her lawyer and her own determination to fight, it was a far from easy time for Joann. "I've never been so low in my life," she recalled. She'd lost a job she deeply cared about. That October she'd received a serious knee injury, tearing her anterior cruciate ligament while working with her athletes on the athletic field she'd told the college was dangerous for her players. By Christmas, she'd moved out of her house and returned home to St. Louis as an unemployed coach. But even through the low times, Joann wasn't willing to give up her fight for justice. "I have to stick with what I'm doing is right. Screw this, they can't get away with it," she thought.

Like Stephanie Schleuder, Joann didn't obtain another coaching job for a long time, 15 months in her case. In the summer of '98 she received an interview with the University of Nebraska, was considered a finalist for the position, but in the end didn't get it. After her situation at New Mexico Highlands University, Joann thought, she'd never get a college coaching job again.

While Joann began working for the certification that would allow her to coach at the high school level, the legal wheels ground slowly on. Finally, in November, 1999, Joann Wolf, Galen Paton, and Peter Cosmiano went to court for their lawsuit in Albuquerque, New Mexico. The lawsuit claimed that New Mexico Highlands University was guilty of discrimination against female athletes and retaliation against the three coaches. At the end of the three-week trial, there was a positive verdict: the university was found guilty on all counts of both discrimination against female athletes and retaliation against the three coaches. The injustices were now a matter of public record. But in spite of the guilty verdict, Joann Wolf and Galen Paton were each only given one year's salary, while former coach Peter Cosmiano received no money, an end result that Joann found disappointing. "I wasn't expecting the lottery," she recalled, "but I was expecting at least two year's pay," the amount of money she'd actually lost.

Joann Wolf finally did obtain another college coaching position. On March 15, 1999, shortly before her lawsuit had been resolved, she signed a contract with Northwest Missouri State University in Maryville, Missouri, where once again she would start a new soccer program. Coaching at Northwest Missouri was a vast improvement over New Mexico Highlands University, and yet Joann was faced with some similar concerns. In her first year, her soccer team had to play on the practice football field. Because of budgetary constraints, she could only hire a graduate assistant to be her assistant coach. And like many other coaches of women's sports, she received only a 10-month renewable contract. Still drained by all of what she went through at New Mexico Highlands University, Joann didn't want to fight any more battles. Yet she felt she had to speak up to the athletic director at Northwest Missouri about the low salaries paid women coaches.

"I don't want to sound like a constant bellyacher," was Joann's self-assessment, "but it's always beating your head against the wall to get anything." In fact, she comes across as still very much a fighter, a strong, determined woman. By the fall of 2001, Joann had purchased a home and was hanging in there with her job at Northwest Missouri State University. Like many other women college coaches, she would continue working in the field she loved and fighting for what she believed was right.

Other Battles

Brown University has a special place in the battle for equity in sports. The 1992 Title IX lawsuit against Brown, based on the unequal access men and women students had to varsity sports opportunities, was the first such Title IX lawsuit to be reviewed in an appeals court. The resulting series of favorable court decisions—favorable for supporters of women's athletics, that is—set an important legal precedent, helping to support other Title IX battles in schools across the country.

Brown University women's ice hockey coach Digit Murphy wasn't involved in the original lawsuit. That was filed on behalf of two women's teams, gymnastics and volleyball, that had been cut as varsity teams in May, 1991. Brown University argued that its male students had a higher level of interest in sports than female students, and therefore Brown should be able to maintain men's athletic programs at a higher level than female athletic programs. But throughout much of the '90s, as Brown continued to lose in court and continued to appeal, the legal battle broadened and many Brown University coaches became involved in some fashion. One of those was Digit Murphy. With her outspoken style as an advocate for women's athletics, she was soon in the thick of the action.

In the fall of 2000, Digit Murphy, whose full first two names are Margaret Degidio, was 38 years old and the senior women's hockey coach among Ivy League and Eastern College Athletic Conference (ECAC) schools. A former star hockey player at Cornell University, for many of her 12 years at Brown University, like many other coaches of women's teams there, Digit had not felt adequately supported or equitably treated.

There wasn't anything especially subtle about the inequities Digit encountered. With men's vs. women's hockey at Brown, the differential treatment of the two teams was of the can't-miss-it variety. For practice times, for example, the men's hockey team received the most desirable time slot, from 3 to 6 p.m., and the women were allotted the later practice time, from 6 to 9 p.m.. In terms of promotion, the men's team had a glossy full-size media guide while the women's team only had a one page team description. The men had glossy game programs listing team rosters; the women had no game programs at all. And after games, the women's team had to shower along with the visiting team, since the women's locker room facilities didn't provide for separate showers.

Salaries was another area of contention. While the men's hockey head coach was able to hire two full-time assistant coaches, Digit only had one part-time assistant, a situation that required her to perform almost all coaching duties by herself. And as head women's hockey coach, Digit received a lower salary than either of the male assistant coaches.

When Digit first started coaching at Brown, she would make polite requests for what she thought she needed. A couple of years later, when her polite requests were not receiving a favorable response, she changed tactics. "I'm not getting anything unless I'm the screechy wheel," she decided. "I stood up for what I believed in and went to battle with them."

We don't have the money to do more for the women's hockey program, Brown administrators would argue, even though money was available to fund the men's hockey program well. Digit didn't accept that answer. "If you had two children, a little boy and a little girl," she argued back, "you wouldn't feed the boy steak and the girl chicken feed."

The question of equity in sports was far from just an abstraction for Digit. At 10 years old, she'd been good at baseball. In sandlot games in her neighborhood, she could hit the ball in grandslam style. But when the neighborhood boys competed in Little League games, Digit wasn't allowed to join them. The fact that she was a fine athlete, better than most of the boys, didn't

Digit Murphy

matter. Digit's gender alone barred her from the chance to compete in a sport she loved.

While growing up in Providence, Digit had always viewed Brown University as a progressive university, including on women's issues. But her experiences as a coach at Brown contradicted that perception. Digit deeply resented the unfair treatment she and her women's hockey team received. "The bee that always stuck in my bonnet was to live in the same environment as a men's team that got everything," she commented. "They were the team; we were the afterthought."

Considering Digit's personal history, it wasn't surprising that she couldn't accept the "afterthought" status. On one occasion she was speaking to her supervisor, a younger man who was new to Brown, in the young man's office. She wanted to have her salary increased, Digit told the administrator. But the young man didn't appear to be hearing her.

Digit felt frustrated that the young man didn't seem to have any understanding of her situation. Frustrated that she had to report to him, rather than speaking directly to the athletic director. She was wasting her time speaking with the young man,

Digit thought. As she sat facing a large picture window in the administrator's office, Digit felt "this overwhelming sense of anger" welling up inside her. Just for a moment, she imagined throwing her chair out the window, and then perhaps throwing the young male administrator out the window afterward. Instead, she stood up and stated simply, "I cannot continue this conversation right now. I need to leave." She had to leave the room, Digit recalled, "because I felt that I'd go postal."

Digit called her physician, concerned about her blood pressure. "I need to come in there ASAP," she said. The physician recommended she see a therapist, a recommendation Digit followed through on because the battles she fought took a heavy toll on her—bringing her to tears, giving her problems sleeping at night. Luckily, in addition to the therapist's help, Digit had solid support from her husband, who understood why she was fighting and what she was going through. She also received support from some of her colleagues, such as from a man who had been a longtime coach of men's and women's track, and from a female physical education professor who became a mentor to Digit.

Digit Murphy would never be described as having a wallflower type personality. She is, according to Harvard ice hockey coach Katey Stone, an "outspoken" person who "can ruffle some feathers." Digit described herself as "a huge rabble rouser and an activist." So when the lawyers representing the plaintiffs in the lawsuit against Brown University contacted Digit, she was happy to talk with them and ready to join their fight. "Good, great, it's about time," she thought. She told the lawyers about how in terms of facilities, ice time scheduling, budgets, etc., women's ice hockey was definitely getting the short end of the stick.

While Brown University had long argued that it was doing what it could for its women's teams, Digit and other coaches of women's teams felt that Brown was not in fact making the "satisfactory progress" mandated by Title IX. In December, 1992, a judge ordered the two dropped women's teams reinstated and prohibited Brown from dropping other women's varsity teams. Brown could simply have complied with the judicial order, but instead for much of the '90s Brown chose to wage a legal battle. In September, 1994, the case once more went to trial.

In November, 1994, a date engraved in Digit Murphy's memory by the fact that she was over seven months pregnant at the time, Digit took the stand as a witness for the plaintiffs. She faced pewlike rows of seats for spectators, that were filled with interested people, some coaches who had already testified, and reporters. Digit wore a black maternity dress and was visibly pregnant.

Digit hadn't ever testified in a court of law before and now was testifying against her employers, so she initially felt somewhat nervous. Yet as one of the lawyers for Brown began to question Digit, part of her began to appreciate her role in the unfolding legal drama. "I run my own show in practice. I'm an entertainer in life. I'm always the one telling stories at the party," she admitted. "So I wasn't intimidated at all... I actually felt it was kind of fun."

Numbers of athletes on teams, that translate to the numbers of men and women who have the opportunity to participate in athletics, are an area covered by Title IX. The lawyer for Brown University asked Digit about her team numbers, trying to make it seem as if the reason she didn't carry enough athletes on her team was a matter of her personal choice rather than the support she received. "The reason I don't have a lot of people on my team is because I don't have the money," Digit responded clearly.

The lawyer for Brown, undeterred, went on asking Digit essentially the same question. "Just keep at her, she'll blow, she's emotional," Digit thought, was the "scouting report on Digit Murphy" the Brown lawyers had received.

Although Digit outwardly kept her cool, the lawyers's repeated questions were getting to her. Rather than blow up at the lawyer, though, Digit found a way to turn the lawyer's repetitive questions to her advantage. While remaining in the witness chair, she turned toward Judge Raymond Pettine. "Excuse me, judge, can I ask you a question?" she asked.

Raymond Pettine, an older Italian man and the father of a number of daughters, readily agreed. "Oh sure, Coach Murphy."

"You see that I'm pregnant, right?" Digit commented to the judge. "Do you think that if this counselor continues this line of questioning, I could have the baby on the stand?" The court room erupted in laughter, and Judge Pettine directed the Brown lawyer to move on in his questioning.

The next morning, the local paper, *The Providence Journal*, headlined Digit's one-liner, describing her as "firing back a slap shot at Brown." "Did you really say that?" Digit's husband asked her. "You're gonna get fired," he told her.

But Digit wouldn't back down from what she had done. "I have to look at myself in the mirror every single morning," she told her husband. She couldn't live with herself if she didn't support women's athletics and the women who played on her team.

The results of the latest stage of the legal battle weren't long in coming. On March 29, 1995, Judge Raymond Pettine ruled against Brown University and in support of women's athletics. Brown University, the judge found, had not complied with Title IX. The court mandated that Brown produce a plan for how it would meet the requirements of Title IX. In response, in April, 1995, the university stated its intention to appeal.

The long legal battle was finally concluded on June 22, 1998. After continuing to lose in court, Brown University signed off on a settlement agreement that required it to maintain all its women's sports teams, and to keep its participation rate in female athletics closely tied to its numbers of female undergraduate students. The university was also required to change women's water polo from a club to a varsity team and to improve funding for water polo and three other women's sports. All in all, years of legal battles had resulted in a clear victory for women's athletics at Brown, and because of the legal precedent established, at many other schools nationwide.

"It was a long road. It was a lot of pain..." Digit commented about the protracted legal battle. Many men's and women's coaches at Brown had been divided by the lawsuit. For Digit's hockey program, however, the benefits have been clear. She now receives far more equitable funding.

"I'm very happy with Brown right now," Digit commented, referring to the positive outcome for her hockey program. During the ECAC tournament held in March, 2000, Brown competed against Dartmouth for the championship. The championship game was held at Brown in an arena was packed with about 3,000 fans. A local cable TV outlet even taped segments of the game. "I never thought I would see that in my life time," Digit commented.

Standing behind the players' bench before the championship game, in the raised coaching box hockey coaches use, Digit looked out at all the people in the stands, at fans giving her a thumbs up for encouragement. She listened to the noise made by all those people and felt a mix of emotions filling her. It had taken a long time to bring women's hockey to this point. And now "All these people ... watching us, cheering us" showed her that "we've finally arrived."

Afterward, when the Brown women had scored a solid win over Dartmouth, carpets were rolled out onto the ice for the awards ceremony. The two teams lined up on their blue lines and Digit and her team captain went up together to receive the championship trophy. She was "a little chilly," Digit recalled, because her players had already marked their victory by dousing their coach with a bucket of ice water. But the ice water shower didn't dampen her own joy in the victory. As she watched her players celebrate their win, she had a clear sense of what that victory meant, of how far she, her team, and women's hockey had come.

Women coaches continue to fight numerous battles and still face many barriers. There's the question of age discrimination, for example, an area of employment discrimination that often hits women harder than men. "I think in general there ... is a tremendous amount of age bias for female coaches," stated Princeton field hockey coach Beth Bozman, a past president of the Field Hockey Coaches' Association. Beth mentioned the case of Temple University coach John Chayney, who was 50 years old when he was hired for his first head coaching job. "They would never hire a woman as a first time head coach at 50,"

Beth commented. "And if they can they're going to hire younger, more vibrant" coaches, a kind of label that reveals a subtle gender bias. "You never hear them talk about vibrant with men," Beth added.

Another factor in age discrimination against women coaches, Linda Carpenter explained, is that "with the experience perhaps comes a perspective that a male athletic director might prefer not having. The older coaches remember the struggles and are probably more sensitive to the presence of discrimination than maybe a young coach might be."

Discrimination is also still a factor in whether women or men coaches are hired and how male or female coaches are recruited. "If they want somebody to coach their men's basketball team," Linda Carpenter described, "they'll find out who the best coach is and ... what it will take to bring them on campus." For a women's team, on the other hand, "they'll say, 'Yeah we'd like to have a woman, but we won't hire somebody if she's not qualified,' and they will lament the fact that they don't get very many résumés, but they won't go out and recruit." Such lack of recruiting, Linda explained, also serves to hold down salaries for women coaches.

In their article entitled "Perceived Causes of the Declining Representation of Women Leaders in Intercollegiate Sports," Vivian Acosta and Linda Carpenter reported that male vs. female collegiate athletic administrators had sharply different explanations for the declining numbers of women coaches. While male administrators typically cited the "lack of qualified female coaches" and scarcity of female job applicants, female administrators mentioned the "old boys club network," the lack of a comparable female network, and the "lack of support systems for females." Looking at the same question in her own article, Mary Jo Kane concluded that the Acosta findings reveal the "direct relationship between the sex of the person being hired and the sex of the person doing the hiring." Similarly, the research of Rosabeth Moss Kanter into corporate hirings, Mary Jo Kane explained, showed that managers typically hire people who are similar to themselves, a finding that "appears to offer explanatory power for the dramatic reduction in the number of women coaches" since the mostly male heads of athletic departments hire fewer women coaches than do female athletic directors.

The women who do obtain positions as head or assistant coaches often still must battle for support for their teams and themselves. However, not all fights deal with tangible items such as money for recruiting or fit under the legal umbrella of Title IX. Some of them might perhaps be better described as skirmishes rather than fullscale battles, moments of resistance by women coaches.

⎯⎯◆⎯⎯

Holly Hatton is an outspoken, 50-year-old woman who has been a coxswain on the U.S. national women's rowing team and is currently the head women's rowing coach at Boston University. At BU, Holly considers her program to be well supported by the university, better supported than the men's program in fact. Since women's rowing teams typically involve substantial numbers of athletes, in recent years the NCAA has been encouraging women's rowing programs as one way to counterbalance the large numbers of male athletes involved in football. Women's rowing is now a growing sport at colleges across the country.

However, when Holly Hatton began coaching women's rowing at Harvard University in 1983, conditions for women in the sport were far more difficult than they are today. In the '80s, Holly commented, the small number of women's collegiate rowing programs received "virtually no money," had to share the men's equipment and typically received "the bottom end of the barrel" overall. They would struggle for a place to row, continually fundraise, stay four or six to a room on road trips, and in general live as the poor relations of the much more well-supported men's rowing programs. "Women were certainly the underlings," Holly commented. "They had to scrape for everything they got."

It's a point of view seconded by Jan Harville, head women's rowing coach at the University of Washington, long a powerhouse of the sport. When Jan herself began rowing, as an undergraduate at Washington from 1970 to 1974, rowing for women was still a club rather than a varsity sport. Women rowers had to purchase their own uniforms, to hold bake sales and car washes, and weren't allowed into male turf: the University of Washington boathouse. Jan was fortunate to begin coaching at Washington in 1980, at a time when both men's and women's rowing at the university were varsity sports and began to receive equitable funding. Conditions were not as rosy, however, Jan recalled, for many other women's rowing programs across the country. "Most women's programs," she described, "had to fight for ... every single little thing."

There was, for example, the memorable protest staged in 1976 by the women rowers at Yale University, who protested their unequal facilities in unforgettable fashion by baring their chests in the athletic director's office, revealing "Title IX" written on the athletes' bodies with blue markers, a gesture of rebellion that was well reported by the media. "Having to strip naked in front of your athletic director to say that we don't have a locker room, we have to sit on the bus and wait for the guys to shower before we can go," Jan Harville commented, was typical of the kinds of battles women rowers had to fight.

Because Harvard University is such a well-funded university, even in the '80s the women's rowing program there was significantly better off than at many other schools. The women did, for example, have their own boathouse right on campus. Yet women's rowing at Harvard was definitely not treated as equal to the men's rowing program. For one thing, Holly Hatton was hired as a part-time coach who often made a poverty-level income. But beyond financial problems, Holly faced the hurdle of negative attitudes toward women coaches and athletes, as well as a lack of support within the Harvard athletic department for coaches and athletes dealing with such attitudes.

It was late spring, in the mid to late '80s, Holly recalled, when she was involved in an unforgettable incident. She was out in her motorized boat, supervising the practice of her rowers, when her boat caused a wake for some of the male Harvard rowers. In response, the male coach for the freshmen men rowers at Harvard used a power megaphone to call Holly the C word—a cunt. Her crew, his crew, and the freshmen men rowers from Northeastern University all heard the male coach's insulting language.

Similar incidents had been previously reported to the athletic department but no action had been taken against the coach. For Holly, however, the situation wasn't one she could tolerate. "I couldn't sleep that night," she remembered. "I couldn't get into the athletic department fast enough to talk about this. I was just absolutely deranged with anger."

Holly expressed her feelings bluntly to the athletic director. "That kind of language is not appropriate to anyone," she said. "But to a co-worker" it was "absolutely unacceptable." It wasn't just the insult to her personally that bothered Holly. She wanted the male rowing coach to publicly apologize to the athletes for the disrespect he had showed by subjecting them to his foul language.

Although the coach did eventually apologize to Holly individually, the athletic department never required him to publicly apologize to the athletes, and he continued to hold his coaching position at Harvard. "No one cared," was how Holly summed up the Harvard athletic department's overall reaction to the incident. Fundamentally, her protest went unheard.

In 1996 Holly accepted the position of head women's rowing coach at Boston University. With her first year at BU providing another experience of inequity, it was , Holly described, "absolutely the worst year of my life." She had very little money for her rowing program, including to hire the assistant coaches she needed, and a lack of support from other areas of the college. "You were the poor relations and you were treated that way," Holly summarized. She'd leave after a year if conditions didn't improve, Holly decided. Then in her second year, because BU had to comply with Title IX, the women's rowing program was upgraded to full budget status while the men's was not. It was an interesting situation, with the lack of equity for once hitting male rather than female athletes.

Although Holly advised her athletes not to brag about, for example, their new equipment, since the women and the men rowers at BU share a boathouse, comparisons and resulting tensions were inevitable. But Holly wasn't going to apologize for the improved treatment the women rowers now received, in good part because she understood the root causes of the inequities that were for a change in the women's favor. "If these universities had done what the law had asked them to do 25 years ago," she commented, "none of us would be dealing with this today." Because football still drains so much money from athletic departments nationwide, and because many colleges only complied with Title IX fairly recently, the increase in funding for women's sports has been unnecessarily difficult.

"I can't feel sorry for these men who have had privileges forever, and now women are getting equal time," Holly added. In four years at Boston University, she built up her women's program from "literally in the bottom of the heap" to a ranking of seventh in the nation. She remains a deeply committed coach who won't accept second-class treatment.

Some women coaches have joined with male coaches to work for change. In 1997, University of Oregon assistant coach Sally Harmon agreed to take part in an antitrust lawsuit against the NCAA. Although Sally felt some trepidation about doing so, she also had very good reasons for joining the lawsuit. A former star athlete at the University of Oregon who had been honored three times as an All-American and who had earned fourth place in the javelin in the NCAA track and field championships in 1985, Sally had then taken an assistant coaching position at her alma mater, specializing in the women's throwing events, and began what would prove to be an outstanding coaching career. But in 1992, along with numerous male and female assistant coaches of nonrevenue sports across the country, she was hit hard in the wallet by the NCAA's restricted earnings policy that limited many assistant coaches' salaries, essentially categorizing these coaches as the equivalents of graduate teaching fellows.

"The salary that I'm scratching and clawing to get up above $20,000 got knocked down for five years to $12,000," Sally described. She had been making $22,000 as a full-time coach, but with her already low salary reduced even further, she was forced to juggle several jobs to make ends meet. While still working year-round at the University of Oregon, she also took on a second job as teacher and coach at an area high school. The grueling combined work schedule left her driving long distances daily, correcting papers until late at night. "It was really a very disheartening period," Sally commented, with ample justification.

The lawsuit against the NCAA was initiated in Minnesota by two assistant coaches, but numerous other assistant coaches soon signed onto the lawsuit. "A lot of people didn't have much to lose," Sally commented. And yet, she added, there was a very real risk for anyone who joined in. They might be "blackballed from ever being hired again, when they tried to resurface, after being the squawkers."

When Sally was contacted about joining the lawsuit, her initial feelings were mixed. On the one hand, she relished the chance to fight back against the NCAA. On the other hand, she felt "scared spitless, absolutely." She delayed filling out the paperwork, afraid to be viewed as an "adversary," afraid that her participation "might be something that could be used against me to replace me." Like many collegiate coaches, Sally was employed on a one year, renewable contract. Ultimately, however, the fact that an assistant coach on the men's team, Stuart Togher, decided to go along with the lawsuit influenced Sally's decision to participate, as did the support of her head coach, Tom Heinonen, and doubtless Sally's own fighting spirit.

In 1998, the restricted earnings cap was lifted, and the lawsuit against the NCAA was finally settled in 2000, with the coaches affected by the NCAA policy receiving the difference between what their salaries would have been before the restricted earnings policy and the lower amounts they actually received. Yet since no allowance was made for inflation or possible raises coaches could have received, it was something of a bittersweet victory. And for Sally Harmon, the resolution of the lawsuit still didn't leave her in a position of being treated with complete equity as a coaching professional.

By the spring of 2001, that was also Sally's 16th year of coaching at the University of Oregon, she'd coached numerous athletes to various championships and awards. Although her salary had now risen to $40,000 a year, it was still, she noted, considerably lower than that of a male assistant coach on the men's track team at the same university, who had only been employed there as a coach for two years. "My argument is why am I making $10,000 less," Sally stated, "and I've cranked out an Olympian, two world championship competitors, three NCAA champions, 16 All Americans, 30 plus NCAA competitors... It just seems very inequitable."

That kind of inequity could, Sally recognizes, be grounds for another lawsuit, but on the other hand she wants to keep the coaching job she loves. "I'm stuck between a rock and a hard spot here," she commented.

———

Margie Wright, head softball coach at Fresno State University, is the winningest active coach in college softball. With a college coaching career that began in 1978, she's also someone who has confronted many of the kinds of inequities that Sally Harmon and other women coaches have faced.

For Margie Wright, those battles began in the 1950s in Warrensburg, Illinois, a small town near Decatur, where a 10-year-old Margie was kicked out of Little League because she was a girl. Twelve was the minimum age to play ASA women's softball, but Margie lied about her age, saying she was already 12, so she could play the sport she loved. She didn't play on varsity teams in high school, since these didn't exist for girls at the time. However, a friend who had made the basketball team at Illinois State encouraged Margie to play basketball there as well. She ended up playing three sports at Illinois State—field hockey, basketball, and softball—without the assistance of an athletic scholarship. Those only began for female athletes at the college in 1975, a year after Margie had graduated.

A talented athlete, Margie played both ASA softball and professional softball in addition to the college game. From 1977 to 1979, she pitched for the St. Louis Hummers of the now defunct Women's Professional Softball League. Since the WPSL recruited all the top women players for their league, the women played top-notch softball. "The teams that we played had the very best athletes," Margie recalled. Her experience in the WPSL would shape her as a coach as well as a player. "It really defined competition for me, " she recalled, "because the level was so high."

Margie Wright

There was a less positive side to Margie's pro experience as well. The schedules were grueling, with the women playing a 120 game season in three months. "It was very very hard," Margie described. "You just kept hanging on. No matter how sore or tired you were, you had to play." And there was another downside as well. To play the game they loved in the WPSL, the women had to accept salaries that were far lower than what their male counterparts in professional baseball received. Pitchers like Margie, typically the highest paid players, made only $2000 or $3000 for an entire season.

At Fresno State, where Margie began coaching in 1986, she fought a long and personally taxing battle for her softball program. When Margie first started coaching there, attendance at softball games averaged about 200 people. Games were typically played in the afternoon, on a old, substandard softball field that lacked an outfield fence, lights, adequate seating, and that the team shared with physical education classes. In 1988, during Margie's third season at Fresno, her young team went to the College World Series and finished second in the championship game—"one hit away from winning it." With that kind of record, Margie felt that her program deserved additional support from Fresno State: "I felt that we had earned the right to have an outfield fence." But when she asked for that modest level of improvement from the college, her request was turned down.

It didn't escape Margie's notice that while softball had been denied additional funding, Fresno State was spending big money on the baseball team. They were the ones who now enjoyed a $200,000 new locker room. Margie considering resigning—her mother had passed away that year, and that personal loss challenged her as well—but in the end she hung in there at Fresno State.

As Margie inspired her athletes to higher and higher achievements, and as her teams won more and more games, their fan base grew as well. Margie helped build that fan base by running free clinics, by speaking almost every day to Rotary Clubs and other community organizations, wherever she could find an audience, and in general by "pounding the pavement to get people interested." With home games now drawing an average of 1,500 fans, it was more and more clear that Fresno State softball had outgrown the substandard home field they were forced to play on. For two years Margie fought for better facilities. On numerous occasions she met one on one with the college president. "Can we get lights? Can we get a stadium?" she asked him. "I'll raise the money myself," she offered. The stadium committee Margie had formed met every Friday morning bright and early at 6:30 a.m. But although Fresno State was putting money into construction for men's sports as well as academic facilities, the university still would not give its approval for the new softball field.

Then in the early '90s, the Office of Civil Rights chose to investigate Fresno State. It wasn't a huge surprise when the investigation revealed that the university was not in compliance with Title IX. After the investigation, one requirement was that Fresno State build a softball stadium comparable to the baseball facility. The only catch was that Fresno State asked Margie to help raise money to pay back the loan for construction funds, a requirement that had not been imposed on any coaches of men's sports. However, Margie and others readily took on the hard work of selling seat options and soliciting donations for the new stadium.

Raising money for her sport was familiar territory for Margie. What she wasn't prepared for was the backlash on and off campus to the Title IX decision. It was a backlash in that Margie herself, as the woman coach with the most successful program and with the longest tenure on campus, became the prime target. In 1995, eight coaches from Fresno State—seven men and one woman—brought their version of the controversy to a local radio talk show host. The women's sports programs at Fresno, the coaches described, were "taking everything" and thus threatening men's sports at the college.

The result wasn't pretty: a talk show segment, that aired in October, 1995, in which, Margie and a female administrator at Fresno "got completely bashed for two hours." The accusations made were so outrageous that even years later Margie found it difficult to describe them. "Margie Wright has ... stole funds from the baseball program in order to have her stadium," was a typical comment Margie recalled. Other comments were equally distorted. They said, Margie remembered, "horrible things. Like ... everybody on the softball team is gay, and she has (had sex) with her players. Horrible, horrible things."

For two years vicious lies like those forced members of the community to choose sides, to consider who and what to believe. As an assistant coach for the U.S. Olympic team at the same time the radio show aired, and with years of excellent coaching to her credit, Margie had numerous job offers at other colleges to choose from if she wished to relocate. But taking another job would mean she would have to leave the new stadium she and others had fought so hard for, a stadium that was now being built. It would mean that she'd let her opponents drive her away. Instead, she decided, she would stay in Fresno and fight. "I had fought all the battles to get the things that I thought women deserved," she recalled. "And I refused to let these guys here run me out of what I had started."

Margie and others asked the university to pressure the radio station to retract their false statements. After the university repeatedly declined to take action against the radio station, Margie filed a lawsuit against the radio station. And then the battle got even dirtier. Just how dirty Margie only found out when a coach she'd been friends with for many years told her about the private investigator who had come to talk to him about Margie. That same investigator, Margie realized, had been coming to games, waiting for her to exhibit any behavior that could be used against her in court.

The long Title IX-related battle took a toll on Margie. "I became a target, and I still to this day am a target," she described. With the Fresno community so polarized, it was hard for her to know whom she could and couldn't trust. Most of the coaches who had spoken against her to the radio show host continued to work at Fresno State.

Although Margie continued to be a dedicated and effective coach, her players saw that the stress of the Title IX battle affected her. When Margie talked with her assistant coaches before practice, former player Erika Blanco recalled, at times it was obvious that Margie was "very emotional," sometimes "very angry and sometimes she would be on the verge of tears." On one occasion, Erika recalled, Margie sat down with her team and told the young women that "she's having a hard time and she's gonna need some support from us."

Finally, in the summer of '97, only a week before the trial would have been held, the radio station settled out of court. At the end of almost two years of struggle, Margie had at last achieved what she described as a "moral victory." The radio station had to admit that they were in the wrong, that they'd given out misinformation, and had to agree that for three years they wouldn't speak out about Title IX. That settlement, Margie described, "was the best thing that ever could have happened" because finally the Fresno community realized that since the radio station "had to settle it ... they must have been lying."

But another, even sweeter victory lay ahead for Margie Wright. In the spring of 1998, she coached an outstanding softball team, a group of "overachievers" Margie sensed had the potential for greatness. After winning all but two of their conference games, they won their regional championship in postseason play and headed for the Women's World Series in Oklahoma City. If they could make it to the championship game there, Margie told her team, "you're gonna win this thing."

The day before the championship would be decided, Fresno State played a high-stakes doubleheader against softball powerhouse the University of Washington. The weather held at a torrid 95 degrees coupled with equally high humidity as Fresno lost the first game to Washington. With only 15 minutes for the team to rest and refocus before the next game, a must-win for Fresno, Margie sent her team into the press box, the only air-conditioned place in the stadium, to literally chill. "OK, that's over," Margie told her team. They couldn't afford to focus on the game they'd just lost. Now, she told her team, "we got to go down and do what we came here to do." As if to illustrate just how strongly they believed in their coach, the Fresno State athletes scored five runs in the first inning and won the second game.

The next day, the high drama of the championship game was accompanied by equally dramatic weather. As a cold front pushed through the area, there were thunderstorms and a tornado warning. At mid-day, when the championship game began, the athletes were refreshed by the now cooler air and Margie felt confident in her team. They could win this game, she thought, even though Fresno State's competitor was top-ranked Arizona State. Margie's players shared their coach's confidence. "Our team never felt like we weren't going to win," Margie recalled. "You could see it on their faces."

In the sixth inning, Fresno State scored a run, making the score one to nothing in Fresno's favor. In the top of the seventh, as Margie sat in her usual place in the dugout, she watched her team get two quick outs and then react to the game's probable outcome, practically missing each other's hands as they tried to give each other high fives.

As Margie waited for one last out, she felt as if "everything was slow motion." In that moment, it was as if her whole coaching life passed before her eyes. She saw one player's face "when we lost a 15 inning game one year to lose the championship." She remembered numerous other players as well. "It was just like, OK, this last out and winning the championship is for every one of them."

After Fresno State won the game, things happened fast. "I

just remember running right to the pitcher and getting just mauled," Margie described. Winning the championship meant a great deal not only to her players but to Margie as well. She might, after all, have chosen to leave Fresno State instead of staying and fighting. Now the softball victory seemed to justify all her hard work, all the battles she had fought. "Just seeing their faces," she commented, "it made everything all worth it."

A community celebration awaited Margie and her team when they returned to Fresno at 11:00 that evening. When the team got off the plane and walked across the airport runway, Margie saw the bright lights of television crews. Inside the airport, there were thousands of fans, so many people that all of the team's supporters couldn't fit into the Fresno airport. Numerous fans wanted to talk to Margie and her athletes, to shake their hands, to get autographs from the championship winning coach and her players. The airport was so crowded with exuberant supporters that Margie needed the Fresno State Chief of Police's assistance to get her bags and leave the airport.

That championship game and the community response showed Margie Wright just how far she and her program had come. They now had a top-notch stadium, they were first in the nation, and the Fresno community had unmistakably demonstrated that they both recognized and valued the Fresno State softball victory. That moment, Margie described, was "one of such accomplishment that it could never compare to anything else." Although her team didn't repeat their championship during the next two seasons, Margie Wright assessed herself a winner too. "I feel like I've weathered all the battles and I'm still surviving," she said. It was a statement that many other women coaches could have made.

Doing It All

The young volleyball player came in for a private meeting with her coach. "I'm pregnant," the obviously scared young woman told Debbie Brown. "What do I do?"

Debbie Brown was then a fairly new head coach at Arizona State, and this was the first time she'd been in this particular situation. But she didn't back away from the the player who needed help. "Let's see. Where do we go from here?" she thought out loud to the student, from the very start acting on the assumption that the two of them were in this together. Her words didn't lie. Debbie went through the pregnancy along with her player—attending Lamaze classes with her, acting as the delivery coach when the young woman gave birth to her baby, and ultimately becoming a godparent for the young woman's son.

It was an emotional moment for Debbie when she attended the young woman's graduation and watched her receive her diploma. Even then Debbie understood that this wasn't an ordinary graduation. But since then the change in Debbie's own life situation has added another layer to her perceptions. In addition to the position she currently holds as head women's volleyball coach at Notre Dame University, Debbie Brown now does another rewarding yet demanding job. Like her former player, she is now a mother as well.

As a mother, Debbie wonders how her former player was able to do so much. After the redshirt year she took when she was pregnant, the young woman competed for two more years on the Arizona State women's volleyball team. She also

Debbie Brown and Family

finished her degree, even though English was her second language, while raising her young son as a single mother. And yet someone could argue that what her former athlete was able to cope with shouldn't surprise Debbie at all. She herself combines being the head coach of a major sport at a prominent Division I university with being the mother of two young sons.

Even without the addition of parenting responsibilities, coaching is a demanding role. When coaches across the country talk about their jobs, one factor comes up again and again—time. Lengths of seasons, pressure to win, and other factors all vary considerably from sport to sport, level to level, and college to college. The fact still remains that for coaches, doing a good job typically means working far more than a 40 hour week. Running a successful program involves so much time and attention to so many areas that it isn't off the wall to compare a head coach to a CEO in the corporate world. Women collegiate coaches make prime examples of professional women holding down high-level, high-intensity jobs.

What Holly Hatton, head women's rowing coach at Boston University, described as her typical schedule is similar to that of many women collegiate coaches, all of whom do far more than just work directly with their athletes. After coaching nine months and working six days a week, like many collegiate coaches, Holly remains busy in the summer. In summer, 2000, Holly worked 12-hour days recruiting, putting together a new brochure, running a camp, preparing for her next season. The huge amount of paperwork that confronts head coaches also takes large amounts of Holly's time. "It's unbelievable the amount of paperwork involved now with the NCAA," she commented.

"The time demands on a coach are tremendous," agreed field hockey coach, Beth Anders. At Christmas one year, Beth's sister-in-law asked her: "Beth, the season's over. What do you do now?" Beth's brother reached over to Beth. "Don't hit her," he joked about the obvious misunderstanding. Beth laughed as she told the story, but also clarified its meaning: "That's what everybody thinks, you just coach and you finish in November, now what do you do?" The reality, she contrasted, is long workdays that include caring for players' needs, dealing with budgets, scheduling, recruiting and other duties.

Because many women's collegiate sports are still not as well-supported as men's sports, either within college athletic departments or in the important area of community booster groups, coaches of these sports must take personal responsibility for tasks such as fundraising or boat rigging or softball field preparation. Athletic departments and booster groups are more likely to fundraise without the involvement of the male coaches who coach traditionally well-supported male sports such as basketball and football. But even women coaches of, for example, well-funded sports like Division I basketball often work marathon hours.

Demanding schedules aren't, of course, something that only female coaches face. While often working seven days a week at her own coaching jobs, volleyball coach Marlene Piper observed that many male coaches did the same. Marlene has heard male coaches in their 40s and 50s lamenting the consequences of those busy schedules. "Gosh, I wish I would have seen my kids grow up. I wish I wouldn't have spent seven days a week coaching my football team," some male coaches have said to Marlene.

But Marlene is well aware of an advantage many male coaches have. Simply put, many male coaches are married men. "The wife can have the supper on when you get home and the house cleaned. I do my own vacuuming," Marlene commented. As a single woman, although she doesn't have the assistance of a wife with domestic duties that many male coaches enjoy, she also realizes that for women coaches with children, the job of balancing coaching duties and home responsibilities is far harder than for single coaches. In the past, Marlene explained, most women had to choose between having a family and being a coach. Even today, when working women are widely accepted, young women considering coaching, Marlene added, will still typically wonder "How can I have time for a personal life? How can I have time for babies and husbands?" Female coaches who are or want to be parents as well must do the kind of juggling act—balancing home and workplace responsibilities—that is surely one of the most difficult aspects of working women's lives.

Today of course, the large number of women in the American workforce—59 percent of women by the mid-'90s—includes many mothers. Yet in most households, as the authors of *Balancing Act* reported, "women still bear the large brunt of housework" while male husbands or partners don't perform an equal share of household work, including childcare. And many American workplaces are still far from family-friendly environments. Even today, certain professional careers seem based on the expectation that employees will put their careers before all else.

Women college coaches are in the same boat as other working women. While countless male college coaches are fathers, these coaches also typically have wives who "stand behind their man." But for a woman coach, having it all is far less possible. There are many women who have chosen to leave coaching rather than try to combine it with being a parent. Yet across the country there are female coaches who do manage to wear both coach and mother hats. Valiantly balancing sometimes conflicting responsibilities, typically with the support of husbands or partners, these coaches show their athletes and others that it is possible to achieve a goal of many working women: doing it all.

———————

As the mother of two young sons, Debbie Brown is one of that still fairly small group of women who are coaches and mothers. "There's not a lot of us out there," Debbie commented. In May, 2000, with Debbie looking forward to her tenth season as head women's volleyball coach at Notre Dame, Debbie's two sons, Connor and Ryan, were only six and a half and five years old. Debbie is a positive person who doesn't complain about the kind of time pressures she faces. Yet even with the help of her supportive husband, Dennis, it's obvious that combining motherhood and coaching hasn't been easy.

Perhaps the fact that Debbie Brown was formerly a world-class athlete used to working hard toward athletic goals is part of what has helped her rise to the challenge of doing two tough jobs simultaneously. As a collegiate player, Debbie was captain of the women's volleyball team at the University of Southern California that won AIAW national championships in 1976 and 1977. She was a two-time collegiate All-American who was recognized as the "nation's best all-around player." In international competition, she was only a teenager when she first played with the U.S. national team at the 1974 World Championships. She was captain of the team that took fifth place at the World Championship in 1978, was then named to the Olympic team, and would have competed at the Olympics in 1980 if it hadn't been for the U.S. boycott.

Debbie's earlier years in coaching may also have helped prepare her for the two jobs she's doing now. When she began coaching at Arizona State University in 1983, her job as a woman volleyball coach was still of the do-it-all variety. With no money for her to hire an assistant coach, Debbie was essentially the entire coaching staff. "The coach had the responsibility to really do everything," she recalled, "including sweeping the gym and getting towels for the opponents and lining up officials and scheduling and travel and just everything."

At Notre Dame now, Debbie not only appreciates the level of support she receives for her volleyball program, she also appreciates the fact that Notre Dame is "a very family-friendly workplace" where childcare is easily available both on campus and at a neighboring college. It's no problem for Debbie or for her husband, Dennis, who also works at Notre Dame, to take a break from work to attend a function at their sons' daycare. When Debbie was pregnant, Dennis could to take time off from work to go with her to doctor's appointments so he could, for example, listen to their young son's heartbeat. "His boss was 100 percent behind that," Debbie said.

Having a supportive husband is a key puzzle piece for Debbie. "It's hard when you're in a dual career marriage," Debbie commented, echoing a thought expressed by many other married women working in the professions. While it's reasonably common for a wife to move for her husband's job, the reverse situation is still far less common. Dennis and Debbie went ahead and made the move to Indiana because of Debbie's job without a firm commitment for a job for Dennis, a situation not all husbands would have accepted.

Dennis' support is crucial in other ways too. "The biggest factor for me," Debbie commented, "is that my husband is so involved in the parenting process. ...It's truly a partnership, and it really has been since we were married. He does take on a lot of responsibility and does a lot of things that I know a lot of men would never dream of doing."

In *The Second Shift—Working Parents and the Revolution at Home*, Arlie Hochschild described the tremendous stress many working women face because in many cases husbands do far less than an equal share of house work and childcare: "Most women work one shift at the office or factory and a 'second shift' at home." This extra burden Hochschild concluded, helps prevent women from achieving in the workplace. It's surely not irrelevant that women who are both coaches and mothers often seem to live with husbands and partners who do share the workload. In Debbie and Dennis' case, rather than dividing their household responsibilities along traditional gender lines, Debbie might take out the trash in addition to performing traditional "women's work," while Dennis often changes diapers, vacuums, does laundry, and cooks meals for the family. Although Dennis has a responsible position as associate director of public relations at Notre Dame, he works fewer weekend and evening hours than Debbie, and travels less on his job, so he is able to keep the home fires burning while Debbie is on the road with her team.

Some working women, of course, cope with packed schedules by sacrificing time at home. As much as Debbie loves coaching, however, she works to keep a balance between her professional and personal life. "I don't want my job to be my life. I love coming home, and my time with the family, the kids, is real important, so I have some guidelines for myself," she explained. She doesn't make recruiting phone calls until her own children are in bed. Unlike many other coaches, she rarely brings videotapes at home to watch, trying to leave that for her time in the office instead.

The frequent travelling involved in coaching has a positive side for Debbie: time for herself away from her family, "really the only time that I ever have to have to myself completely." She enjoys the chance to read, or listen to music, and to connect with old friends, such as former teammates on the national team who have also gone into coaching. Yet as a mother of young children, Debbie also finds that leaving home can be a very difficult part of her job.

"Oh, Mom, we don't want you to go," Debbie remembered her young sons pleading. "Oh my gosh, it kills you," she admitted. In a worst-case scenario, one time Dennis, Connor and Ryan not only went with Debbie to the airport, but then accompanied her all the way to her gate to see her off on a trip. The boys were crying, asking again and again for hugs and kisses. Through trials and errors like that, Debbie and Dennis have learned to make goodbyes less emotionally wrenching. She'll say goodbye to her sons at home, or Dennis and the boys might take her to the airport but leave right away after dropping Debbie off outside.

At other moments, home and work life are more in harmony. Debbie, Dennis and the boys attend numerous women's sports events at Notre Dame, and Debbie appreciates the fact that her young sons will grow up understanding that sport isn't just a guy thing. When her two boys attended a clinic Notre Dame female athletes put on for children, Connor, the oldest boy, learned how to catch a lacrosse ball with a stick from one of the young women on the lacrosse team. "Be sure to come watch one of our games," the young woman encouraged Connor. "Oh, I will," he told her enthusiastically. "Mom, Mom," Connor insisted afterward, "We got to go to a women's lacrosse game."

Just as women athletes can make positive role models for Debbie's young sons, she herself provides a special kind of role model for the young women on her team. "It's important for them to see that you can work, and you can be a mom," Debbie asserted, "and you can ... have a balance in your life."

———•◦•———

But finding that balance isn't easy. "It's a challenge," Stephanie Gaitley said bluntly about combining coaching and parenting. Until recently she played the dual roles of head women's basketball coach at St. Joseph's University and mother of three fairly young children—in May of 2000 their ages were 12, 7 and 1. "The only way you can really do it," Stephanie added, "is that you have a lot of support.

Stephanie's husband, Frank, her mother, and her husband's mother and sisters have all been important parts of her "support system," as have other adults. When the St. Joseph women's basketball team played road games, the two older sons would often stay at the home of one of their coaches, while the youngest child would be cared for by Stephanie's mother or mother-in-law. She had a "built in babysitting system," Stephanie commented appreciatively.

For most of Stephanie's coaching career, she and her husband coached together. "We both had a passion toward the sport and we both loved what we did. And the kids could enjoy all of that with us," Stephanie said. However, because of the demands of parenting, Stephanie explained, beginning with the 2000-2001 basketball season, Frank decided to give up coaching, so, for example, when the women's basketball team was on a road trip, Frank could still be at home.

Like many working women, Stephanie has thought about the impact of her job on her family. "I don't want anyone in my life to suffer because of me pursuing a career that I love," she stated emphatically. In that way she shares the attitude of many professional women, who make their families and children a "primary priority," Stanford professor Laraine Zappert reported in *Getting It Right*. While Stephanie's job limited the time she could spend with her children, her workplace provided "a big playground" for them. After their school day ended, the two older boys would often watch practices, or head to Stephanie's office area and use the computers there to do their homework. And Stephanie's coaching position was a plus for her kids in other ways as well. "I'm the most popular kid in the school because my mom is the coach at St. Joe's," Dutch, Stephanie's oldest son, told his mother one day.

Yet even with a supportive partner and family, combining coaching and parenting still wasn't easy. "How do you do it?" a number of Stephanie's coaching colleagues asked her. For Stephanie, part of the answer lies simply in who she is. She's from a large family where both her mother, her father, and her siblings were involved in sports. For her coaching is "in the blood so to speak." She's also, she admitted, a distinctly type A personality. "I'm very very self-motivated and very driven," she described. "I'm the kind that says if you tell me that I can't do it, I'm probably going to do it twice as good."

The typical schedule Stephanie maintained as a coach illustrates just how high-energy some working women have to be to make all the parts of their lives work together. Stephanie usually rose at 6 a.m. and worked out on a treadmill, frequently combining exercise with watching a video and making notes for an upcoming game. After she and her husband got the kids ready for school and babysitting, she might take an hour at home to do laundry, clean the house, or maybe even read a book and find "an hour of peace for myself." Around 10 a.m. she would head to work and remain there the rest of her day, meeting with staff, watching more game or practice videos, meeting with players, running practices. In the evening, in addition to spending time with her family, she often needed to make recruiting phone calls.

On top of everything, there was the time Stephanie spent promoting her team. In the spring of 2000, when the women's basketball Final Four was held in Philadephia, she met with the sports editors of the two major Philadelphia newspapers, offering them ideas for stories, and she appeared often on Comcast, Philadelphia's local version of ESPN. "I'm the type that'll go anywhere and do anything," Stephanie commented. By the end of the 2000 Final Four, one of the sports reporters from Comcast jokingly asked her if she had an apartment near their TV studio, since she was on the air so much.

That jam packed life had its costs as well as benefits. "You'll never see her," one of Stephanie's friends told a neighbor. And in fact, Stephanie had little time to get to know people in her neighborhood. But Stephanie mainly focused on the positive aspects of her situation, and agreed with Debbie Brown that coaches who are also mothers can provide important role models for their players. "I feel it's important for the women of today," Stephanie argued, not to "limit your dreams and aspirations."

Unfortunately, Stephanie's own coaching aspirations took a hit in April, 2001, when she was fired from her coaching job at St. Joseph's. The firing resulted from a complaint made by a former player on Stephanie's team, who accused Frank Gaitley of sexual harassment. Stephanie was let go even though each of the Gaitley's, their attorney reported, "emphatically" disagreed that there was any truth to the accusation.

Post-firing, at a press conference in early April, Stephanie's pain and anger was clear. "After 13 years of unwavering commitment and honesty, ... after bringing nothing but accolades and admiration to this university, I was given only 16 ½ hours to decide the fate of my career and the direction of my family's life," Stephanie stated while "holding back tears," the associated press writer described. She had decided to be fired rather than resign to protect her "reputation, character and integrity..."

By September, 2001, after a very difficult period of time, Stephanie Gaitley had settled with the university and was taking a year off to spend with her family and consider her options. She would continue to do some camps and clinics, some involving travel to exotic locations like Bosnia and Israel, and she would also do "a lot of soul searching" about her professional future and its potential impact on her family. If she did return to coaching, she felt, the tough times and resulting personal growth she'd experienced "will truly make me a better coach." For the time being, though, Stephanie had largely stepped away from her personal/professional balancing act.

———

At some moments home and work life can come together for women coaches. Volleyball coach Laurie Corbelli also finds that her children can get involved with her coaching career. On one evening at home, when Laurie was going to make a recruiting phone call, her 9-year-old daughter actually quizzed her mom about the potential recruit. "Is she any

Laurie and John Corbelli

good?" Laurie's daughter, Rachel, questioned. Rachel then added some heartfelt advice. "If she's any good, call her now. If she's not that good, Mom, just stay with us." It was a family situation that coach and mom Laurie found "hilarious," her daughter attempting to evaluate Laurie's recruits.

For Laurie and her husband, John, who coach together as head coach and associate coach at Texas A&M, combining the multiple roles of coaches and parents to a son and a daughter has been doable so far yet certainly not easy. When Laurie and John were newly married but hadn't yet started a family, they coached against each other at Santa Clara and San Jose State. Initially, Laurie described, their biggest challenge was recruiting from the same pool of young players, but once they added baby Rachel to the mix, their home and working lives became much more complicated. Laurie might be downstairs taking care of their baby daughter, with John upstairs making recruiting phone calls. Then she and John would pass each other in the stairway, he would take the baby, and Laurie would go upstairs to call potential recruits. The fact that Laurie and John would often be travelling with their respective teams at the same time only added to the confusion. "It was a zoo," Laurie described succinctly.

Obviously, something had to give, and if the Corbellis had been living out the traditional roles for husband and wife, that something would probably have been Laurie's coaching career. Instead, Laurie and John found another solution—combining their coaching efforts in one college's volleyball program, at Texas A&M—so that they could have the flexibility to arrange their work and family schedules in a more complementary fashion. Since the Corbellis knew that many schools were looking to hire women as head coaches for their women's teams, and since Laurie was more comfortable than John with the multiple speaking engagements head coaches typically have, it made sense for her to be the one to apply for head coaching positions. At Texas A&M, she initially hired John as her assistant, but later requested that the school change his title to associate coach.

"We know that we are in this together," Laurie said about coaching along with John. Since both she and John are "opinionated" and "stubborn" people, at times they inevitably disagree with each other over coaching matters. But for Laurie, the bigger adjustments were and continue to be combining her roles as parent and coach. "I think where I have the most difficult time," Laurie stated, "is splitting myself up as a wife and a coach and a mom, and keeping the priority as wife and mom, because I love my players and I want to give them the best experience I can."

She worries, Laurie admitted, about whether she gives enough to her players, and to her husband and children. She tells her players that she cares about them and that she wants to be there for them. For her children, as Laurie sees it, both she and John are good role models of working parents happy about their work, yet like many working mothers, Laurie sees the potential conflict between her dual roles. "I want them to see that we're doing what we love," she said about her children, "yet I don't want them to think that we love it more than them."

There are numerous moments when Laurie's roles as coach and mom seem to come together well. Daughter Rachel, who plays volleyball herself, enjoys sitting on the team bench during Texas A&M games. After a Texas A&M victorious home game, both Corbelli kids take part in Aggie rituals like sawing off University of Texas rival Varsity's horns. On the flip side though, there's the "emotional drain" of Laurie's demanding schedule as head coach. In September, 2000, already busy with her volleyball season, Laurie had also spent a great deal of time with four recruits over the weekend, and as a result had had very little time with her two children. "There's no downtime; we don't have weekends," Laurie commented about a schedule she described as "brutal." Although she loves and is committed to her coaching job, for the sake of her family she can envision giving up her coaching job at some point and moving into athletic administration or perhaps running a volleyball academy. "But I'd have to be ready to leave it," she said about her coaching job, "because what I'd be giving up is so huge."

———•—•———

As many working women have discovered, doing it all doesn't always work out. Among the numerous women who have left the coaching field, many have chosen to leave in order to devote more time to their families. Lisa Beckett, formerly the head tennis coach at Pomona College, is one of these women. Her last coaching season at Pomona was the spring of 1998. In May, 2000, with her three children—Holly, Denni Jo and Henry—at the still fairly young ages of 10, 8 and 6 years old, Lisa was no longer coaching but instead working in a part-time administrative and teaching position at her college.

Leaving the coaching profession wasn't an easy decision for Lisa to make. For a number of years, she'd hung in there with coaching even though balancing the responsibilities of three kids along with coaching left her remembering the spring tennis season as "kind of a blur." It helped that until 1996, Lisa's husband worked out of a home office and could, she described, "pick up the slack" during her especially busy coaching times. But once her husband began to travel a great deal for his job, Lisa felt that something had to give.

"It just got to be too much," Lisa felt, both for her own schedule and for her kids. She would leave home for work early in the morning, knowing that she wouldn't return home until close to dinner time. "I would have this sort of achey feeling inside," she described. "And it kind of sounds clichéd but it's true. It was a nagging feeling that I just wanted to spend more time with (her children)."

Like many working mothers, Lisa was often forced to make difficult choices. In the fall, for example, she would need to make recruiting calls yet also wanted to help her oldest daughter with her homework. Lisa's schedule was so jam packed that it was hard to find quality time with her children. "Instead of being with the kids and just having fun...," she recalled, "it was ,OK, let's get everything ready for tomorrow because tomorrow's a busy day." Lisa was living out the home speedup described by Arlie Hochschild as typical of many working mothers.

Leaving coaching was the right thing for her to do, Lisa felt. As a part-time teacher and administrator at Pomona, she appreciated the chance to spend time with her children and to coach some of their teams. Yet she admitted missing coaching, and the strong "connection" she'd felt with the athletes on her team. "You miss the thrill," she added, "I loved the competition, the excitement, and I loved being successful."

In fact, next to having children, Lisa described, "the most exhilarating experience I've ever had," was in 1992, when her Pomona women's tennis team became the first Division III team to win a triple NCAA title, winning in singles, doubles, and in the team competition as well. So it wasn't surprising to learn that her answer about whether she would return to the coaching profession at some point was a definite maybe. "I wouldn't rule it out," she said simply.

———✦———

When Notre Dame basketball coach Muffet McGraw had just had her baby son, Murphy, a few of the seniors on her team came to see her in the hospital. The players were excited to see the newborn baby, but their coach was worn out from childbirth. "I think I told them not to ever get pregnant," Muffet recalled, laughing at the memory.

Muffet also laughed at the joke told by volleyball coach Paula Petrie, a joke common among women coaches. "You guys have to time this perfectly," Paula said, referring to how female coaches may try to plan their pregnancies for the best fit with their sports seasons, a woman coach's version of the life strategy common among professional women of planning childbearing around career demands. In fact, Muffet and her husband did plan for their son's birth—he was officially due in May but Muffet gave birth to him on April 29—to occur after the end of the basketball season. What that pregnancy "schedule" meant was that Muffet was visibly pregnant during much of the season, an aspect of Muffet's coaching life that turned out to have a benefit unattainable for male coaches. With the referees seeing not only a coach but a pregnant woman, Muffet didn't have a single technical foul called against her.

From the time her son Murphy was born, he was a part of the Notre Dame women's basketball team. Even as a toddler, Murphy would spend time in the Joyce Center while his mom's team practiced. "It's like he grew up in the Joyce Center arena," Muffet commented. "He learned to walk in there and ate a lot of old popcorn from underneath the stands."

All along, the young women on Muffet's team have been like big sisters for Murphy. In May of 2000, Murphy had just turned 10, and was busy enough with school and other activities that he no longer travelled with the team as much as he had when he was younger. But he still went along on some team road trips and would sit in the back of the bus with the young women on his mom's team, continuing to learn from them "about different kinds of people, and music, and different ways of saying things."

Like Debbie Brown, Muffet McGraw not only coaches at family-friendly Notre Dame but has strong support from her husband, Matt, who owns his own business and works out of their home, giving him the advantage of a flexible schedule. But most important, it would seem, is Matt's willingness to be a full partner on the home front. "He does everything," was how Muffet summed up her husband's multiple roles. "He cooks, he does the laundry, he takes care of Murph.

...And he likes doing it. There's never 'OK, you're home now. It's your turn.'"

Although many women coaches who are also mothers have the assistance of supportive partners, Muffet is well aware that her home situation is far from the norm. "It's really interesting to have the role reversal kind of thing," she commented. "Because most of the time it's the man coaching and the woman is home." More typically, Muffet described, that male coach will blithely tell his wife, "Hey, I'm bringing the team over for dinner."

As Muffet has combined building a powerhouse women's basketball pro-

Muffet McGraw

gram with being a wife and mother, obviously, many of the stars have been in alignment for her in her personal horoscope. Yet she understands the difficulties women coaches with children face with balancing their multiple roles. "I think there's always going to be conflict for any working mom," Muffet asserted. Recently, for example, when her son wanted her to go on a field trip, she told him that she couldn't because of a prior engagement to speak at a luncheon. But when she was at the luncheon, she described, "the whole time I was thinking, gosh, is this really important or could I have (gone on Murphy's trip)?"

Muffet obviously cares a great deal about her son's well being, yet she's also someone who describes coaching as "my true calling" and herself as an "intense and competitive and ... fairly demanding" coach. At the mid-life age of 44, like many other working mothers, she felt that she wouldn't be as happy personally if she gave up her job in favor of being a full-time mother. "And if I'm not going to be happy, he's not going to be happy," she added about her son. "So that's probably what I consider the tradeoff."

Overall, Muffet McGraw comes across as positive about her multiple roles. Clearly, the multiple facets of her life mostly work in harmony. In many ways, the same is true for other women coaches who are also mothers. It certainly isn't easy to combine those two roles. Like Lisa Beckett, numerous other women have left the coaching profession in order to spend more time with their children. Compared to the large number of male collegiate coaches who have families, the numbers of their female counterparts are far smaller. But obviously, with a favorable enough situation, some women coaches do combine being a coach and being a mom. Sometimes, in fact, that can lead to a very exciting ride for all involved.

On the evening of April 1, 2001, the Savvis Center in St. Louis was packed with enthusiastic fans there to watch Purdue play Notre Dame in the women's Division I NCAA basketball championship. While dualing bands from the two colleges helped turn up the noise volume in the arena, and fans eagerly anticipated a contest between two of the best women's collegiate basketball teams, the head coaches also prepared for the game. It was perhaps a sign of the times that not only were both of the head coaches women, but both Kristy Curry from Purdue and Muffet McGraw from Notre Dame were mothers as well.

For Purdue head coach Kristy Curry, in some ways her entire life had led to this moment. She grew up near the small town of Olla, Louisiana, in a family of coaches, with her father, mother and grandfather all members of the coaching profession. "I went to practice every day, was practically raised under a bleacher," Kristy described. After school,

Kristy would ride the bus to LaSalle High school where her mother coached. Kristy's mother provided an early example that a woman could be both a mom and a coach.

In college, Kristy majored in physical education, planning to coach and teach at the high school level like her mother. But after working at two Louisiana high schools, Kristy soon began to move up the college coaching ladder, with assistant coaching positions at Tulane, Stephen F. Austin, Texas A&M, and Louisiana Tech, where she worked for the well-known coach Leon Barmore. Finally, in April, 1999, Kristy accepted the position she currently holds as head women's basketball coach at Purdue.

"It was a family decision," Kristy said about coming to Purdue. She appreciated the fact that Purdue made women's basketball a priority, that Indiana was a strong basketball state, that the town of West Lafayette wasn't a gigantic city. As head coach, she would be able to hire her husband, Kelly Curry, as an assistant coach. "I wasn't gonna leave him with Coach Barmore," Kristy joked.

In May, 2000, after her first full season at Purdue, Kristy was looking forward to the birth of her first child in August. "I've always wanted to do it all, be a mom and be a basketball coach," Kristy commented. On August 28, she and Kelly became the proud parents of a healthy baby girl, Kelsey Curry. During Kristy's second season at Purdue, a high-profile season where Purdue piled up the wins, Kristy was not only a second-year head coach but a new mother.

"It's been an incredible year, both personally and professionally," Kristy summed up. Both she and her husband, she explained, have the dual goals of being successful coaches and good parents. With their extended family far away—in Louisiana and Texas—certainly Kristy and Kelly couldn't have managed without the full-time assistance of a woman they hired to care for their baby. But Kristy described another kind of help as well, other women basketball coaches who can serve as role models and in fact what sounded like a kind of mini baby boom among women coaches. "There are so many babies in the Big Ten," Kristy commented.

Kristy, Kelly and Kelsey Curry

Among the coaches she often encountered professionally, Kristy mentioned two other women coaches with babies, two women whose children are already in high school, and also Muffet McGraw at Notre Dame, whom Kristy referred to as "a great mentor and example" for being a good mother and "a great basketball coach."

Being a mother, Kristy found, had a positive impact on her as a basketball coach, making her "more patient" and more aware that each of her players is "somebody's daughter." Even so, combining parenting and coaching isn't easy. "Make sure that you keep everything in perspective; the most important thing is your family," a woman coach who is also a good friend advised Kristy. No matter how busy you get at work, "don't forget that there's a little girl waiting for you at home."

All season long, Kristy and her husband Kelly worked hard to keep that balance, bringing their young daughter, Kelsey, to home games and along on most team road trips. After games, as soon as Kristy had spoken with the press and checked in on her team, her next priority was to go up and hold her baby daughter. So it was only fitting that at the Savvis Center in St. Louis, in early April, 2001, Kelsey was in the stands, sitting just a few rows back from courtside along with both of her grandmothers, one grandfather and other family members.

Working mothers have been disparaged for taking the "mommy track," accused, not always unrealistically, of having divided loyalties. But as Kristy Curry stood in front of her players shortly before the championship game, with TV cameras focused on Kristy cheering on her players, Kristy herself seemed completely focused. "We can overcome anything," she told them, her voice and body language conveying intensity. "You keep the dream alive."

Muffet McGraw's final pregame words to her team in the locker room were similarly upbeat. "The game's 40 minutes but the memories last a lifetime," Muffet told her players. "Just enjoy playing like we have all year."

Appropriately enough for such an important contest, both Kristy Curry and Muffet McGraw were formally dressed in black suits, with Kristy's gold blouse and Muffet's yellow top echoing the colors of each other's teams. Poised and professional, the two women smiled as they shook hands with each other before the game. The game itself lived up to its billing as a contest between two elite teams, the kind of nailbiter, with neither team able to decisively pull away, that didn't disappoint the fans in attendance or the many more fans watching on national television. At the half, the teams were only separated by 6 points, with Purdue in the lead at 32-26.

The game featured such high-octane basketball that at a couple of moments, rather than focusing on her own team alone, Muffet saw the game as a spectator would, she told reporters, thinking to herself, "This is such a great game..." She'd had a similar perspective at moments in the semi-final game against the University of Connecticut. "This is fun," she'd thought, "what a great game to be a part of."

In the end, Notre Dame pulled out a narrow victory, winning by a thin, two-point margin, 68-66. As Muffet and the Notre Dame players began to celebrate, for a moment the TV camera focused on the losing coach, Kristy Curry, rubbing her eyes. Afterward, in the privacy of the locker room, she cried just as did her players. "We were pretty devastated," she commented. And yet both at the time and looking back, she felt considerable pride in the accomplishments of her team.

Muffet of course was all smiles. "It's definitely euphoria," she told the media about winning the championship.

"It's the greatest moment in our basketball history at Notre Dame." Muffet's husband, Matt, and son, Murphy, were witnesses to the moment, at the game along with the rest of Muffet's family fan club, sitting a few rows back behind the Notre Dame bench. Once the game had ended in a Notre Dame victory, Matt and Murphy ran onto the court. "I think Matt was like my second hug," Muffet recalled. Murphy joined the players' celebration, but "he was kind of waist level," Muffet commented, laughing about the size disparity between her tall players and her son, "so I'm not sure if they even knew he was there."

There was no doubt in Muffet's mind, however, that her son was excited and happy about what his mom and her team had accomplished. They had, of course, brought football legend Notre Dame its first ever women's basketball championship. As Muffet received the trophy, holding it up with a brilliant smile on her face, it seemed fitting that she thanked not only the Notre Dame family but her own family as well.

In the hectic weeks after the championship game, when Muffet and her players visited the White House, both Matt and Murphy would accompany the team, and Matt also came along for the team's trip to New York, husband and son once again showing their support for and involvement in Muffet's coaching life. Post-championship as well, Muffet and her players would be caught up in a whirlwind of activities. But surely the high point for players and coach, and probably for Matt and Murphy as well, was Notre Dame's victory in that championship game.

"We were just so happy," Muffet recalled. She and her players and assistant coaches "just wanted to celebrate being together. It was just a real emotional moment. Kind of on the verge of laughing, crying, smiling." And although it probably didn't cross Muffet's mind at the time, it was also a moment that demonstrated just how successfully a working mother and coach could combine both roles.

A Question of Attitude

Even with the national championships her teams have won, as an African-American woman, University of Texas track coach Beverly Kearney has to deal with prejudice. "I still get comments such as, "You speak well," she described, "and I'm pretty sure most coaches don't get that as a compliment." People will say to her, as if the fact is surprising, "Boy, you're intelligent."

On one occasion a clueless white male reporter asked Bev if she was sure she had actually received her master's degree. "You know how sometimes you said you had a master's for so long that you forgot you didn't get it," the reporter said to Bev. Since he obviously assumed she was such a fool, perhaps he was taken aback by Bev's perfect comeback: "You're a reporter. Why don't you call the school and ask."

Although the male reporter's thoughtless comment offended Beverly, it didn't surprise her. The racial prejudice the reporter's remark reflected was something she has frequently dealt with. "You just get (prejudice) so often, and it comes out of nowhere in the questioning process," Beverly explained, "that I've just learned to call attention to it and move on, because you don't want to get angry, and you don't want to get upset and you can't afford to constantly get offended. It's not a productive state of mind."

As an African-American coach, Beverly Kearney is one of a still small number of African American women in coaching. A *Hartford Courant* article entitled "Progress? Not for Black Women Coaches" reported that only four of the 64 teams in the 2000

NCAA women's basketball tournament had African-American head coaches, and altogether among Division I schools, only 6.4 percent of the head women's basketball coaches are African-American, a number that compares unfavorably with the almost 20 percent of Division I men's basketball coaches who are African-American men.

In *Men and Women of the Corporation*, Rosabeth Moss Kanter described how in the '70s women executives in the corporate world were "highly visible, much more so than their male peers" precisely because at the time they were a distinct minority compared to male executives. "The upper-level women became public creatures," Kanter wrote. "It was difficult for them to do anything ... on their jobs, or even at informal social affairs that would not attract public notice." Among today's women college coaches, the small number of minority women head coaches are similarly visible. They face the kinds of special pressures, such a the need to represent their group and to perform especially well, which Kanter described. "You represent everything and everyone," was how Bev Kearney put it, "and that's a heck of a responsibility to carry on a day-to-day basis."

There are a small number of African-American women who have achieved anything like Bev Kearney's level of success in coaching. On one occasion she called up African-American coach C. Vivian Stringer for advice, even though Vivian Stringer coaches basketball rather than track, because like Beverly, Vivian is a highly successful African-American female coach, and there was no African-American female track coach with that level of success whom Bev could talk with.

As Beverly sees it, the situation may not change anytime soon. About her African-American players, she commented, "A lot of them, especially the African-American women, don't want to go through what I've been through. They see how difficult it is. It's still a very lonely field because there's not many of us in it."

Among the numerous challenges women collegiate coaches face is a question of attitude. Not the positive attitude that a player may display, for example, on the basketball court, but attitude in the sense of the still common presence of prejudices and stereotypes. Negative views about race and ethnicity, for example, are a common denominator minority coaches must deal with. Although racial and ethnic prejudices have become far less acceptable than they were formerly, Beverly Kearney's experiences, which are echoed by other minority coaches, show that such prejudices are still out there. They may manifest themselves in more subtle ways than in years past, but prejudiced beliefs continue to affect the lives of athletes and their coaches.

Another sort of attitude that has a significant impact is the lingering stereotype that females who are involved in sports are likely to be lesbians. Female athletes in sports such as figure skating and gymnastics, sports which are typically considered "feminine," are likely to be exempt from such stereotypes. But in supposedly more "masculine" sports, such as basketball, ice hockey and softball, athletes who compete in these sports not uncommonly face the suspicion that many of them are lesbians.

These sorts of attitudes affect not only athletes but women collegiate coaches as well. Regardless of their own sexual orientation, women coaches may encounter homophobic views from fans or members of the media, or from some of the women on their teams or members of the athletes' families. Both lesbian and heterosexual coaches must deal with common held suspicions about the sexual oriention of women who go into coaching. Additionally, lesbian coaches face the difficult question of just how open to be about their sexual orientation.

Frequently or infrequently, women coaches face the kinds of attitudes that can get in the way of their doing their jobs. Women coaches recognize these damaging beliefs and in varying ways respond to them.

———

Syracuse University basketball coach Marianna Freeman, who is president of the Black Coaches Association (BCA), has a keen understanding of the history of racial prejudice in the United States and how that history has affected numerous individuals. In her own life, she understands that the coaching opportunities she's received have come in part because of earlier struggles against racism. "I benefitted from a lot of sacrifice ... I reaped the benefit," Marianna commented. "I don't know what it was like to live in the Jim Crow era where you had to sit in the back of the bus."

Marianna took the position as president of the BCA to work for positive change. "I got involved because I'd like to see there be more representation of African-American men and women in positions of authority within sport," Marianna stated. "Because I don't think that we should be limited to (being) the participants."

In 1998, according to the "Racial and Gender Report Card" prepared by The Center for the Study of Sport in Society at Northeastern University, 11.1 percent of the female Division I athletes were African-American. In contrast, among the assistant coaches for women's teams at Division I universities, 8.6 percent were African-American women but only two percent of head coaches were African-American women—a shockingly low number!

The answer to why so few African-American females hold coaching positions is undoubtedly complex. More young women of all races need to be encouraged to consider the coaching profession, many coaches will argue. As the *Hartford Courant* reported, many people in the coaching field cite a need for "consistent lobbying to promote black coaching candidates," a need for more networking among African-American coaches, "a perceived lack of interest" among minority athletes who could potentially go into coaching, as well as "the inability of black women to break through the existing network of university administrators, which is populated largely by white men."

Prejudices held by some of the athletic directors involved in hiring coaches are very likely a key stumbling block for minority coaches, just as they are for women coaches in general. "I'd like to be able to break down the myth of there aren't enough qualified black men and women for those roles," Marianna Freeman commented. "There are. The people who are in the posiion to hire and fire must be able to step out of their comfort zones so they can see those people."

Intensified efforts to understand differences and backgrounds and perspectives could help too. "Unless you walk a mile in my shoes," Marianna added, "you're never going to understand the subtleties of racism that happens every day." She could walk around with a chip on her shoulder about this pervasive prejudice, but she chooses to resist in a different way, by making an effort to treat the people she deals with simply as fellow human beings. "Sometimes I think I'm an alien," she commented humorously, "because I do that. Like why can't other people do the very same thing?"

Like Marianna Freeman, Marian Washington has also served as president for the Black Coaches Association. As the first female to head up the largely male BCA, Marian wanted the organization to represent the interests of both male and female coaches. She worked hard to understand "the plight of our black male coaches in all sports," including the many challenges facing black male football coaches, and also "wanted to be sure the association was very aware of the challenges of the black female."

Anyone wanting a personal view of those challenges could have looked at Marian Washington's own history in the coaching field. As the head women's basketball coach at the University of Kansas beginning in 1973, and as Director of Athletics for Women from 1974 to 1979, Marian felt isolated by her color as well as by her gender. As an athletic administrator, Marian knew only one other black woman in a similar administrative position. And as a coach, especially early on, Marian "didn't have anyone to really talk to because I was one of the few women of color that was in that position."

For the few women corporate executives in the '70s, Rosabeth Moss Kanter described, one of the barriers that they faced was the isolation they typically experienced from male executives. Marian Washington experienced the same type of barrier. "As a young black coach," she recalled, "I never felt that there was a coaching group that really embraced me." For the most part, she had to learn about her profession on her own. Fortunately, Marian found some coaches, mostly African-American men such as John Chayney and Jim Clemons, who encouraged Marian in their mutual profession. "Hey Marion, you know, come on out, we'll sit down and just talk," these coaches would say.

That kind of support helped Marian to continue coaching and cope with the racism she experienced, such as in recruiting and officiating, while doing her job. Close friends and family members helped her cope too. And just as the church has served as a source of strength in many other African-American people's lives, Marian's religious faith helped her carry on as well. "I just really believe that God will enlarge your territory in ways that you don't even always realize. ..." Marian explained. "Yes, it was challenging, but I did get through it. I feel good about what I was able to contribute."

As president of the BCA, Marian worked and struggled with USA Basketball to help bring about today's system, where "there's a person of color on every coaching staff that goes out now," a policy which did not exist in the past. Another area that concerned her as president and continues to concern her is the very low number of African-American women in head coaching positions. "It's an ongoing challenge to get those numbers moved up," Marian commented.

Part of the problem, she explained, is that many young black coaches have been hired primarily to work on recruiting, and therefore don't receive an opportunity to learn about all aspects of the coaching profession. The exploitive situation Marian described seems parallel to that of athletes brought in to compete without any consideration for whether the athletes will actually graduate. To counter that type of dead-end situation for assistant coaches, when Marian speaks with young black people considering coaching, she emphasizes that "they need to be sure, if they're going to work for somebody, that they leave the program understanding the game as well as, of course, doing the job of trying to bring in players."

Marian Washington is an open, caring person who describes herself as "someone who embraces everyone." But the tough times she's had personally as an African-American female coach and administrator lead her to be "especially concerned about the limited number of people of color in our business" and "especially interested in any young coach of color to help them any way I can." When young minority coaches contact her, she'll give them "any support or encouragement" that she can. "I want to share with them," Marian affirmed, "because I didn't have that opportunity."

<hr />

Younger African-American women in coaching talk about their need for role models and support from other women of color in coaching. Deitre Collins, an African-American woman in her late 30s who coaches volleyball at the University of Nevada-Las Vegas, described her appreciation for UNLV track coach Karen Dennis as a "strong black female" presence and "probably the closest thing to a mentor that I have." Deitre also mentioned calling up African-American basketball coach Vivian Stringer, even though Vivian coaches a different sport, to get Vivian's perspective on what it would be like for a black woman to live in Iowa, the location of a potential job for Deitre. And even earlier in her life, Deitre recalled, watching Vivian Stringer on TV had made an impact. "When I was growing up and seeing women's basketball," Deitre described, "I used to think, if I ever am going to coach, I want to be like C. Vivian Stringer because she has such style as a female in coaching." Even as a coach herself now, Deitre still looks up to Vivian Stringer. "She's an exciting role model for me," Deitre commented, "and she has no idea."

Traci Waites, another African-American coach, was 34 years old in May, 2001, and completing her third year as head women's basketball coach at the University of Pittsburgh. She also may have been lucky to have her job. As the *Hartford Courant* article on minority coaches reported, "white women with no previous head coaching experience are 30 times more likely to land a Division I job than

Deitre Collins

black women with no experience." In fact, Traci Waites has solid basketball credentials—competing in two Final Fours as a player, and serving as both a head and assistant coach at two other colleges before coming to Pittsburgh—but she also has an understanding of the fact that few other African-American women are head coaches. "I just feel very blessed and fortunate to be in that small number," Traci commented. "But what comes with that is a lot of responsibility. You want to do well."

Traci does work very hard as a coach, trying to teach her players the values of discipline and responsibility, sending those same players weekly notes when coach and players are separated in the summer. Coaching, Traci believes, is "a very special career," but most definitely not a 9 to 5 job. "I sleep with it; I think about it all the time," she described. The rewards come from watching her players grow as people, like the young woman who expressed her deep appreciation for her coach: "Coach Waites was like a friend to me. She didn't give up on me when I wanted to quit."

Like Deitre Collins, Traci was inspired by Vivian Stringer. When Traci was competing for Long Beach State against Vivian's University of Iowa team, Traci noticed Vivian coaching from the sidelines. "Wow, maybe one day I want to do that," Traci thought. Similarly, one of Traci's wishes is that she can herself can encourage a minority young woman to consider coaching. "When I walk away from this game," Traci envisioned, "I hope I am able to look back and see more (minority) coaches than there are now, because of me." The coaching profession "has to be something they see that they can attain."

Pat Kendrick, the head volleyball coach at George Mason University, grew up in the integrated society of today's U.S. army bases, and feels comfortable with the diversity at GMU, a public university whose student body includes international students from numerous other countries. Yet like most minority coaches, Pat has experienced prejudice and is well aware of the stereotypes she and her players can face.

There are, for example, the times when she's on the road with her team—a diverse group of athletes—and the team eats together at a restaurant. In the back of Pat's mind is the common stereotype, "that a bunch of black people get together and they get loud." So Pat will take a form of evasive action. "We need to settle down here," Pat will tell her players. "We're female athletes," she may add. "We're black or we're Hispanic or we're from other countries. People are watching." In other situations, Pat simply recognizes stereotypes. One white volleyball coach who was interested in trying to locate African-Americans who could serve as assistant coaches would call Pat up for help with the search. "Like I knew where they all were," Pat commented sardonically. To her, the white coach's assumptions were glaringly obvious.

On another occasion, when Pat and her assistant coach were both at a volleyball tournament in Las Vegas, Pat spotted a prominent white female coach there as well, a woman whom Pat recognized but who didn't know Pat. Shortly afterward, the white female coach called the George Mason volleyball office, inquiring about the African-American woman who was the George Mason assistant volleyball coach. Who was the coach asking about, Pat tried to clarify, and where had she seen her? Pat's assistant coach was actually an Asian-American man. At the Vegas tournament, the other coach responded.

"Was she wearing a green and gold jacket?" Pat asked. The white female coach answered in the affirmative. "That was me," Pat told the other coach simply. She didn't accuse the white woman of making a racist assumption, yet Pat herself was per-

Pat Kendrick

fectly clear about what had happened. "It never occurred to her," Pat commented about the white female coach, "that I would be the head coach."

A friendly woman with an engaging smile and a quick sense of humor, Pat herself has an easy acceptance of diversity. It's probably no accident that the players she has recruited for her team at George Mason are diverse racially and in other ways as well, with players from Europe, South America, Puerto Rico, and varied locations in the U.S. "We've got a bunch of everything," players on Pat's team will tell others. Pat's own accepting attitude is mirrored by her athletes. She mentioned no team problems caused by the diversity on her team.

Pat's personal background can lead to some interesting situations. Since she grew up moving around the country from army base to army base, she doesn't speak with a particularly regional accent, certainly nothing that might be identified as either southern or African-American. One day, when Pat was making a recruiting phone call to an African-American woman who was the mother of a potential player, the mother kept stressing that she wanted her daughter to attend a "diverse university" with a "good social balance."

"Mason is like that. I went to Mason," Pat replied.

"I really don't think you understand exactly what I mean by the racial diversity," the mother replied.

"I know exactly what you mean," Pat replied. Then suddenly she realized that the mother probably didn't realize that Pat herself was African-American. "I know exactly what you mean," Pat repeated. "I'm black."

There was silence at the other end of the line. "I thought the woman passed out on the phone. You're talking dead air," Pat recalled, laughing about the incident. "Oh," the mother said at last, finally hearing Pat's assurances in a new light.

It may be in part because she's a minority coach that Pat is sensitive to other sorts of prejudices as well. During the year when she was an assistant coach for a USA volleyball team then in training in San Diego, one day after practice Pat was the driver for a van full of young women athletes. One of the young women, who was around 21 years old and planning to be married the next year, explained to the other athletes why it was so important for a woman to be married by her early 30s. "Any coach that's not married by the time they're 30 or 32," the player said, "they're a lesbian, you know that."

Although Pat looked younger than her actual age, she was not only unmarried but already older than 32, so she fit the player's stereotype to a T. "I just kind of laughed to myself," Pat remembered. She let the stereotype roll off her back, surely a good survival strategy at times, and kept on driving.

The kind of homophobia Pat Kendrick encountered with the USA Volleyball athletes is rampant in women's sports. Society's prejudice against gays and lesbians hits female athletes and coaches especially hard, since male athletes and coaches are commonly assumed to be heterosexual unless proven otherwise. Athletic women on the other hand, and women who work professionally within the sports field, are often stereotyped as lesbians. In fact, homophobia has a strong impact on both heterosexual and lesbian women in the coaching field.

Unmarried female coaches are especially vulnerable to being stereotyped as lesbians, a stereotype that can then be used against them in the important area of recruiting. However, basketball coach Tara VanDerveer argued that any woman, regardless of her marital status, can be the target of antigay insinuations. "There's always room for people planting that negative seed," Tara commented. Coaches who either are or are perceived to be lesbian may lose their jobs or have difficulty finding employment. "Who's going to put that down as a reason (for firing a coach)?" retired volleyball coach Barb Viera questioned rhetorically. "Nobody. But it happens."

"Homophobia is in the bone marrow of women's sports," asserted sports sociologist Mary Jo Kane. It affects hiring of women coaches overall since athletic directors "don't want to have to deal with the so-called lesbian presence in sport. So it's used as an excuse not to hire women coaches." Homophobia affects recruiting as well, Mary Jo added. "It's often the case that the lesbian innuendo is used as a way to stigmatize and hurt recruiting."

Donna Lopiano, Executive Director of the Women's Sports Foundation, often makes the humorous yet also serious comment that for a women coach applying for jobs, "the best employment position to be is to be divorced with no children." Whereas a single woman might be assumed to be gay, and a mother either single or married could be assumed to be too busy to have her work be her main commitment, a divorced woman appears to be both heterosexual and "willing to work like a dog if there is no man to take care of you." In her article "Attracting Women to the Coaching Profession: Recruiting, Education and Retention," Donna referred to the "common and insidious underground campaign that stems from the lesbian or unfeminine stereotype applied to women who engage in sport or previously all-male professions..."

Women in the military, for example, have often been stereotyped as lesbians. In *Ground Zero*, Linda Bird Francke described how "lesbian-baiting became a military art form," and how "'witch-hunts' for lesbians" became commonplace in the military. Homophobia in the army, as Captain Carol Barkalow described in her book, *In The Men's House*, makes it difficult for women in the army to meet together for mutual support since "something as simple as two women officers having lunch together more than once might spark rumors of lesbianism" and "even rumored homosexuality can damage an officer's career."

In the coaching field, such rumors can also have an impact. "Some coaches have been told to shut up about Title IX. Otherwise the athletic director is going to announce that they're lesbians. Whether they are or not," Linda Carpenter reported. After speaking with numerous coaches, Vivian Acosta and Linda Carpenter are convinced that homophobia is a factor both in recruiting and hiring. A male softball coach, Vivian described, while on home visits to recruit athletes, might say, "You don't want to go to such and such a school because you know their coach is lesbian. You don't want your daughter to be under her influence." Regardless of the female's coach's actual sexual orientation, Linda added, the negative recruiting strategy can still be used.

During a 1984 study, Vivian and Linda asked both men and women in sports about the trend toward lower numbers of women coaches. Although homophobia wasn't mentioned as a possible cause on the list the study supplied, respondents were allowed to write in additional items. Fairly often, Linda described, male respondents wrote in "being a lesbian" as the reason "why they'd never hire a woman." Those type of attitudes, Linda and Vivian agree, are still prevalent today. According to the numerous coaches they speak with, Linda reported, homobia is a "big problem."

Retired softball coach Judi Garman knows firsthand just how blatant the homophobia in sports can be. "There's the dykes on spikes," the football coach would say to his players when he spotted the softball players on their way to practice. "That was his favorite joke about our team," Judi recalled.

On one occasion, Judi had to threaten a lawsuit against a youth coach who had told a young woman interested in playing for Cal State-Fullerton, Judi's college, "what a terrible mistake" it would be to go there because "everybody on our team is lesbian." On another occasion, Judi was on a recruiting trip, sitting in the stands watching potential players. A man sitting in front of her, the father of one of the players, talked about his daughter. "She was going to go to Fullerton. They have the best program," the father said. "But because everybody there is lesbian, I'm glad she's going somewhere else."

"I'm so tired of this," Judi thought. After the father left the softball park, she went up to him, introduced herself, and told him what she'd overheard him saying. "Do you know any of our players?" Judi asked the father. She mentioned players who were engaged to be married, as a way of refuting the father's stereotype, but she didn't duck the question of lesbian athletes. On her team, Judi said, "I do have a couple of kids who have indicated that they're gay." Those players, she continued, "are as special to me as the rest of these players. They're part of our family."

"I don't appreciate you sitting up here and talking about all of our players this way," Judi told the father. "I'm sorry your daughter's not coming to Fullerton. She would have had a great opportunity."

On that occasion, Judi's forthrightness paid off. The father admitted that he hadn't been well informed about the Fullerton softball program. As Judi talked with him, the father's attitude about what his daughter should have done visibly changed. "I'm sorry she's not playing for a coach like you," the father ended up telling Judi.

Numerous other coaches, both lesbian and heterosexual, have worked to counter prejudices. "Treat everyone with respect and everyone has the right to be who they are," is the basic message which Portland State University softball coach, Teri Mariani, gives to her team about the various kinds of diversity her athletes can have, including sexual orientation. As a longtime coach, Teri is well aware of the impact of prejudice on players and coaches. In the past, she described, women in sports were commonly labeled either as a tomboy or a lesbian. Nowadays, although women in sports are far more accepted, prejudices can still have an impact. In the past couple of years, when Teri and Mary Haluska, her assistant coach, have gone together to visit parents and potential recruits, "somewhere in the course of the conversation," Teri described, "I've always made sure that they know that Mary's married and has a daughter, so they don't think the two of us are partners."

It was the recent negative experience of a woman then coaching basketball at PSU, Teri speculated, that made her extra aware of the damaging effect homophobic insinuations can have. Basketball coach Jenny Yopp, currently the head women's basketball coach at Illinois State, vividly recalled the incident that occurred in her second year of coaching at PSU.

It was late in the day when Jenny met in her office with one of her players, along with the player's mother and father. His daughter should get more playing time, the father argued. As a coach, Jenny was holding his daughter back. Then the father sharpened his attack. "You told my daughter that she couldn't go out" with a particular boy, he accused.

Jenny had no idea what the father referred to. "What exactly is he talking about right now? What exactly did you tell him?" she asked her player. "I don't even know who she's dating," Jenny said to the player's father.

When the father asked his daughter and his wife to leave the room, Jenny felt nervous enough to turn on her tape recorder. The father's implication, she realized, was that since she was, as he thought, telling her daughter not to date guys, "Therefore, I must be gay." Although the father didn't spell out his accusations, he made the fact that he was threatening Jenny perfectly clear. He stood up, towering over Jenny, holding, in the best McCarthy-era witch-hunt style, a manila envelope which supposedly contained damaging evidence in his hand. "I just want you to know that I'm going to find out everything that I can about you," he told Jenny. "I've hired a private investigator. I've got a lawyer."

"I have absolutely nothing to hide," Jenny replied. "I'm disappointed that this is your interpretation of what we're doing in our program." Although she isn't a particularly anxious person, after the father left she was "literally shaking" and a "nervous wreck." She called her athletic director, who advised her to talk to the college attorney, but fortunately the father never followed through on his threats.

The entire incident opened Jenny's eyes. "I am a single female that is working with ... very young adults," she commented. "The longer I do this and remain unmarried," the more, Jenny realized, she was open to stereotyping. Although Jenny is a warm, friendly person who works to be approachable by her athletes, the lesson she learned has had an impact on her as a coach. To protect herself when the situation warrants it, she now has an assistant coach with her when she's going to meet privately with a player or with a player's parents.

Other coaches have had similar experiences. Sometimes homophobic attitudes are expressed subtly; other times they come across in a particularly blatant fashion. But homophobia remains part of the attitude that female coaches must deal with.

"How many lesbians do you have on your team?" a reporter once asked New Hampshire ice hockey coach Karen Kay, at a media conference for the women's national ice hockey team. "You've got to be kidding me," was Karen's incredulous reaction. Since she had to maintain her professional demeanor, the reply she actually made was more circumspect. "I really couldn't give you the answer to that question," she replied. "because I'm the coach, and I teach the sport. And those are personal issues. And how (the players) lead their life is their business."

On the one hand, Karen Kay's response was right on target. On the other hand, as former coach Pat Griffin has documented in her book *Strong Women, Deep Closets*, for women coaches sexual orientation goes beyond a personal issue. A female coach's actual or perceived sexual orientation affects how she presents herself to parents and potential recruits, how she chooses to address or not to address the issue of sexual orientation with her team, and last but not least, how open she chooses to be about her own personal life. Lesbian coaches, Pat Griffin described, typically choose from a range of "identity-management strategies," from being completely in the closet, to letting selected people know about the coach's sexual orientation, to being completely open to anyone. "Few college or high school coaches are publicly out," Pat Griffin summarized. "Most lesbian college coaches and professional athletes are passing as heterosexual or covering their lesbian identities with the public and media," although they may be more open in some situations. Many lesbian coaches, as Pat Griffin described, feel that they simply cannot afford to be open about their sexual orientation.

A retired coach, for example, who identified herself as a lesbian but preferred to remain anonymous, described the intimidating prejudice she encountered both as a coach and as a college physical education major in the late '40s and early '50s. When this coach graduated from the University of California in

1952, many women faculty members were lesbians but "very very closeted" and students who wanted to graduate from the program needed to be closeted themselves. In California during the '50s and '60s at all levels of education, any gay teachers whose sexuality became public knowledge would quickly be fired. "People just disappeared...," the retired coach recalled, and "if you are an animal that's hunted you hide." At the two California colleges where she worked, although many women among the faculty and students in the physical education department were lesbians, they couldn't be open about their identities. And although the kind of prejudice she and others faced in the past has become less prevalent today, "physical education and athletics," the retired coach concluded, "is undoubtedly one of the last holdouts for homophobia."

Since most college coaches lack the protection of tenure, it's not surprising that so many lesbian coaches choose to stay in the closet. As Pat Griffin pointed out, lesbians who coach prominent sports like basketball and/or who coach in Division I programs, because they have especially strong pressure to win, to recruit top athletes, and to present themselves as public personalities, are least likely to be able to be open about their sexual orientation. Across the country, in fact, very few female coaches or athletic directors have openly acknowledged being lesbians. Yet there are a very small number of women who have done so.

———◦◦◦———

At 56 years old, Beth Bricker shows her years on the job; her formerly reddish-brown hair is now intermingled with gray. Currently the head women's lacrosse coach and associate director of athletics at the University of Puget Sound, Beth is originally from New Jersey, but her coaching career has moved her across the country to jobs at the University of Rhode Island, at Idaho State, and most recently at the University of Puget Sound in Tacoma, Washington.

"I've always been an activist," Beth characterized herself. Yet in her professional life for many years she kept silent about her sexual orientation. And there was, of course, good reason for that silence. Earlier in her coaching career, Beth described, coming out as a lesbian coach "would have been a death knell for that profession."

But times began to change and Beth personally experienced some of the changes, both in the late '70s, when she was a student at the University of Oregon in the liberal small city of Eugene, Oregon, and during the mid-'80s when she worked as an athletic trainer in the San Francisco area. By 1989, when she accepted a coaching position at the University of Puget Sound, she described, "I probably would have come out right away, but I wanted to make certain that the climate was accepting."

Beth acknowledged her sexual orientation to gay and lesbian student groups at her college and to a number of her colleagues. Then in 1992, at a prejudice training event for faculty and staff at the University of Puget Sound, Beth came out publicly to her colleagues throughout the college. The prejudice training session was planned as a confidential event for faculty and staff at Puget Sound where people could speak freely. "It seemed like a perfect opportunity," Beth said simply.

Considering the still very strong amount of homophobia in the sports community, Beth is amazingly matter of fact about her decision to come out as a coach. "I was thinking I was getting old enough to quit worrying about this stuff," she explained. She was "tired of trying to remember who knew and who didn't." Subsequent to the prejudice training session, Beth included her partner's name along with her own in the college directory, and she continued to identify herself as a lesbian at trainings for residence hall assistants, at new student orientations and at other college events.

The reactions Beth received at the University of Puget Sound were uniformly positive. "I saw you put your partner's name in the directory. That's great," a co-worker might comment. Colleagues would ask Beth about her partner and how she was doing, Beth recalled, "rather than just totally ignoring the fact that I might have someone that I'm living with for my lifetime." However, in contrast to that support, Beth has encountered homophobic attitudes in the area. When she was still coaching basketball at Puget Sound, a father asked her whether any of the girls on her team were lesbians. Some coaches told Beth about negative recruiting directed at coaches who were perceived to be lesbians. Experiences like these help Beth understand why numerous coaches haven't followed her example of being publicly out, especially coaches at Division I colleges. "I think there are too many people that would use that against them in recruiting," she commented. "I really think that's the key."

Since Beth herself was profiled as an openly lesbian coach and athletic administrator in a 1998 article in *The Advocate*, a magazine with national distribution, she can't exactly go back in the closet. Fortunately, she has no regrets about the decision she made to come out. Among other benefits, there's the fact that being open about who she is makes it far easier for her to be supportive of gay or lesbian athletes at her college. "I really cherish the ability," Beth said, "to be a role model in that way."

Like other minority coaches, Helen Carroll, a former coach who until recently held the position of athletic director at Mills College, is also willing to be a role model. And as with Beth Bricker, Helen Carroll is one of the few women professionals within the collegiate sports world who has elected to be completely open about being a lesbian. In fact, Helen quit her job at Mills College partly because she saw the need for someone to devote a large amount of time to speaking out on the issue of gays and lesbians in college sports.

"Somebody needs to kind of take the charge and help direct all the good work that is being done so it can have a powerful impact," Helen commented. She's currently working with the Women's Sports Foundation, and is project manager for the Martina Education Fund on Homophobia in Sport. Helen envisions a national organization, comparable to the Black Coaches Association, that would provide support for gay and lesbian coaches, administrators and athletes, and that would also help all coaches deal with the topic of sexual orientation.

Like Beth Bricker, Helen Carroll wasn't always able to be so open about who she is. Forty-eight years old in February, 2001,

Helen grew up within an athletic family in her home state of Tennessee. After competing as a multisport athlete, began coaching basketball and tennis at the University of Tennessee-Martin, then coached basketball and track at Wayne State College in Nebraska, and later coached basketball at the University of North Carolina in Asheville, where her team won a national championship in 1984. Coaching mostly in the south, Helen was perfectly clear that she couldn't discuss her sexual orientation. "I would never talk about my personal life to anyone in athletics," she explained. She might choose to be open with "maybe another coach who's a friend that I'm at the beach with," but that openness wouldn't extend to opposing coaches, or other coaches at the colleges where she worked, and certainly not to the athletes on her team. At the time, she took an approach to her own sexual orientation that is still typical among coaches today: that the topic is "just irrelevant ... has nothing to do with coaching the game, and ... doesn't need to be talked about."

The homophobia that Pat encountered reinforced her personal silence. While she was coaching at the University of North Carolina, for example, there was the male coach at another southern school who told parents not to send their daughters to UNC "because the coach was a lesbian." Instead, the coach advised, the parents should send their daughters to him because "he has a good family atmosphere at a good Christian college."

But Helen would still talk with her athletes about questions of race, sexual orientation, and other potentially divisive topics, making use of what she described as "teachable moments." When, for example, a player's boyfriend made fun of two other players on the team, because he thought they looked "butch," Helen discussed the situation with her players. "How did that make you feel that your boyfriend said that about two of your friends?" she asked the player. "How do these two women feel? And what does it mean to the rest of the team?" she asked all the young women. When Helen was moved into athletic administration, she advocated that other coaches use that same approach. Rather than ignoring topics such as race and sexual orientation, Helen argued, coaches should deal openly with them. "Put it in there just like you teach a layup," she advised.

In 1988, Helen interviewed for the position of athletic director at Mills College, a liberal university located in Oakland, California. "How would you treat some athletes that you knew were lesbian?" the Mills interviewers asked her. It was a question that Helen was ready for. She talked about how people needed to respect each other and understand each other's differences. No doubt her clear, forthright answer was part of why she was hired as Mills athletic director.

While she was at Mills, Helen became increasingly public about her sexual orientation, moving from being open personally to actively working for a climate where lesbian coaches and athletes could feel free to be

Helen Carroll

open. The student athletes at Mills proposed workshop topics each semester, with lesbians in sport and racial issues always among the topics suggested, and Helen spoke at and in other ways supported these workshops. For her personally, speaking out about her own identity was a liberating experience. "I just got this sense of relief," she described. "People are still going to like who you are and ... they're not gonna say that you can't be a good basketball coach, you can't be a good athletic director, because you're lesbian."

But Helen isn't naïve about the kinds of pressures many lesbian coaches still face. She's working with the National Center for Lesbian Rights to compile stories of lesbian coaches fired for their sexual orientation. "It happens all the time," she commented, although the official reason given is typically different. But Helen continues to work for positive change. At workshops she leads she gives coaches information on how, for example, to discuss the issue of sexual orientation with parents. In the near future, Helen is optimistic that growing numbers of lesbian coaches will be able to be open about their personal lives.

———•+•———

In spite of Helen Carroll's and Beth Bricker's positive experiences, the situation of an assistant coach at a Division I university, a woman who felt she needed to speak anonymously, illustrates exactly how difficult their working lives can be for lesbian coaches. Although the coach has done very well in her profession, in order to keep her job she doesn't feel able to tell a single other coach at her university about her sexual orientation. "I'm not in any way ashamed (of my sexual orientation)," the coach explained, "but I am really concerned about my job being in jeopardy."

The fact that she needed to stay in the closet was made completely clear for this woman right away. Her initial interview for the job she still holds had gone very well, but at the end of that interview, the head coach asked the woman to close his office door. "It has been rumored because of your associations that you're a lesbian," the head coach told the woman. "I could feel the blood curdling up to my neck, and rushing through my face," the woman recalled, "that hot nauseous feeling, with the adrenaline rushing." What should she say, she thought quickly. Perhaps the less the better.

"I don't know what your sexual status is," the head coach continued, "but I want to remind you that you are a public figure and as such I would like you to conduct yourself as to not bring controversy or shame to the program."

"You are perfectly understood," the woman replied. She left the head coach's office as quickly as she could, with no doubt in her mind about what the head coach meant. He'd give her the job, but the price she'd pay would be to keep her personal life a secret.

"It's an isolating disease, and it's insidious, and it's chronic and it's sad," the woman summed up her situation. Although she was able to be open with a very few of the athletes in her program—typically young women who had initially come out to her as a coach they felt would be sympathetic—the coach had to monitor her own behavior so as to keep her secret. For this coach, the unwritten part of her job was to continually wonder if she was "fitting into the norm ... in the way you conduct yourself, the way you walk, the way you wear your hair, if you wear makeup or not, if you say too many swear words..." It's a continual effort that has taken a toll on the coach's personal life in many ways, and as a result she has considered leaving the coaching profession. "But blood runs deep," she commented, "I have a passion for what I do."

Head softball coach Jenny Allard also feels deeply committed to her profession, but fortunately at Harvard University, Jenny found a supportive atmosphere for coming out. In February, 2001, along with two Harvard athletes and two other sports figures, Jenny spoke at a Harvard forum about sports and homosexuality, an event that was reported in the Harvard paper and elsewhere, and that put Jenny in the unusual position of being a Division I coach who had publicly acknowledged herself as a lesbian.

When Jenny introduced herself to the full house at Harvard Hall, she gave her name, and said that she'd been coaching at Harvard for six years. "I was asked to be on the panel because I'm a coach who's been out to my players for the past four years," she told the audience.

Not long after Jenny came to Harvard, she became a proctor, a position as advisor for students that meant she lived in a student house on campus. After Jenny met Maureen Jones, the woman who became her life partner, and after Jenny and Mo, who also found a job at Harvard, established a home together on campus, Jenny felt that the time had come to tell her team. The fact that Jenny wasn't the first gay proctor to live in Harvard Yard, and the fact that Harvard's nondiscrimination policy includes sexual orientation all made a difference. But most of all Jenny didn't want her players to whisper and wonder about who their coach was living with, or for her partner to have to hide her presence at a Harvard softball game.

Jenny Allard

In a sign of the times, Jenny first came out to her players via e-mail, although that wasn't, she thinks, the ideal method. But in August Jenny's players had begun calling the home on campus where Jenny and Mo now lived together. Since the players weren't on campus yet, a group e-mail message, Jenny figured, was a quick way of communicating with her team. She promised her players that they would talk more on the subject fact to face, but let her players know that she and her partner were now living together. "I want you guys to be aware and not be caught off guard or by surprise," Jenny wrote.

At the first team meeting, Jenny followed up on the team "conversation" she had promised her players. "I want the respect of all of you and you deserve my respect," Jenny said. "I think it's fair for you guys to know that my partner Mo has decided to move to Boston ... and we will be living together." She didn't want her players to be whispering about who Mo was, Jenny said. "I'm telling you this not because I feel that you need to know this person," Jenny explained. "You just need to know so that I'm honest with you."

Jenny had been "very apprehensive" about telling her team, even though she felt strongly it was the right thing to do. Somewhat anticlimactically, most of her players didn't say much about their coach's announcement, although Jenny did receive a supportive e-mail from one player: "Good for you, coach. I'm really happy for you." But the overall impact on her team, Jenny feels, has been positive. "There's just this ... acceptance and genuineness amongst players," Jenny described, which she attributes in part to her openness as a coach.

At Harvard overall, Jenny has met with positive reactions

as well. "Hey, thanks for speaking like that," some people told her after the Harvard panel on gays and sports. Jenny appreciates the "very tolerant and very accepting" atmosphere of the Harvard community and doesn't regret the step she took. "I know that I'm not going to be comfortable if I have to hide things or pretend," she commented. "That's not who I want to be."

Now a professor at the University of Massachusetts in the Social Justice Education Program and involved in educating others about homophobia, Pat Griffin came out herself in 1987, at a professional conference, not accidentally just after she'd received tenure at her university. Someone needed to speak openly on the subject, Pat felt, and for herself personally "it felt to me as if there was no way I could do this (education re homophobia) kind of work if I didn't come out myself."

Homophobia, Pat commented in June, 2001, is still very much out there. The example she gave, of "code words, like, we create a whole family environment for our team," served to illustrate the sometimes subtle yet persistent presence of prejudice. Such prejudice, Pat feels, is one reason for the low numbers of women coaches, with certain athletic directors avoiding the chance of hiring a lesbian coach by hiring a male coach instead. Yet Pat also feels optimistic that things are changing for the better. "There are more and more young athletes who come to college already out," Pat commented. "They're not going back in. I think they're really pushing coaches and their teammates to broaden their horizons." As Pat travels the country to lead workshops on homophobia in sports, she tries to show coaches they need to "create athletic environments where everybody is safe and respected."

A number of coaches, regardless of their own sexual orientation, are doing just that. At a team meeting, for example, ice hockey coach Shannon Miller discussed the fact that the makeup of her team was very diverse. She talked about the presence of international players on the team, the differences in race and ethnicity, and sexual orientation as well. "This (college) is a place of education," Shannon told her team, "and part of education is accepting social differences."

Along the same lines, when field hockey coach Beth Bozmen first came to Harvard, she couldn't help noticing the lack of diversity. "When I got here," Beth described, "everybody was blonde haired, blue eyed, from Greenwich, Connecticut, and I was the only nonrepublican." As she's built the field hockey program at her college, Beth's teams have included players from Holland, Germany, Australia, and Canada, with other kinds of diversity as well. Beth deliberately works with her players to foster an acceptance of the differences among them, including those of sexual orientation. Among her players, Beth described, homophobia is "a nonfactor now. ... Our straight kids joke about taking (a lesbian player) to house parties."

Softball coach Rhonda Revelle has found that the overall supportive atmosphere she creates allows players to speak openly about a variety of topics with her, including about their sexual orientation. "I've had kids out themselves to me, I've had kids say I don't know if I'm anything. I've had kids say I think I'm both things ..." Rhonda described. "I think my persona is that I'm ... pretty open door."

"The lesbian label and the accompanying homophobia have been major influences upon coaching careers and recruitment decisions of women coaches," wrote Susan Wellman and Elaine Blinde about their study of Division I women basketball coaches.Certainly, stereotypes and prejudices of all sorts—including about race, ethnicity and sexual orientation—still abound in the collegiate sports world, just as in other areas of society. But numerous coaches across the country, whatever their race, ethnic background or sexual orientation, continue to find positive ways to confront prejudices. While the question of attitude is still very much out there, numerous women coaches are giving their own kind of "attitude" back.

Ways of Coaching

The stereotypical coach, perhaps a man with close-cropped hair and a steely expression who coaches football or basketball, shouts and curses at his athletes, exhorting them to kill their opponents, to do or die for the good of the team. Another hypothetical coach forces athletes to spend minimal time on their college classes and to push themselves past pain to the point of injury. Although abusive coaches definitely exist, fortunately the reality is often different. Coaches don't all lead their athletes as if they were clones from a grade B Hollywood football film. Many women college coaches put into practice a very different vision of coaching.

The gender of the athletes, many coaches say, affects the kinds of approaches coaches will find successful. Since less than two percent of women coach male college athletes, it seems likely that many women coaches tune their coaching approaches to the female gender of their athletes. When a male golf coach at Portland State University was going to coach female golfers for the first time, he asked longtime softball coach Teri Mariani for advice. "Don't expect it to be the same as coaching your men," Teri told the male coach. "You really can't coach them (males and females) the same," she explained. "Women take things a little more personal" than men, Teri cautioned. They often need to be motivated differently.

"A coach's approach to men and women is definitely different," University of North Carolina women's soccer coach, Anson Dorrance, wrote in *Training Soccer Champions*. Male athletes, he described, are more likely to respond to "strong personalities who lead with a powerful presence and will." They respond well to a coach they can "respect." Female athletes, in contrast, "have to feel that you care about them personally or have some kind of connection with them beyond the game. Woman want to experience a coach's humanity." While male athletes are more likely to challenge their coach's authority, female athletes are more likely to take critical comments personally and to watch and listen for the subtle nuances in a coach's voice and body language. Since the gender roles girls learn growing up make it more difficult for girls than for boys to compete against teammates who are often also friends, as a coach Anson Dorrance has to teach his female players that competing hard against each other helps everyone on the team.

While the gender of the athletes is undoubtedly a factor for coaches, what of the gender of the coaches themselves? Needless to say, women coaches aren't all cut from the same cookie cutter mold. As Donna Lopiano summarized, "How a coach gets an athlete to perform to his or her potential varies considerably and varies as (much) within gender as well as between genders." Or as former University of Massachusetts swimming coach Pat Griffin described humorously, "There are (female) coaches that if you put a bag over their head or their body, you couldn't tell them from the baseball coach or the football coach." And yet in coaching as in other areas of life it doesn't seem off the wall to consider coaches' gender as one aspect of their working lives. When we consider the very different histories men and women have with sports in the United States, as well as differences in gender role socialization, it's not surprising that many female coaches seem to speak the same or at least similar languages when they talk about their personal approaches to coaching.

Chris Shelton of Smith College, a former tennis coach who now teaches women who will become coaches, is concerned about the manner in which these future coaches will practice their profession. Many of the women she teaches have only had male coaches. "If you have women coming through programs coached only by men," Chris argued, "most likely they're going to come out coaching like these men, and if there is a style that you could label a gendered style of coaching, to me that would be the disciplined, authoritarian, bossy, totally controlling coach, military model that men have had as their models."

That stereotypically macho style of coaching, Chris was quick to point out, is one that many coaches, both male and female, are now rejecting in favor of a more "compassionate style" and a "more humanitarian treatment." Athletes today, Chris argued, want more ability to make their own decisions, want more explanations of why they should do things a certain way. "The military style coach, the screamer coach," Chris commented, "like a Bobby Knight or Pat Head Summitt, slowly are having to come up with a different style" to use with a new generation of players.

When Indiana University's men's basketball coach Bobby Knight, a male coach famous for his macho, confrontational style of coaching, was fired, it made headlines around the country. For years, Bobby Knight was known for verbally and physically abusing players and others. Among other incidents, he had thrown a chair on the court in a game, kicked his son when he competed on the Indiana basketball team, and choked a player during a practice. In May, 2000, Indiana University imposed a "zero-tolerance policy" on Knight based on his repeated abuses, then finally fired him in September of the same year after he grabbed a student and cursed him for, the student reported, "his lack of respect."

Mary Jo Peppler, former volleyball star, college coach, and now teacher of coaches, considered the Bobby Knight situation in a humorously critical light. "He's coaching from another century," Mary Jo commented about Knight. "Before there were human rights."

Mary Jo Peppler's years of involvement in the athletic world give her words considerable weight. As her résumé states, she has "coaching and playing experience in four decades at every level of volleyball competition: international; professional; collegiate; junior, open; beach." In the late '70s and early '80s, she was co-head coach at the Utah State University and the University of Kentucky, and she's been a coaching consultant for a number of other universities. For years, she's given clinics for coaches at all levels across the country. Mary Jo also has a star-studded list of accomplishments as an athlete. During the '60s, she competed on the USA National women's volleyball team, including in the 1964 Olympics. At the 1970 World Games she was honored as an "outstanding player." She later competed in a professional co-ed volleyball league and in professional beach volleyball as well, often acting as a coach as well as a player. "She's one of our best coaches ever in the United States," commented volleyball coach Stephanie Schleuder.

Currently, Mary Jo Peppler is the director of coaching at Coast Volleyball, a junior volleyball club in San Diego. Her main role there is to train high school and college coaches. "Coach training has been my passion," Mary Jo commented. "I really believe that players want to do their best. And I hate watching a coaching style where players are abused or they're cancelled, or they're labelled, prevented from doing their best."

Women are among the coaches Mary Jo teaches at Coast volleyball, but the bulk of her coaches-turned-students are men. Often with these men she has to specifically confront the authoritarian, macho style of coaching these men have typically learned, and to suggest other options in coaching styles. Mary Jo has to set some ground rules for coaching. "Getting mad is not an option," she tells her coaches in training. "You're the problem solver. You can't get mad. You have to find out what's in the way" for an athlete or team.

When Mary Jo herself was coaching at Utah State, a man teaching psychology at the college would come to matches and observe. It had been very interesting to watch the different coaching styles, the psychology teacher eventually told the coaches. His label for Mary Jo and her assistants' styles of coaching was "humanitarian."

It's a label that Mary Jo embraces. "I really do think that the arena belongs to the players," she commented. "That the coach is there to assist them to reach their goals." For herself as a coach, she explained, "my primary asset is problem solving, to find ways to open new doors" for the athletes.

How do individual women coaches open those doors? For volleyball coach Marlene Piper, relating to her athletes in a manner that maintains her "respect for human dignity" is central to her coaching approach. Some of her athletes, accustomed to a hard-nosed style of coaching will ask for the same from Marlene. "Yell at me, scream at me," the women will say to Marlene. "I'm sorry I can't because that's not my style," Marlene will reply. Regardless of the inevitable anger and frustration a coach can feel at times, one of Marlene's hard and fast coaching rules is that "I don't throw chairs, and I will not berate my players. I will not cuss at them. I will not treat people with indignities."

University of Texas track coach Bev Kearney takes a similar approach. As a coach, she works to create "as much of a family relationship" as possible with her athletes, a job description that many other women coaches echo. For Bev, treating her athletes as she herself would want to be treated is an important part of her coaching philosophy. "I don't think you can demand anything from an athlete that you're not willing to give," Bev affirmed. "If you expect them to respect you, then you must respect them. If you don't want them screaming and cursing and hollering at people, then you don't treat them like that."

Laurie Corbelli, a former USA Volleyball player who now coaches volleyball at Texas A&M University, leads her players in a style that could be labeled both disciplined and maternal. "I tell them I love them," Laurie commented. "I tell them how important they are to me and I'm there for them." But on other occasions, she can demonstrate a no nonsense, I'm-the-boss approach. "Give me three shuttle runs in under 15 seconds each," she might demand. Since she knows volleyball players dislike the sprints from sideline to sideline, they can be an effective tool to sharpen her players' attention.

"I yell a lot," Laurie admitted, "but it's mostly to challenge them. It's not to diminish or degrade." As a woman coach, sometimes she wants to break away from gendered behavior, to be "less nourishing and more rough ... more assertive" about her expectations. Yet she most definitely doesn't want to echo the style of a male coach she played under for USA Volleyball, a man who never really listened to or trusted his players.

Laurie Corbelli

Unlike that coach, Laurie Corbelli has a strong rapport with her players. During a match, for example, if a player isn't doing well and needs to come out of the game, Laurie will typically have the player sit next to her on the team bench, then put her arm around the player. "It's yukky out there right now," Laurie might say, rather than chewing out the player. "You're having a heck of a night," she might sympathize. "I just want you to take a deep breath. Let's just sit here together and watch this, and we'll figure it all out." While many coaches in the same sitaution will yell at their athletes, Laurie's approach is to "only get in their face" when she can see that an athlete is not giving full effort.

During the years she's been a college coach, Laurie has gradually evolved a fairly flexible style of coaching. On one road trip, for example, a player told Laurie that she'd forgotten her white jersey, expecting her coach to implement the team rule and say, "Then you are not playing." But instead Laurie talked the matter over with her two team captains, both seniors. "What do you all think we should do?" Laurie asked. "I have an emergency jersey. What do you think the team would respond with?"

When the captains concurred that using the emergency jersey made sense, Laurie allowed her player to do so, explaining to the young woman that she wasn't "a repeat offender." Her decision in that case, Laurie evaluated, worked out well. Certainly, it was a good example of the collaborative style of decision making that women leaders often use. It also revealed how a coach can empower athletes by allowing them input into team decisions.

In contrast to the softer approach used by Marlene Piper and Laurie Corbelli, there are female coaches whose overall approaches to coaching are more in the tough love mode. Ice hockey coach Digit Murphy, for example, who described her coaching personality as "competitive and intense," argued that since ice hockey is "a sport where you have to be tough, I feel I have to coach in a tough way to bring out the best" from her players.

Digit's belief in toughness doesn't mean she holds in warmer feelings in a stereotypically male style. Like Laurie Corbelli, Digit Murphy is not only a mother but someone comfortable with expressing the affection she has for her players. "I love you guys," Digit will tell her players. But all along, even from when she's recruiting potential athletes, she'll also tell the young women: "I'm going to be in your face. I'm going to be someone you're going to hate." If a player can't handle that approach, Digit warns she shouldn't come to play at Brown University. "You need to understand," Digit will explain to her players, "that it's my job as a coach to bring out the best in you. You gotta get thick skin."

In situations where some coaches might go easy on their athletes, Digit refuses to cut her players any slack. On one occasion, after her players had played poorly and badly lost a game, even though Digit knew that the players were going to a party to celebrate a teammate's 21st birthday, she scheduled a 6 a.m. practice for the next morning and skated her players for about an hour without a puck. Perhaps it isn't surprising that Digit's oldest son, Kevin, described his mom as "tough."

"You gotta raise the bar," Digit commented about her expectations for her athletes. "The day I stop pushing you is the day I don't coach anymore," she told her team captain one day. "You know ... that I'm not a big person to tell you guys how good you are," Digit added. "Oh, we know that," her captain quickly replied. Yet at the team banquet held at the end of each year, Digit will not only praise her athletes but tell them again how much she loves them. In fact, Digit's tough approach may work with her female athletes in part because of the basic level of caring she establishes.

Like Digit Murphy, Pat Head Summitt from the University of Tennessee is well known for being a tough coach. In her book *Raise the Roof*, Pat characterized herself as a "yeller" whose "voice gets so hoarse it sounds like tires crunching over gravel." She needed to raise her voice with young players especially, Pat argued, because she needed "to break young players down in order to build them up again, properly." Although Pat didn't make the comparison, that's basically the same plan of action which the military uses with new recruits.

On the other hand, clearly Pat Summitt has changed her approach to coaching over the years. In 1975, when Pat began coaching at Tennessee, she believed that she "wouldn't be able to do my job if I cared about (the players) too much." For years, her attitude had been that "the only time a coach should be close to her players was when they needed a talking to, eyeball to eyeball." But by the start of the 1997-98 season, Pat was ready to be more open with the young women on her team. In October of that season, Pat held a team meeting where both players and coaches talked about themselves and their families. "The more trusting my relationships with players," Pat realized, "the better teacher and coach I could be to them."

Lori Dauphiny, head women's open crew coach at Princeton University, finds it effective to blend toughness and a softer approach while working with her rowers, a coaching mix that many women coaches use. "One of my jobs is to push people to their limits," Lori described. "And I think that's one of the hardest things that I have to do. ...I'm always supportive, but at the same time I have to push pretty hard. I have to be tough with them." Lori needs to find the "very delicate balance" between encouraging athletes to stretch their physical limits yet not pushing her athletes hard enough that they risk injury.

At times, when working with her rowers, Lori might feel like saying to a young woman, "Oh, honey, I can see that you're tired. We need to go in." Sometimes she does take that approach. But at other moments Lori comes across as less nurturing. "You know what," Lori might say, "you've got to step it up right now because at the end of the race you're going to feel like this, and you're going to have to be a little bit tougher."

Whatever their personal approaches to working with their athletes, women coaches are all people whose jobs place them in positions of authority. While this is, of course, true for male coaches as well, women coaches are authority figures within a larger culture where women are still more commonly found in subordinate roles in the public realm and authority figures are typically male.

For Pat Kendrick at George Mason University, becoming a volleyball coach at the same university where she had competed as a player made expressing a coach's authority difficult initially. After an outstanding athletic career at GMU, during which she excelled in track and field and volleyball, Pat took the position of assistant coach with the women's volleyball team. Her change in status, from peer to coach, meant that she had to give up social activities such as going to movies with women who had been her teammates. It would be very difficult to discipline players if she and they maintained their relationship as friends. As Pat adjusted to her new leadership role and became the head women's volleyball coach after two seasons, maintaining that line between player and coach became easier.

Pat isn't the sort of rigidly authoritarian coach who maintains a stiff distance between herself and her athletes. At 39, she was still competing in volleyball tournaments when her coaching schedule permitted, and one of her strategies for staying in shape was to work out with her team in the weight room and on the track. A former sprinter and hurdler, Pat knew that she provided a kind of moving target for her players to compete against. When her players did track workouts, Pat commented, for "some of them, their goal is not let me beat them." She laughed at the idea, clearly not threatened by it. "Hopefully that's a little incentive for them to run a little faster."

Pat isn't the sort of coach who leaves her sense of humor at the locker room door either. On one occasion during a team practice, when a player acted in a childish manner, Pat's response was, "Somebody didn't get their nap this morning." In 1997, during a tough tournament match against American University, Pat's players performed poorly, losing their first two games, but Pat managed to preserve her sense of humor. "Someone has kidnapped our team," she said to her assistant coach. "I mean, who are those people?"

Her female gender, Pat is well aware, affects the way she communicates with her players. "To some extent they expect a male coach to be a little meaner," Pat commented. Yelling and screaming from a male coach, Pat explained, is perceived as more OK than from a female coach. Yet Pat Kendrick most definitely speaks with the voice of authority to her players. A player, for example, might talk back to Pat during a practice. "This is stupid," a player might say, "Why do we have to do this?" Pat's response is typically clear and emphatic. "See that door?" she might say. "No one is holding you back."

Her players' responses to her as an authority figure, Pat has found, are connected to the players' own family histories, especially to the players' relationships to their mothers. If a player has been raised by a mother who is clearly an authority figure, Pat described, "I tend to not have as much trouble with them." Pat's coaching style is influenced by her relationship with her own mother, a woman whom Pat respected growing up but didn't see as one of her friends. "When she told me to do something, I did it," Pat remembered. Like a savvy, no-nonsense mother, Pat isn't swayed by the actions of some of her less than mature players. "I've had players that have just thrown tantrums," Pat recollected. "I sub them out, and I just chew them a new one," she described succinctly.

Pat doesn't always play the heavy, though. Like many other good coaches, she's skilled at adapting her coaching approaches to the particular group of athletes she has on each team. In 1995 and 1996, for example, when Pat coached a team of highly self-confident individuals who nevertheless needed a large share of coaching attention, a group Pat humorously described as "the high maintenance girls," she would typically try to "pump up the competition," to encourage her team to play their hardest.

In 1997, by contrast, Pat's top players had previously been over-shadowed by the top athletes of the previous years' teams. "There's nobody else ahead of you. You're the seniors. It's your turn," Pat encouraged these players.

As a coach, Pat Kendrick is a strong leader who exercises her authority without fitting into the stereotypical yeller-screamer coaching mold. And like many other coaches, Pat sees her connection to her players as an ongoing one, something very much like an extended family connection. She keeps in contact with many of her players, receiving invitations to their weddings, photos of them and their babies. "You might graduate off this team, but you're never off this team," Pat tells her players.

———

Sports isn't just about relationships, of course. It's about winning and losing games and meets and matches. Numerous women coaches have commented on both their own competitive natures and the importance of competition for themselves and their teams. And as the older model that discouraged competitive sports for supposedly too delicate females has become more and more discredited, and sports opportunities for girls and women have greatly increased, many women coaches now face the kinds of pressures to win that coaches of men's teams have long experienced. As that trend very likely continues, how will women coaches respond? Will some of the abuses seen in men's athletic programs be replicated on the women's side? Will women coaches and women's athletic programs adopt the win-at-all-costs approach that certain male coaches have used?

Realistically, the answer is probably yes, some of the time. As a case in point, Andrea Durieux, an assistant basketball coach at Portland State University, preferred not to name the female head basketball coach but mentioned that the coach had lost her job when it was learned that she'd been "negligent " about injuries to her players, forcing the young women to continue playing. An April, 2000, an Associated Press article described the "dizzying pace" of coaches of women's basketball teams with a losing record themselves losing their jobs. For women's basketball coaches, the sportswriter asserted, "the pressure on coaches has never been greater, the profession never so volatile." And because women are "aware of their tentative status in the men's gym," Mariah Burton Nelson argued, "some try to play by the men's rules, including destructive competitiveness and tyrannical coaching styles."

However, female athletes as a group, according to researchers Mimi Murray and Hilary Matheson, may be less willing than male athletes to accept winning at any cost or the kinds of aggressive sports behaviors that cause injuries. And numerous women coaches, while emphasizing that they do want to win, have made abundantly clear that they only value wins that come in a good way. Although Princeton field hockey coach Beth Bozman agreed with football coach Joe Paterno "that you learn more from winning than from losing," she clarified that for both herself and her players, "we don't like losing but we will not win at all costs."

As an example of the kind of approach she doesn't respect, Beth described a game a few years ago, where the opposing team "intentionally took out one of our players ... physically hurt her." In front of the Princeton team bench, and in clear view of the opposing coach, some opposing players "hit (the Princeton player) with the stick, took her down, and then hit her when she was down." Beth brought the matter up with an official, then after the game she spoke to the woman who coached the opposing team. Beth asked why didn't that coach do anything about the deliberate injury. "I don't know what you're talking about," the other coach stonewalled. "I left the game embarrassed to be in this profession," Beth described, "and thinking at the time that if that's what it takes to get to the top level, that's never gonna happen here because I won't compromise to do that." In her own experience, though, she's found that "you can get to the top level and maintain your integrity."

A coaching colleague and friend of Beth Bozman, and someone with similarly high ethical standards, is Beth Anders of Old Dominion, whom Beth Bozman praised highly as "the best coach in the country" and someone with "a brilliant field hockey mind." Beth Anders can clearly express her authority as a coach, like many coaches using her voice as a tool. With her players, she described, "My voice dictates what they should be thinking and feeling... If it's soft, they probably should be relaxed. If they need a little kick in the rear, it might get a little bit intense or harder." An outstanding athlete, Beth led the U.S. field hockey team to a bronze medal at the 1984 Olympics as she scored all but one of her team's goals, setting an Olympic record in the process. But while Beth certainly enjoys winning, she also highly values good sportsmanship. The winning-at-all-costs philosophy is one that she completely rejects.

Beth Anders

In one field hockey match, Old Dominion was credited with a goal but Beth Anders felt that the official had made an incorrect ruling, that the goal really shouldn't have counted. Beth stood on the sidelines, inwardly debating what to do, knowing she had to make a rapid decision. Although she chose not to intervene, she was glad when her team scored another goal because she "didn't want to win like that."

Beth Anders tells other coaching stories that reveal the kind of values she teaches her athletes. In 1992, the night before the national championship game, Beth spoke to her team in a hotel room. Beth had seen the pressure mounting on her players; she'd seen how nervous they were about the upcoming game. "We're all going to face a challenge together," Beth told her players, "and we're going to do it together, and whether we win or lose this game won't make a difference in our life, but how we play is going to make every difference."

The ethical approach to competition expressed by Beth Anders, Beth Bozman, and many other women coaches has some of its roots in what Chris Shelton of Smith College described as a model of sport different from the male model. In contrast to football, for example, where aggressive, win-at-all-costs competition is seen as the norm, there is, Chris described, "another model of sport" that "has abounded in women's sports for a hundred years." According to Mary Jo Peppler, the win-at-all costs, stereotypically male model is one where sports are seen as disengaged from the rest of life. "You're trying to win. You take every advantage that you can ... then walk away from the court and it's over." Many women coaches and athletes, on the other hand, Mary Jo has observed, take a different approach. "What we call the female model," Mary Jo described, "is everything you do in that competitive arena is affecting your relationships to people on the team, to your opponents, to the refs, even to the fans. It's a piece of your connected life." The good news, according to Mary Jo, is that attitudes about sports are changing. "I think both men and women have come to a more balanced view of what sport is," she argued. Within the past 10 years she's seen a "remarkable change in attitudes" about coaching styles and the meaning of competition.

In *Are We Winning Yet?*, Mariah Burton Nelson described what she called a "new model of sport." In contrast to the "military model," with its emphasis on winning, hostile relationships between opponents, and warlike language, Mariah characterized the "partnership model" as "a compassionate, egalitarian approach in which athletes are motivated by love of themselves, of sports, and of each other" and in which "teammates, coaches, and even opposing players view each other as comrades rather than enemies." This approach to sport has strong similarities to that espoused by earlier women physical educators, who thought that sport should encourage comraderie between participants, but adds the dimension of high-level competition.

When Pat Griffin coached the women's swim team at the University of Massachusetts, she implemented what she described as "feminist coaching principles." With the women swimmers she worked with, Pat explained, "I really tried to promote an attitude that their competition was their strongest ally." On one occasion during a swim meet, Pat's swimmer and a University of New Hampshire swimmer were "stroke for stroke coming down the last lap," Pat recalled, until at the end the UNH swimmer "just barely touched out my swimmer." After the race, Pat remembered, the woman on her team "just sort of erupted from the water, and reached over and grabbed this woman and said 'thank you, thank you,' and the woman was stunned." The opposing swimmer's surprised reaction fit with the conventional model of sport, where losers don't typically thank winners. But the reaction of Pat Griffin's swimmer made sense according to a different, less antagonistic model of competition. Pushed by the high-level competitor, Pat's swimmer had just swum a personal best.

Although Mills College cross country coach Sharon Chiong enjoys winning as much as other coaches, like Pat Griffin, Sharon Chiong appreciates an approach where individual wins are not the highest goal. At Mills College, Sharon commented, coaches are encouraged to "focus on the whole individual, not just on athletic performance." It's an orientation that Sharon strongly agrees with. "I didn't want to be coaching someone just to run faster or throw farther or jump higher," Sharon commented. "I wanted to work on the whole person."

"Holistic" is the one-word label Sharon gave for her emphasis on the "whole individual." In her view that approach is harder to maintain at a Division I university where coaches face a higher level of pressure to have a winning record if they want to keep their jobs. At Division III Mills, in contrast, Sharon is confident that she could have a number of losing seasons and not lose her coaching position, because rather than emphasizing the number of wins, the emphasis is on a positive experience for the student athlete. Similarly, one benefit of Sharon's job at Mills is that the somewhat less high pressure position, although often involving long hours of work, also allows Sharon to live a more holistic lifestyle than is possible for some coaches. She has the flexibility to take personal time to be with her family and to run with her dogs on the wooded trails near Mills.

Even though cross country is an individual sport, in part because of her Asian-American background, Sharon highly values and works for "team cohesion." If her runners feel comfort-

Sharon Chiong

able with their track program, their teammates, and their coach, Sharon feels, "the performance will take care of itself." It's an orientation that some people might label as "lackadaisical" but Sharon's response to that potential criticism is to point to the success her runners have had, such as the California Pacific Conference championship the Mills cross country team won in fall, 1999.

Before coming to Mills, Sharon served as the head men's and women's cross country coach at Depauw University and at Florida Atlantic University, making her one of the very small group of women who have coached male college athletes. When Sharon started out at Depauw, she was only 23 years old and felt concerned about how the males on her team would react to her as coach. "What are these guys gonna think," she wondered, "taking directions from a female?" Luckily, the male athletes Sharon worked with at Depauw and FAU had no problems with a woman as their coach, and Sharon found that she basically didn't change her coaching approach when working with male vs. female athletes. She wouldn't yell at her male runners, for example, even though she knew they might accept that style of communication more than female runners would. "I try not to see men and women ... I try to see human beings," Sharon commented.

With very few male athletes coached by females, however, women who coach male athletes can take a fair amount of flak for doing so. In *The Quiet Storm: A Celebration of Women in Sport*, authors Alexandra Powe-Allred and Michelle Powe describe the reaction Air Force Academy diving coach Micki King received from members of the media about her role as a female coach for male cadets. Over and over reporters asked Micki about how, as a woman, she could handle coaching the male divers. Finally Micki had had it with that kind of question. "Well, first I'm going to cut out the locker room talks," Micki said to a member of the media, "since I'm not allowed in, then I think I'll paint the diving board pink with a pink trim around the pool." The reporter's assumptions were absurd, Micki King's up-yours response made perfectly clear.

Yet not all women coaches have had Sharon Chiong's positive experiences when working with male athletes. When Jane Paterson took the position of head tennis coach for men and women at Bowdoin College, some of the men on her team would argue with Jane or refuse to comply with her instructions. Their attitude was that "I'm just a female and what could I possibly know about the men's game of tennis," Jane recalled. Undoubtedly, it didn't help that the previous tennis coach at Bowdoin was a man who had a "get-in-your-face, yell, scream, shout" coaching style very different from Jane's own more positive, open approach. "What the heck's this all about? You don't give a rip because you don't get mad," is how Jane thinks some of her male players especially perceived her. Some men and some women as well quit the tennis team in Jane's first year of coaching at Bowdoin, a year she described succinctly as "hell." After Jane finally had to kick one antagonistic man off the team, the letters he wrote about her to people at the college, Jane described with some restraint, included a "character assassination" of her that was "fairly graphic and just extremely upsetting."

The negative reactions she encountered, Jane recalled, "made me do a lot of soul searching as to whether I really did know what I was talking about." In fact, Jane's strong background in tennis competition in her native Britain and in U.S. collegiate tennis, and her previous coaching experience at other colleges had prepared her well for the Bowdoin head coaching position. During that difficult first year there, Jane was also helped by her conversations with other female coaches, especially Chris Davis, whom Jane had worked under at Smith College as an assistant coach, and Carol Weymuller, the men's and women's tennis coach at Hobart College, who had had similar difficulties with male athletes when she first began coaching there. "Stick with it," Carol advised, saying that Jane would be able to recruit new players who felt good about her coaching style.

Presently, Jane commented, on her team she has "some wonderful guys that I think extremely highly of." She does use a somewhat different approach with her male and female athletes because she's found that works better. With a young woman, Jane described, "I'll go out there, and we'll talk about what she's thinking" and "I'll try and encourage her" whereas at times with a young man Jane might simply say, "take your head out of your backside and let's get going." Overall, Jane tries to adapt her coaching style to each individual, and now happy at Bowdoin, she enjoys those coaching moments when she's working with her athletes and "you see the light bulb go on."

———◦◦———

Although coaches are stereotypically viewed as firm, no-nonsense coaching authority figures, some women coaches demonstrate how coaching can involve a much lighter touch. One of those is Smith College tennis coach Chris Davis, who deliberately uses humor as one of her coaching tools.

The women Chris coaches at Smith are typically high achievers who put a great deal of pressure on themselves. A few years ago the women on Chris's team had been having problems with their serving, and Chris could sense a growing tension among her players. Chris's response was to make creative use of some swimming flippers she found in the basement of the gym. While Chris's assistant coach had trouble keeping a straight face, Chris told each of her players to put a flipper on their nondominant foot. "I'm really sick to death of you guys foot faulting ... and we've got to stop it," Chris said with mock seriousness.

The players, convinced their coach meant business, took their assignment seriously, asking her questions like "Now do we line the end of the flipper up to the baseline?" After the players had all hit their serves, Chris let her players in on the secret. It was all an April Fool's joke. The young women, who by then were as relaxed as Chris had wished, responded in kind to the joke by chasing after their coach with their flippers.

On another memorable occasion, Chris brought in a collection of plastic drink glasses, complete with a set of drug testing instructions she had typed and rolled up within each of the plastic glasses. Everyone on the team would need to provide a urine sample for drug testing, Chris told her team at a practice. "You have to be careful and read the directions very carefully," she emphasized. One by one her players took the "specimen glass" to the bathroom and read the instructions, including the last line: "This is an April Fool's joke. You've been had."

While humor can be used in a negative way, that is definitely not Chris's intent. She wants to develop her players as whole people, to let them know that "your self worth is not related to how you hit a tennis ball," and that winning and losing tennis tournaments isn't the only important part of life. Although Chris doesn't want to impose her personal religious beliefs on her players, she does find them influencing her coaching philosophy. Chris and the young women on her tennis team talk, for example, about "grace," which Chris defines as "being there for each other," and being "forgiving of themselves as well as of those that are around them." The idea of grace, Chris explains, also includes "being gracious" toward opponents. "You can still be very competitive, but be a gracious competitor," she tells her players.

The balanced perspective and the ethical behavior that Chris teaches, in her case in part with humor, is both an approach used by many other women coaches, and an approach that has strong similarities to the holistic view of sports advocated by early women physical educators. The joke that the Wellesley College tennis team played on the Smith College tennis team on one occasion seemed to illustrate that these types of lessons were taking hold.

Chris Davis and her players were driving along the Tatonic Parkway, enroute to Vassar College for the Seven Sisters Championship, when they purchased an inflatable rabbit at a gas station. The players blew up the pink and white plastic rabbit and hung it in the front window of their team van. After they reached their hotel and forgot to lock the van, however, players from Wellesley College stole the rabbit, deflated it, and hung it by the ears in their own team van. The Wellesley players then called up Smith players to report on the theft. "Smith College, we have your rabbit," a Wellesley player said in a low-pitched, mock-criminal voice.

While play days and sports days are a thing of the past, an emphasis on friendship as well as competition can still be found in women's collegiate sports. At the Seven Sisters tournament, Chris described, one goal is "to create comraderie within the teams and with the coaches as much as possible." At the joint team banquet before tennis matches, players from various teams are encouraged to mix with each other, and each team provides some kind of entertainment. "We try to take it out of the realm of the tennis competition," Chris explained, "because we want to value the fact that each individual has a lot of skills that go well beyond tennis." In the inflatable-rabbit year, the players from Smith and Wellesley indicated that they understood the spirit of the tournament by holding a mock-ceremony to exchange the pink and white rabbit at the tournament's end.

Through experiences such as these, Chris Davis believes, players build the kind of memories and friendships which can last a lifetime. As a coach, she values those types of experiences as highly as the competitive tennis skills she teaches. And although the kinds of jokes Chris employs only work for some coaches, her holistic perspective on sport and approach to coaching is put into practice by many other women coaches.

Challenges and Rewards

It was a sunny Sunday in late April, 2000, an unusually balmy day for the Pacific Northwest, where spring weather is more typically cool and soggy. Many fans in the bleachers wore summer attire, shorts and T-shirts. On the field, the young women playing for Teri Mariani's team looked appropriately dressed in their black shorts and dark green short sleeved shirts with "Portland State" written in white letters on the front.

The game was held in Erv Lind Stadium in Portland, Oregon, a stadium named after the Erv Lind Florists, a legendary local women's softball team. It was a team that Portland native Teri Mariani had played on years ago. But today she was here, as she had been for many years, as the coach of the Portland State University women's softball team.

For Teri, the game wasn't a gimmee. She's too experienced a coach to take that attitude with any game. But this Sunday's doubleheader, the sequel to a Saturday doubleheader against the same team, were nonconference competitions that Teri had set into PSU's schedule in the hope that PSU would have improved more this year than their opponent, Southern Utah. These four opening weekend games could get the PSU players off to a good start in an important season for them—their third year in NCAA Division I and their first year in a conference.

As the Southern Utah players took their first at bats, Teri watched from a far corner of the PSU dugout. The PSU players got three quick outs, "Born in the USA" played on the stadium loudspeakers, and Teri moved to her accustomed position, standing along the third base line, sometimes squinting against the

Teri Mariani

sun as she watched the play. With her comfortable stance, green team T-shirt and steel wool gray short hair, Teri looked exactly what she was—a longtime softball coach.

Teri Mariani has been coaching long enough that she's experienced many of the challenges involved in coaching a women's sport, as well as many of its rewards. And although female coaches like male coaches often opt to move up the career ladder by relocating to other colleges, Teri has accumulated all her college coaching experience in one place. The 2000 season was Teri's 24th as a head softball coach at PSU. Teri's "veins run green and white," the PSU colors, commented Teri's former coach and current coaching colleague, Marlene Piper, adding that Teri is "the true epitome of team loyalty."

In 1986, Teri was honored by her selection to the Portland Metropolitan Softball Association Hall of Fame, an award that recognized her achievements as a collegiate softball coach and as a former star player as well. Teri got her softball start in American Softball Association (ASA) summer programs, playing practically all the positions. Teri competed in three sports at Portland State University, basketball, volleyball and, of course, softball. She played for top notch Portland softball teams as well, including Hanset Sheet Metal and the Erv Lind Florists, a team that had twice won national championships. Marlene Piper, who had both played alongside Teri and coached her in softball at PSU, remembered Teri as an "excellent infielder and a great, great player."

In the late '70s, Teri had the opportunity to play professional softball for a short-lived women's pro softball league. The league, Teri described, had "a great level of competition" and top level talent. She remembered the crowds of 1,500 or 2,000 people—good attendance at the time for softball—who would come to games. But the salaries players received were low. Teri signed one contract for the grand total of $2000, another for $4,500. And media were typically not interested in covering a women's sports league. The league, Teri commented wistfully, was "just ahead of its time, I think. If you had the same players playing now in a pro league, you could pack the place."

It was all a useful background, all grist for Teri Mariani's coaching mill. The high level softball competition she experienced her up-close-and-personal knowledge of the game, undoubtedly influenced the high expectations she's had all along for her players. Her experiences with adversity—low salaries, little media interest—were good preparation for the many challenges she's faced in coaching an often poorly supported women's sport. Yet paradoxically, Teri's background as a high-level athlete also posed some problems for her as she faced the first and biggest challenge of her professional career: learning how to coach.

When Teri began her coaching career at Portland State, she was only 23 years old, a green young coach attempting to lead players who were only slightly younger than her, many of whom had recently been her teammates. "I'm a good player, so I should be a good coach," Teri assumed. But knowing all about the game of softball, Teri discovered, didn't translate into coaching know-how. "You're a young coach and you're trying to go on a power trip and make sure everybody understands you're the coach," was how Teri described her initial coaching style.

As a new coach, Teri was far too rigid about rules and expectations, once demoting a player from the varsity to the JV team because the player missed a practice in order to attend her parents' 25th wedding anniversary. "I expected perfection and couldn't handle anything less than that," Teri recalled. It was the style of coaching she had sometimes experienced herself as a high-achieving athlete. "I've had coaches come up and just grab me by my shirt and say what the heck do you think you're doing out there," Teri described.

Although Teri hadn't minded that approach herself, as a new coach she had a lot to learn about being flexible when the situation warranted and about treating her players as individuals. "Let's not be afraid to listen to our players," was the heartfelt advice Teri gave recently at a clinic for Little League coaches. In Teri's first few years of coaching, it was her players who helped Teri grow into her job. "We need to talk," the young women on Teri's PSU softball team told her one day before a practice. They sat down with her and described the way she communicated with them. "Treat them as people and understand that sometimes they're going to make a mistake," was the message Teri received from her players. It was advice Teri took to heart. "There's no way I'd be the coach I am today if I had not listened to my players," she commented.

The inevitable moments when Teri messed up also helped with her personal coaching education. Early in her career, it was still legal for her to coach her PSU players during the summers on an ASA team. During the sixth inning of one unforgettable tournament game, Teri sat in the dugout along with a few of her players, including one young woman whom Teri had told to sit out of the game because the player had "thrown a temper tantrum" in the previous game. Teri's team was up by a run and only needed one more out to end the inning, but first her pitcher and then her catcher made crucial errors, resulting in the other team scoring a run and tying the game.

With the player she had sitting out for a show of temper watching her, Teri's own temper got the better of her. She hit the chain link fence with her hand, hard enough that the bats dropped off a bat rack, falling noisily onto the cement floor of the dugout. By now both angry and embarrassed, Teri began picking up the bats. She shoved one bat into the rack hard enough that the rack vibrated. The first bat clattered down to the cement again as Teri tried to put a second bat back in the rack. "You gotta make this a teaching moment here," she somehow managed to think. She turned toward the player whom she'd benched: "You see how a temper never gets you anywhere?"

Many years later, Teri is able to laugh about the incident, which she described as "one of my most embarrassing moments as a coach." If it were possible, she might prefer to rewind her personal coaching tape, do some of it over again. In fact, one of the most rewarding moments of her coaching career came in August, 1999, at the World Masters Games in Portland, when Teri had the opportunity to once more coach some of her early group of PSU players, the young women who had helped to teach her about being a coach. On the day of the championship game, the summer heat was intense, and since the game was the 11th in four days for Teri's team of over 35-year-old players, all of her players were battling some sort of an injury. Even so, Teri recalled, the women's "true love and passion for the game" was clearly visible. "You could just see it, you could see it in their eyes..."

While Teri has experienced many rewarding moments in her years of coaching, there have been plenty of tough times as well. For one thing, in the rainy Pacific Northwest, nature often doesn't cooperate with pre-planned softball schedules. "You get all psyched up to play a game," Teri commented, "and then it gets rained out." In March, 2001, when Teri reached the personal landmark of having coached her 1000th game, she knew that she could have reached that point even sooner. "You add up all the rainouts, and this should have happened 400 games ago," Teri joked to a reporter. But as a Pacific Northwest native, she's used to weather throwing a wet sort of punch. "You can't control the weather," she'll tell her players philosophically.

Teri displays that patient, philosophical attitude toward a very different kind of adverse conditions. Until three years ago, she and her team didn't even have a home field to call their own. For practices, Teri recollected, "we were bouncing around all over the city. The team might have to practice in a church parking lot. They weren't able to practice in Erv Lind Stadium, and until recently, even PSU games scheduled there might be bumped to an outside, less-than-adequate field. One way Teri coped with this situation was by simply refusing to focus on it in a negative way. To her players, she never described their lack of a permanent facility as a problem. "If you don't talk about it being a problem, then it doesn't become a negative in their eyes," she commented.

But Teri did more than just make the best of the situation. She also, Marlene Piper described, "fought for years," to have the right to use Erv Lind Stadium on a consistent basis. She fundraised and put in money from her never huge softball budget for new backstops and dugouts. Finally all the hard work and negotiations paid off. Teri's team was allowed to lay down a tarp at Erv Lind so they could protect the infield dirt and use the field for both practices and games.

Lack of a home field is far from the only difficulty Teri has had to deal with. With increasingly competitive play in collegiate athletics, recruiting is vital to a team's success, yet Teri recruits with a built-in handicap. In contrast to well-supported softball programs, none of Teri's players receive full-ride scholarships. Instead Teri must divvy up the limited number of scholarships she receives—only six in-state scholarships by the 2001 season. At the highly competitive Division I level, Teri only receives, Marlene Piper commented, "a bare bones budget." Marlene agreed that Teri's long-established reputation as an outstanding coach assists her with recruiting. "Now we're cutting good players," Teri herself commented. Teri's warm personality undoubtedly helps too. "I'm a hugger," Teri tells her players. "That's the Italian nature of me."

What also helps Teri is the long perspective she has. In her early years of coaching, she can recall, her teams wouldn't travel much, typically only making short trips, and the level of play was far lower than it is today. The first scholarship allotment Teri received for her team totaled only about $900, an insignificant sum by today's standards. Yet even at Portland State University, an urban university that no one would describe as a big sports school, the women's basketball team, unlike softball, is fully funded for scholarships. At PSU, Teri acknowledged, women's basketball is simply higher than softball in the athletic department's pecking order. "I feel you've got to prove that you're worthy," she commented. "And we're doing that." It's an impressively philosophical attitude after her years of coaching.

For many of those years, Teri was the only female head coach at PSU. In addition to coaching, she's also held administrative positions in the PSU athletic department, at various times serving as associate athletic director, interim athletic director, and senior woman administrator. "It was pretty lonely in my position ... as an administrator and as a coach," Teri commented, in "a very male populated department." Those sort of experiences undoubtedly helped motivate Teri to work with the Oregon Women's Sports Leadership Network, a group that promotes both women's sports overall and women working in the field.

In December, 2000, Teri took on the job of senior woman's administrator again, in addition to her coaching duties, to help with her college's gender equity plan. While she described her personal vision, that men's and women's sports at her college will reach parity in the next five years, she also mentioned how in the previous five years she observed the gender equity "gap get wider, without a thought for the equity side of it." Men's basketball, for example, was added back at PSU in a champagne budget style, with four assistant coaches to aid the head coach. "Did they need that right from the start?" Teri questioned. "I mean there are other programs that could use that, too."

Yet Teri remains loyal to the college where she got her coaching start. In the '90s, when PSU was considering making a move from Division II to Division I, and joining the Big Sky Conference, a conference that didn't include softball, as interim athletic director Teri had to "take off the softball hat and look at what's good for the (entire athletic) program." She had no illusions about what the move meant for her own sport. "If you're not in a conference in Division I, especially in softball, you're screwed," Teri said simply. Yet she supported the move to Division I because she felt that was the best decision for the PSU athletic program overall.

For Teri, her loyalty to the players she's coached may be her most unshakeable committment. Watching and helping those players to grow, both as athletes and as people—has been the primary reward of coaching. And just as her players have taught her so much about coaching, over the years Teri has taught the young women on her teams not just about softball but about life—how to work together for group goals, how to work well with a variety of personalities, how to be responsible, even about the importance of getting places on Mariani time, which, Teri joked, is about 15 minutes early.

Inspired by Teri's example, many of her former players have gone into coaching themselves. Fairly recently, while the PSU team played its games at Portland's Delta Park due to construction at Erv Lind Stadium, Teri could see her coaching influence in action. It was a sunny spring day, and after PSU had finished playing, Teri and her assistant coach, Mary Haluska, checked out the high school games in progress on the various softball fields. At every one of them, a former Portland State softball player was now coaching. At a couple of fields, both of the coaches were former PSU players. "That makes you feel special," Teri commented. Seeing her former players coaching their own teams provided a living illustration of how much she herself has given to countless young women.

The millennial year softball season was exciting for Teri because it was the first year her team played in a conference. Previously, as an independent, Teri had scrambled for whatever home dates she could get, with her team forced to play most of its games on the road. So when Teri read in the newspaper that the Western Athletic Conference was splitting up, she immediately saw the opportunity. That very day Teri phoned WAC headquarters. "If you're looking for somebody," Teri said, "we're looking for a home." Teri's strategy proved successful, and PSU became an affiliate member of the WAC. For the first time her players could be officially recognized for their achievements within a conference. For the first time her team would play significant numbers of home games.

On the warm, sunny Sunday in April, 2000, Teri could witness all her hard work bearing fruit. After winning two games the day before in Sunday's doubleheader, the Portland State women continued to play well. The first game ended with PSU on top 5-1. In the second game, Teri's players seemed to play with even more confidence than before, exactly the result Teri had been hoping for. Her players high fived each other as the PSU runs mounted up. The game was ended by the softball mercy rule after the fifth inning, with PSU up by 11 to 1. During the tough, mostly on-the-road schedules Teri's teams had played in past years, they had not infrequently been on the other end of the mercy rule. This was the first time Teri's players had ever been so far ahead in a Division I game.

At first Teri seemed to take the two solid wins in stride. After the play ended, rather than celebrating she walked off alone to open up the outfield fence. Teri, her assistant, and several players rolled out a giant blue tarp to protect their infield surface. As the tarp billowed out, looking something like the tarp that devoured Cleveland, players dived on top to flatten it, then Teri and her players rolled out a series of tires to hold down the tarp.

Only after their ground crew work was finished, work they were obviously well experienced with, did Teri talk with her team. The games on Saturday and Sunday, Teri told her players, were "the best four games in a row that any Portland State team that I can remember have played." It showed the whole team, Teri told her players, just how well they were capable of playing. "Good job, ladies," were Teri's parting words to her team. Her players left the field chatting and smiling. As their coach, Teri felt happy, too. "I was beaming after that one," she recalled.

All told, for Teri, the Saturday and Sunday doubleheaders had been a coach's dream. "We couldn't have drawn this up any better," Teri told her assistant coach, Mary Haluska. "Beautiful weekend. We played great and won four games. It was everything you'd want it to be."

Like Teri Mariani, coach Jenny Yopp is a warm person who connects easily with people. Originally from North Carolina, Jenny is in her mid-thirties, speaks with a soft Southern accent, and is well aware that she's benefitted from the hard work and battles fought by veteran coaches like Teri. Unlike Teri, however, Jenny has moved around from job to job. Formerly the women's head basketball coach at Portland State, and before that an assistant coach at the University of Maine and Tulane University, Jenny Yopp is currently the head women's basketball coach at Illinois State University in Normal, Illinois.

Jenny didn't always understand what her career moves would involve. As the top assistant coach at Tulane, Jenny considered the job of head coach with some naïveté. "Hey, being the head coach can't be that much harder," she thought. Her experience in two head coaching positions has since taught her better. A head coach, she now knows, is "held accountable for every single decision, down to the colors on my uniform and what we order for pregame meals." The job, Jenny described, is a "24-hour-a-day responsibility" that "keeps me up at night" and at times leaves her feeling like "a little stress ball."

When Jenny accepted the head coaching position at Portland State, she was only 29 years old. She took over from a male head coach who had not related well to his players, and as a woman coach felt that her gender helped her with the process of "mending a lot of scars." During the three years she coached there, the university moved from Division II to Division I. "Let's build some respect here and get this thing turned around," Jenny thought about the challenges that involved. Together, Jenny and her players built a solid team, and in Jenny's last year at PSU, she led her team to a surprisingly strong second-place record in the Big Sky Conference.

After that successful season, like other women's collegiate basketball coaches, Jenny would be attending the women's Final Four. "Jenny, what are you gonna do if someone talks to you about another job?" people asked her.

"I never wanted to look at Portland State as if it was a step-ping stone," was Jenny's self-assessment. But after Jenny's strong coaching performance at PSU, a new career opportunity presented itself. At the Final Four, Jenny ended up sitting high up in the bleachers with Jill Hutchison, the women's basketball coach at Illinois State who was now retiring from coaching. Jill talked up the program there and informally interviewed Jenny, who couldn't help feeling both flattered and distracted by the interest shown in her by such a veteran, highly successful coach. Although several teams were practicing at the time, afterward Jenny could barely remember anything about those practices.

Illinois State wanted to make its hiring decision quickly. When Jenny left the Final Four and headed back to Portland, she knew she needed to do some serious thinking. Was she ready to leave PSU? Was that what she wanted to do? Illinois State was closer to her parents' home in North Carolina; it represented a new coaching challenge. Yet Jenny loved the city of Portland and hated to leave a team she'd worked so hard to build.

After only a weekend back in Portland, Jenny flew back to Illinois State on Monday afternoon for a Tuesday job interview. On the way back to Portland again, during a layover at the Minneapolis airport, Jenny called Jim Sterk, then the athletic director at PSU. "Jenny, this is really hard for you isn't it?" Jim said sympathetically. At that point she realized that she'd made her decision.

Early on Wednesday morning, sleep-deprived and emotional, Jenny arrived back in Portland. She scheduled a morning meeting with her players, wanting to tell them personally of her decision before they heard it from anyone else. In the no-frills locker room, with her players gathered around her, the normally articulate coach found it hard to speak. The players, she felt, sensed her emotions. "Coach Yopp, you're leaving, aren't you?" one player questioned.

"Yes, you're right," Jenny affirmed. In response several of her players put their heads down, faces in their hands, to hide their tears.

Jenny tried to explain how she'd been offered a new job, and why she had chosen to take it. She told the players how deeply she cared about them, how proud she was of them, how difficult it was for her to leave. They might be angry at her, they might not understand her decision, she said, and yet she knew "that they were as supportive of me as I was of them." Her players cried and Jenny cried, also. When she told her players how tough it was for her to leave them, she was not lying.

Jenny's fast-track life moved forward. That Friday she spoke to media at a press conference held at Illinois State. On Saturday she left on a pre-planned cruise to Mexico, Belize, Key West, and Fort Lauderdale. Not surprisingly, it took her at least a couple of days on the seven-day cruise just to unwind from her rapid-fire life changes.

After her vacation, Jenny began the challenging job of taking over a team of players. As the new coach, she had inherited the players who had been coached by Jill Hutchison and the new players who had been recruited by Jill. That spring, Jenny had her first meeting with half of her team—the veteran players. As a college player herself, she had twice experienced coaching changes. "Would the new head coach accept her as a player?" she had wondered. So at the meeting, Jenny tried to reassure her new team. She told the players about herself and why she had decided to accept the Illinois State job. Although the team had finished the season in ninth place in their conference, Jenny told the players that their future as a team was bright. She wanted to convince the returning players that "I was going to embrace them as if I had recruited them." But looking at the watchful faces of her new players, Jenny wondered if they believed what she was saying.

Over the summer, one of Jenny's most important jobs was to re-recruit her players, to ensure that they wouldn't leave Illinois State and go elsewhere. That summer, with her players scattered geographically, she built up frequent flier miles travelling to players' homes to meet with them and their families face to face. The fact that Jenny had hired two of Jill Hutchison's assistant coaches undoubtedly helped, as did the fact that Jill had had an influence on the decision to hire Jenny. But still, Jenny had no illusions about the uncertain terrain she was standing on.

In spite of the many difficulties she faced, and the moments

Jenny Yopp

of anxiety she experienced, Jenny welcomed the challenge of her new job at Illinois State and of building up her team after some recent losing seasons. For one thing, Jenny Yopp is a self-described "champion of the underdog." As a child, she recalled, the only physical fights she was involved in were on the school bus, defending other children being picked on. But if Jenny's first year coaching the Redbirds at ISU had been scripted in Hollywood, the plot description could have read something like, "New coach deals with adversity."

Right away, Jenny lost one player, who returned pregnant from her summer break. In the fall, two talented freshmen went on the injured list, one woman to a season-ending ACL tear, the other to a stress fracture in her foot. Then still another freshman, a leading scorer and rebounder for the Redbirds, tore her ACL at the beginning of January. As if all that weren't enough, in early February Jenny lost both her point guards, one to a lower back injury, another to a separated shoulder that kept the woman, Jenny's senior point guard, out until the last game of the season.

At times Jenny only had six and a half players to put out on the floor, the half being a post player who managed to hang in there with a broken bone in her foot. As coach, naturally Jenny questioned herself. Could she have done anything differently as a coach to help avoid the injuries? But basketball was a "very high risk sport," Jenny knew. It was a fact of women's basketball life—compared to male players, women players typically have a higher rate of injuries such as ACL tears—which Jenny and her players were experiencing firsthand.

Jenny toughed it out as the losses mounted up. Throughout that difficult first year, she dug deep into her personal reserves of energy and guts, working hard to stay positive herself, and to communicate that hang-in-there attitude to her team. She tried to redefine success by setting "motivating goals" that the players could meet, regardless of the team's win-loss records, such as taking care of the basketball, fighting for lose balls, and taking a charge. She even created a MIP, "most intense player" award.

Looking back on that difficult first year, Jenny demonstrated that she had two of the character traits that successful coaches need—resilience and optimism—by remaining positive about coaching and looking forward to the upcoming season, when she expected both newly recruited and returning players to help the team succeed. With a new athletic director at Illinois State and a winning reputation at the college, the expectations facing her, Jenny felt, were that she would turn her program into a winning one "relatively fast." Jenny seemed to simply accept that pressure. "I think I'm humble enough to recognize," she commented, "that if I don't get it turned around, there's somebody who can."

Jenny's typical "non-stop" schedule didn't seem to faze her either. During the coaching season, she often watches basketball videotapes until two or three in the morning. "But I love my life that way," she said. The players on her team "make it all rewarding," she added. "They sacrifice so much, and they work so hard."

Although Jenny Yopp is still a fairly young coach—she was 33 years old at the conclusion of her first season at ISU—she doesn't lack for a sense of history. "I'm very fortunate to be coaching in the new millennium," she added. She feels personally empowered by the strong women coaches she played for or worked with as an assistant coach, women who are in many cases now her friends and mentors. "We can't say thank you enough," Jenny commented, speaking for herself and other younger coaches. "I know that I've really benefitted throughout my playing career and now my coaching career," Jenny said, not only because of Title IX but because of "the women before me that have battled and battled to gain resources and respect for their teams."

About both the challenges and the rewards of coaching, Jenny remains upbeat. She described her difficult first year at Illinois State as "the most interesting year that I've ever experienced, absolutely." The job mobility that many coaches undergo hasn't been easy for her, yet she's happy in her new job at Illinois State, has bought a home in a small town fairly close to the college, and speaks humorously about her adjustment to the flat terrain of the Midwest: "When I was driving back from Oregon, I could see Bloomington-Normal from Kansas," Jenny joked.

<hr/>

To the north of Normal, Illinois, the first-ever Women's World Ice Hockey Championship took place in Ottawa, Canada, in 1990. Karen Kay, an assistant coach for the United States National Team, watched the U.S. players warm up. As game time approached, more and more people entered the arena. From her slightly raised vantage point on the U.S. team bench, Karen looked around the rink. The game was sold out, she knew, with 10,000 fans there to watch a women's hockey game.

After Canada scored the first goal of the game, "the whole roof sounded like it was going to come off," Karen recalled. It didn't matter to Karen that most of the fans were Canadian. The main thing was that all those fans were there. "We've arrived now," Karen thought. Women's ice hockey was "not going to go away. It's just going to get better."

Now head women's ice hockey coach at the University of New Hampshire, Karen Kay has a personal understanding of the still fairly short history of women's and girls' ice hockey in the United States. Although Karen comes across as a straight-forward, non-egotistical person, she knows that she's one of the pioneers for the sport. The fact that in September, 2000, heading into her ninth season as head coach at New Hampshire, Karen Kay was only 37 years old says a lot about the relative newness of her sport in the U.S. One of the challenges for Karen, as well as one of the rewards, has been her personal involvement in developing girls' and women's ice hockey.

While she was growing up in the Boston area, Karen watched NHL games on television with her father, who was a fan of the Boston Bruins. She wanted to play hockey, Karen told her father, but she didn't know if girls could do that. Karen's father bought her hockey skates and Karen worked hard to build up her hockey skills, skating every day of her summer break at a local rink. By the fall, she felt ready to try out for a boys' hockey team, at the time her only option.

Some of Karen's girlfriends tried ice hockey and gave it up because they felt girls weren't welcomed in the sport, but Karen and one other girl continued to play on boys' teams where being the only girl was a mixed experience. The boys on her own team respected Karen as a good player and acted toward her like "a bunch of brothers," sticking up for her against opposing players. But for boys on opposing teams, Karen remembered, "I was a girl on the ice and they'd know what number you wore and they'd be out to get you."

In 1981, Karen entered Providence College, then home to one of the handful of women's varsity ice hockey programs in the country. Karen joined the ice hockey team at a time when only a very few university teams—Providence, Northeastern, New Hampshire, and then Brown—provided a reasonably high level of competition. Fan support was low as well. Mainly friends of Karen and her teammates would come to their home hockey games, with about a hundred or fewer people typically there to support the team.

Looking back on that earlier period now as a head coach, Karen can see how far women's ice hockey has come. When she first took the job as coach at New Hampshire in November, 1992, one change she pushed was to charge admission for women's hockey games, arguing that "it's free, so come and watch it" wasn't a good approach for marketing women's hockey. By the end of her eighth season as hockey coach, the support for women's hockey still wasn't as strong as Karen wished. "It's a constant battle. We're always working at it," she

Karen Kay

commented. Yet she described a game against Harvard that drew 1,800 fans and a game against the national team that 2,400 fans attended.

Judy Ray, the athletic director who hired Karen at New Hampshire in November, 1992, was supportive of women's hockey, and Karen also benefitted from a history of positive relationships between the men's and women's hockey programs. Male and female hockey players at New Hampshire share a weight room, a training room, a media room, and their identical locker rooms are adjacent to each other. The men's coach, Karen commented, "doesn't allow his players not to respect our women as athletes." All of that, Karen knows, has made her situation far easier than at some other schools where male coaches and athletic directors actively oppose women's hockey. Nevertheless, Karen had plenty of work to do in her new coaching position. She worked to recruit top players from the the U.S. and other countries, to boost attendance at games, to create a booster group for women's hockey.

Karen's workload increased sharply when in January, 1993, only a few months after she took on the head coaching position at New Hampshire, she also began coaching the USA Hockey women's team. In 1994, at the Women's World Ice Hockey Championship, held in Lake Placid, New York, Karen had the singular distinction of being the only female head coach there. At the time, that wasn't something she gave much thought to. Busy with preparing her team to compete, she was somewhat taken aback when in the middle of a press conference, a reporter asked her about being the only woman in her position.

Although Karen viewed the fact that she was a female head coach for international hockey as not "such a big deal," and although some of her fellow coaches were supportive, she also encountered some people who clearly resented a woman coach. "There were some countries just looking at us, like how can you guys have a woman coach," Karen recalled. "There were some coaches that made no effort to communicate with me but would talk to my male assistants."

After serving as head coach for the women's national team in 1995 as well, Karen was, she admitted, "very disappointed" when she was not chosen as head coach for the team which would compete in the 1998 Olympic games held in Nagano, Japan. Busy with her own collegiate season, Karen didn't travel to Nagano. Instead, she got up at 5:30 am to see the gold-medal game on television at home, wanting to watch it by herself. The gold-medal game had a special meaning for her because she had coached all of the athletes on the U.S. team in national team events, or at the collegiate level, or in youth hockey.

Since Karen no longer coached the national team, she was free to concentrate all her coaching energies on her program at New Hampshire. In 1998, at the first women's ice hockey national championship competition, that extra intense coaching focus yielded dividends for Karen and her players. For Karen, it was especially exciting that the championship game would be held at the Fleet Center in Boston, the same arena where as a child she had watched the Boston Bruins play.

Karen wanted her athletes as well to understand how special the competition was. She searched for something that would give her team a winning edge of motivation and chemistry. She chose a Garth Brooks song popular with some of her players, "How You Ever Going to Know." Just before the semi-final game in which New Hampshire played against the University of Minnesota, during Karen's pre-game talk, she read part of that song to her players, then played a CD of the entire song after she was done speaking.

The New Hampshire Wildcats went on to beat the University of Minnesota in the semi-final game, held at Harvard University. In the championship game, held at the Fleet Center in Boston, Karen's team faced a top-notch Brown University team coached by Digit Murphy. But after the second period, when Karen went into her team's locker room, she saw her players sitting together and holding hands. The Garth Brooks' song she had chosen to motivate her team was playing and the young women on her team were singing along. "At that moment," Karen recalled, "you just knew we were going to win... and I didn't have to say anything."

Karen's whole family was in attendance at the championship game, as were the athletic director and president of the University of New Hampshire, both of them women. After New Hampshire beat Brown 4-1 in the championship game, the celebration began. Two of her players "got the typical Gatorade jug and doused me," Karen described, "so then I had to go up and accept the trophies and everything and I was drowning." But she didn't really care that the nice black wool suit jacket she was wearing was ruined by the Gatorade. "You don't mind those sacrifices when you win," she commented wryly. The gatorade shower in the middle of the Fleet Center was only one more sign of how far the women's game had come.

About the future for that game, Karen knows that building fan interest remains a challenge but sees plenty of possibilities. "I think it's a tremendous time now. There's so much growth," she said enthusiastically. As a women's hockey coach during this period of growth for her sport, Karen Kay is well aware of the pressures on her and responsibilities she faces. "I always try to make sure that I'm more prepared than what I need to be," Karen commented. "People are going to judge women's hockey or how women can coach based on what I do."

Karen is also aware that she works harder and longer than many men's coaches need to do. She works to keep building a fan base, to find additional sponsors for her team, to encourage hockey opportunities for girls, to change people's ideas about women playing hockey. "Why do I still have to do more than what a guy has to do?" Karen described some women coaches as asking. But for Karen, the answer is simple: "Because we're not there yet."

———————

Deitre Collins is a fairly new head coach with an impressive personal background as an athlete. A former star volleyball player at the University of Hawaii, Deitre competed on the U.S. National volleyball team from 1985 to 1988, including at the '88 Olympics, and then from 1991 to 1992. She also played professional volleyball in Italy and France. For Deitre frequent relocations are one challenging aspect of the coaching profession. Along with other challenges, however, she's found numerous rewards to being a coach.

Thirty-eight years old in May, 2000, Deitre calls Lancaster, California, her hometown. Both of her parents, who were themselves quite athletic, supported her athletic interests. When describing her father, Deitre laughed about how he "was one of those parents your coach was wishing wouldn't show up, always wanting to give his two cents." Although Deitre hadn't planned to become a coach, her experience working in summer volleyball camps at the University of Houston led to an assistant coach job there. She moved on to assistant coaching positions at Northern Arizona and at South Alabama. In June of 1995, she began her first coaching job at the University of Nevada-Las Vegas.

Moving around so much had its drawbacks. The locations of her second and third assistant coaching positions, Flagstaff, Arizona, and Mobile, Alabama, Deitre described, "were both very difficult lifestyle adjustments to me." Flagstaff, she found, was a city that "for an African American ... didn't have a lot to offer. " With few other African Americans in Flagstaff, Deitre found it hard to find a place to get her hair done, or a church she felt comfortable in. Living in Mobile, Alabama, she said, was challenging in a different way. "I had never really dealt with racism before," she commented, at least not the Deep South's style of overt racism.

Las Vegas, the location of Deitre's new, head coaching job, provided both a location Deitre felt reasonably comfortable with and plenty of new challenges. Since UNLV had dropped women's volleyball in 1985, when Deitre began coaching there, she was essentially starting up a program. She was given a year to recruit players before her first competitive volleyball season would begin, but found the "sin city stigma" of Las Vegas created some difficulties. In general, Deitre described, "recruiting the level of athletes that I want, to be as successful as I want to be" has been the toughest aspect of coaching. "Just building reputation is really, really hard," she added.

Since one of Deitre's goals is to win a national championship at UNLV, she appreciates the fact that her program is fully funded with scholarships, but would like to see even more support for women's volleyball. "I tend not to complain too much," she explained. "I just try to get what I can and deal with what I have." In a different way, Deitre tries to look on the positive side in relation to her players. Although she cares a great deal about winning, she has come to realize that not all of her players want to replicate their coach's experience of playing at the Olympics. "If they can win and walk away saying that they had a good experience and they learned something about life," Deitre said, "wow, what an impact you've had."

"I'm strict, but I'm fair. I treat players as individuals," Deitre said about herself as a coach. As an African-American coach, she herself has felt fairly treated too, even in the predominantly white sport of college volleyball. The fact that she was "a fairly successful athlete and decently known in the field," she explained, is a good part of why she hasn't felt much racial prejudice as a coach. She does, however, describe how sometimes

Deitre Collins

"People ask me to speak because I'm black, but they want to hear that I've had a hard luck story. Like they expect everybody black to have been raised poor and didn't know where the next meal was coming from." That wasn't her own family background, Deitre clarifies, obviously annoyed at the the "sad misconception," aka racial stereotype, she has sometimes encountered as a coach.

For Deitre, other rewards and challenges of coaching have nothing to do with race. With her busy coaching schedule and the relocations coaching has involved, it can be difficult to keep up a personal life. "I miss that I don't live where my friends are," Deitre commented. She also wishes she had "a lifetime companion," and mentions that some of her male friends have told her that men can feel intimidated by the fact that she's a head coach. And when Deitre thinks about having a family, she wishes she was earning a higher salary as a coach. "Sometimes I'd consider being a single mom if I financially could afford it," she added, in a poignant statement about the dreams she has and possibilities she sees.

When asked what the most rewarding aspect of coaching is for her, Deitre quickly replied, "my relationships with the players," who are, she described, "people that I truly care about." On the other hand, she also mentioned the stress of her previous season's fairly evenly split win-loss record as "really really disappointing and extremely stressful." After her successful career as a player, it can be difficult to accept the fact that ultimately, a coach can't control her players on court.

And there's one additional challenge Deitre described: the fact that numerous women are leaving the coaching profession. With a number of women volleyball coaches among those leaving, Deitre feels "now more than ever" the pressure of representing, in a sense, women coaches as a group.

But for all the challenges, Deitre has one bottomline assessment of her own future in the coaching profession. "Now," she commented, "I couldn't imagine myself doing much else."

A New Generation of Coaches

Where to place the chronological boundary around a particular generation is a subjective decision and generational markers can seem fluid and insubstantial. Yet there are, of course, historical events that impact particular generations with particular force, such as the impact of World War II on the young people who came of age then, or the political tumult of the '60s and '70s, that strongly affected the baby boomer generation. Likewise, in the women's sports world, Title IX has had such a huge impact on the younger women in coaching that it marks them as a new generation.

Title IX-inspired progress for female athletes took place in a patchwork fashion across the country in the later '70s, the '80s, and the '90s. Yet it's safe to say that among women collegiate coaches, those who were in their 20s and 30s by the millennial year 2000 had benefitted not only as coaches but also directly as high school and/or college athletes from the many changes brought about by Title IX. Growing up with the new possibilities available for female athletes, or experiencing the enhanced opportunities at some point in their high school and college careers, these young women saw themselves as athletes in a somewhat different way than had previous generations of girls and women. And now, as coaches themselves, these women work with still younger female athletes who continue to reap the benefits of Title IX.

Although many of today's girls and young women don't understand the history behind the sports opportunities they have, the women who coach them do see the changes for women's sports in a historical perspective. But younger women coaches may view that history in a different light than that of women coaches in their 40s, 50s, and 60s who fought somewhat different battles and experienced significantly different conditions. Some of the younger women coaches have mixed feelings about Title IX; others strongly support it. Among the new generation of coaches, many women have fought and continue to fight battles for equity.

As with the relationships between fathers and sons and mothers and daughters, the relationship between older and younger women in coaching isn't always an easy one. There certainly can be intergenerational tensions or simply a recognition of key differences. "The older coaches, the people that are my age, the Sue Gunters, the Jody Conradts, the Pat Summitts, Billie Moores, all of that 48 to 60 age group ... we were very very close. We socialized together. We would go out and take three or four days and play golf together," described former coach and former Women's Basketball Coaches Association CEO, Betty Jaynes. In contrast, the younger women basketball coaches, Betty commented, probably in response to the pressures of today's more competitive recruiting for players, are not friends with each other in the same way.

These younger coaches may also be less aware of the fights for equity that have occurred in the past, Betty Jaynes remarked, yet she praised the "really good leadership coming up" among young coaches and mentioned the need for older female coaches to mentor younger women. In fact, many of the younger women coaches speak strongly about the help they've received and the valuable lessons they've learned from older women in coaching. While it makes sense to consider younger women as a new coaching generation, these younger women are often connected by loyalties and affections, by common experiences and lessons learned, to the older women who preceded them into the coaching profession.

On March 19, 1999, just before the championship game of the KIA Klassic Tournament, two women softball coaches were involved in a ceremony that represented a symbolic passing of the coaching baton from an older to a younger generation. The tournament was hosted by Cal State Fullerton, where the long-time softball coach there, Judi Garman, would be retiring from coaching. It was mid-afternoon on a warm spring day perfect for softball, and Judi had already thrown out the symbolic first pitch. Then just before the game began, microphones were brought down to the field. University of Washington coach Teresa Wilson, along with University of Arizona coach Mike Candrea, stood at home plate and spoke to the crowds of fans about what Judi Garman had meant to them.

Younger coaches like herself, Teresa said, had greatly benefited from the struggles of older coaches like Judi Garman. "Those of us in the athletic world today," Teresa told the fans, "have what we have because people like Judi Garman paved the way for us. They fought the battles ... They forced the rest of the country to take women's athletics seriously." After a long day of softball games, Teresa described, Judi would have to take her team's uniforms to the laundromat; when it rained, Judi would bail water from the puddles on her field to get it back to playing condition. "For those of us who are fortunate enough to have wonderful grounds crews and managers who travel with us to do our uniforms, and who don't have to fund raise anymore," Teresa continued, "we have people in Judi Garman's generation to thank for that."

While she spoke, Teresa watched Judi, imagining the older coach remembering her early days in coaching and other memories of her long coaching life. It was a heartwarming tribute, Judi recollected later, clearly moved by the event. After the speeches concluded, Teresa and Mike hugged Judi, and Judi walked off the field arm in arm with a former player. Recalling the event, Teresa Wilson was clearly moved as well. "It was poignant," she said, "in that it signified another era of time almost passing."

Thirty-eight years old in the year 2000, Teresa Wilson represented the older end of the new generation of women collegiate coaches. She was old enough to have personally experienced times when conditions were less favorable, to have fought some similar battles to those experienced by Judi Garman and other older coaches. In Teresa's first coaching position, when she was a half time head coach at the University of Oregon, she recalled fund raising "endlessly," and having to hire bulldozers to literally build their own softball field from an abandoned baseball field. As a new coach, Teresa recalled, "I was basically told that you'll compete locally and regionally, you'll run an ethically sound program, break no rules, and that's about all we expect from you."

When Teresa called her first team meeting at Oregon, only four players showed up. "Where is everybody?" Teresa asked. "Practice has been optional here before," her players told her. It was a policy that Teresa didn't need to spend time evaluating. "Well, guess what," she told her players. "Practice isn't optional any more."

While Teresa worked to build her program, she had to cope with a miniscule recruiting budget; she and her assistant coach drove team vans to almost all their road games; she saved money on team uniforms by getting them made cheaply in Korea. "We went to some great lengths to survive," Teresa commented.

The kinds of difficult conditions Teresa experienced at the University of Oregon may well have reminded her of her own days as an athlete. Growing up in a poor farming community in Missouri, when Teresa competed in high school softball, she and the other girls wore blue jeans for uniforms. As a college athlete, Teresa benefitted from Title IX by receiving an athletic scholarship. But she still experienced the low level of funding for women's sports that meant that on road trips about 25 people plus all of their luggage would be crammed into two vans.

As a coach, Teresa moved from the University of Oregon to the University of Minnesota, and finally to her current coaching position at the University of Washington, where she was hired in 1992 to start up a women's softball program. By then, with the post Title IX era well advanced, conditions had improved greatly for women's sports. Teresa told the athletic director what she needed to build a top program at Washington and made her own position clear. "If that was not the goal, to challenge for a national championship each year," Teresa said simply, "then I was not the person they wanted to hire."

The University of Washington did want to stand strongly behind their softball program, as they have done in recent years for other women's sports. At Washington, Teresa's team is fully funded for scholarships, a condition she feels is vital in today's highly competitive women's sports scene. The University of Washington, Teresa commented, has "been a model for how to start a program across the country."

In 1989, Teresa was honored as the NCAA Coach of the Year for Softball. By the end of the 2000 season, her Huskies softball team had posted an impressive 62 and 9 record, and added to their string of appearances in the College World Series with their fifth trip there in as many years. Because of those coaching achievements, even younger coaches have begun to approach Teresa at conventions or to call her up for coaching advice, a situation that she has found somewhat surprising, since she considers herself young to be a coaching mentor.

Teresa understands the importance of mentoring younger coaches, however, in part because she can recall the time when she herself, as a 22-year-old, brand new head coach attending a coaches' meeting, felt that some of the older women coaches at the meeting regarded her suspiciously as a member of a new generation and "didn't give me the time of day." After finding some of the older women coaches to be far from friendly, Teresa appreciated the fact that softball coach Mike Candrea, the man who ended up as Teresa's opposing coach at the KIA Classic Tournament where Judi Garman was honored, was much more forthcoming. Teresa and Mike sat together at the meeting and Mike, who was a few years older than Teresa, talked openly and helpfully with her about the game. Although Teresa looks up to a number of older women who are or have been coaches, including Judi Garman, it's Mike Candrea whom she regards as her most important mentor. Teresa also mentioned how the baseball coaches she's met—all of them men—have been much more open to her than some women coaches. "You go to a baseball convention," she described, "and talk to a guy you've never met before, and he's telling you his five favorite plays."

A male coach may be especially willing to open up to a young woman who is not a direct competitor. Yet Teresa's experience of friendly baseball coaches vs. some less friendly older women coaches also illustrates how gender does not always affect coaches in a simplistic fashion and how the generation gaps found within the ranks of women coaches can certainly lead to tensions. Similarly, when Teresa contrasts her own perspective with those of the younger women she coaches, a generational tension is evident. "Kids are not even close to being as appreciative as they were in the past," Teresa commented. The girls on her team, for example, receive all their uniforms and equipment free, and sleep one person per bed when they travel. It's all much more luxurious than the conditions Teresa herself experienced as a college athlete not too many years ago. "You have to remind (the young women)," Teresa added, "and make sure they're aware that there was a time when this didn't happen. This is something to be appreciated." It's a type of comment that many older coaches also make.

Teresa is strongly appreciative of the new opportunities that she and the young women she coaches find today. "Softball's at a real period of growth right now," Teresa described, "and there's a window of opportunity which we have not seen in this sport." But like many other younger women in coaching, Teresa hasn't forgotten the past and how her sport made the progress that it did.

When she's "sitting with the pioneers," 38 year old softball coach Rhonda Revelle commented, she tries to acknowledge "that I understand that they really had to go through the fire, even to have opportunities available." Similarly, Teresa Wilson continues to speak respectfully about the struggles undergone by older women coaches, continues to be interested by their battles. "You listen to them" Teresa commented, "and you get a sense of history and you really appreciate what they did."

———◆———

Assistant volleyball coach Shannon Tuttle is one young coach who feels a strong connection to an older woman coach. In her junior year at Notre Dame, Shannon was working out in the weight room when she suffered a severe shoulder injury. At the start of her senior year, no longer able to play volleyball herself, Shannon began thinking about a way to stay involved in the sport she loved. It was then that Shannon's coach at Notre Dame, Debbie Brown, became a mentor for the young woman, doing a great deal to facilitate Shannon's entry into the coaching profession.

In August, 2000, Shannon Tuttle was 25 years old. As someone who still wasn't very many years removed from her own playing days, she could vividly recollect exactly how she had made the change from player to coach. And as a coach herself now, she had come to appreciate in a new light just how much her former coach, Debbie Brown, had helped her. "Being a coach now for four years," Shannon stated, "every day I appreciate more the opportunity she gave me both as an athlete and ... the doors that she opened for me to get into the career that I'm in."

All along during Shannon Tuttle's four years at Notre Dame, head coach Debbie Brown had been an important person for her. Debbie's open door policy meant that whenever a player came to see Debbie in her office, Debbie would put aside whatever she was doing and talk with her player, a policy that Shannon often took advantage of. In Shannon's freshman year, when she found the small amount of playing time she received to be a difficult transition to college athletics, she sought out her coach to find out why that was happening. When Shannon struggled with a chemistry class her freshman year, she talked with Debbie about that, too. Shannon isn't someone who cries easily, yet almost every time she spoke with Debbie in her office, Shannon would end up in tears, even though Debbie, Shannon recalled, "never gave me any reason to want to cry."

It's an aspect of their relationship that she and Debbie laugh about now. But at the time, Shannon's tears made a kind of emotional sense. "It was so important to me what Debbie thought," Shannon remembered. "I wrapped it up into so much emotion."

After Shannon's shoulder injury, her talks with Debbie became important in a new way. At home in California, Shannon learned that she would need to have shoulder surgery, and that she wouldn't be able to return to playing volleyball. She felt isolated and depressed, her identity as an athlete suddenly ripped away from her. "The emotional part of it was much more difficult than I ever imagined anything ever being for me," Shannon recalled. The telephone conversations she had with Debbie were difficult for Shannon—it was hard to speak about her injury and what it meant—and yet they were a link between her past and future lives.

During Shannon's senior year, once she had told Debbie that she was interested in the coaching field, Debbie converted her open door policy into an open office policy for Shannon, converting herself into Shannon's coaching mentor. "She opened up her files for me," Shannon described, "and let me go through everything to see what I wanted ... made copies for me of everything." Shannon talked with Debbie about the process of applying for coaching positions, about what she should look for in a coaching job, about the importance of working for a head coach who was someone she could learn from and whose coaching style would be compatible with her own.

Debbie's own position in the volleyball community and the network of people she knew, also greatly assisted Shannon. "She has a great reputation in the coaching world and is very well respected," Shannon summarized. The fact that Shannon had played for such a well thought of coach was a distinct advantage when Shannon applied for coaching jobs. But Debbie helped her former player more directly too, serving as a reference when Shannon applied for the assistant coaching jobs she held at the University of Wisconsin—Milwaukee, at Kent State University, and finally for her current position as an assistant coach at Georgia Tech, where the head coach was both a friend of Debbie's and someone she had coached with for the U.S. national volleyball team.

While Shannon was a college athlete, she didn't consciously think of Debbie as a role model. And yet now that she's in coaching herself, Shannon can see how in many ways her former head coach has been an important influence. The openness to her players that Debbie modeled is clearly reflected in Shannon's own coaching style. On one occasion during Shannon's assistant

Shannon Tuttle

coaching career, for example, when an injured player came to Shannon for advice, Shannon talked openly about her own career-ending shoulder injury, in order to help the player understand and cope with the range of emotions she would likely be experiencing.

In other ways as well, Debbie remains a role model for Shannon. Although at 25 Shannon was still single, she could envision a time when she might combine her coaching duties with having a family. The fact that Shannon saw Debbie do exactly that—Debbie gave birth to both her sons while Shannon was at Notre Dame—encourages Shannon. "I saw her go through it and make the time and be able to be good at both, " Shannon commented. "It's going to be tough," she added, "but I envision that I'll be able to do it."

While Debbie and Shannon have maintained their close ties, it's still possible to see generational fault lines between the two women. Coaches who are, like Debbie Brown, approximately at middle age, have a keen appreciation for the changes Title IX has brought about for girls' and women's sports. Yet Shannon sees the landmark law from a different chronological perspective. "I really had no clue about it while I was in school," she admitted. It was not until she was a graduate student at Kent State and did a presentation on Title IX that she fully realized the overall impact Title IX has had and how it helped provide the opportunities she enjoyed as a multisport athlete in high school and as a varsity player on an athletic scholarship in college. In spite of that realization, Shannon admitted to having "pretty mixed feelings about Title IX."

"I think that it has done great things for female athletes and it has provided an unbelievable amount of opportunities," Shannon stated. "I love that the benefits are there," she added, "I just am not real fond that the benefits are there as a result of taking them away from other athletes." Men's so-called minor sports, such as wrestling and men's volleyball, Shannon described, have been cut at the same time various women's sports have received increased funding. It's not surprising that this situation has brought about tensions between coaches whose sports have been Title IX beneficiaries and coaches whose sports have not. In an odd historical reversal, Shannon has heard male coaches "joking around about how great it would be to be a female athlete because you get ... the VIP treatment as opposed to the scrub treatment."

Other experiences, however, link younger and older women coaches. Post Title IX, Shannon has still encountered some of the negative attitudes about females in sports that older coaches are familiar with. There is, Shannon described, "the perception that a female (college) athlete is less of an athlete than a male athlete." When Shannon herself was playing college volleyball, a football player brought up the classic argument about revenue versus nonrevenue sports, telling Shannon that "if it wasn't for us, you guys wouldn't be here." It's experiences like these that have led Shannon to believe that for women's college sports overall, "gaining the type of respect that the male sports have" is both "an uphill battle" and "a long battle."

Along with her awareness of these challenges, Shannon Tuttle maintains the enthusiastic attitude about coaching expressed by many coaches of all ages. She's happy in her current position at Georgia Tech and hopes to move on to a head coaching position within a few years. "I really can't picture myself doing anything other than coaching," Shannon commented.

———•◦•———

Ice hockey coach Katey Stone was similarly upbeat. "You can wake up every day and have a new challenge," she said. At 34 years old, Katey held the position of head women's ice hockey coach at Harvard University, a job that she obviously loved, and which was a good fit for a "very competitive person" like herself. Katey described herself as excited by the challenge of developing women's hockey and the bright future she sees for her sport.

Becoming a coach was a natural choice of career for Katey. "It's sort of the family business," she commented. Her father, two older brothers and her sister are all coaches, and she's had strong family support all along for her athletic interests, including when, prior to high school, she competed as the only girl in an otherwise all boys hockey league. Just as hockey coach Karen Kay experienced, many of the boys on Katey's Stone's team were supportive, but that positive attitude wasn't shared by boys on other teams. As the only girl on the ice, Katy recalled being "gunned for a lot of the time, but it was certainly worth it to have an opportunity to play." In college, Katey competed in both hockey and lacrosse at the University of New Hampshire. After graduating from UNH in 1989, Katey's coaching career took off fast. She coached and taught physical education at Northfield Mount Hermon School, at Phillips Exeter Academy, and then at Tabor Academy. In 1994, she accepted the position of head women's hockey coach at Harvard.

With Harvard's high academic standards, one of the challenges Katey faces there is "identifying qualified student athletes and having the admissions office admit them." The fact that Ivy League colleges don't offer athletic scholarships could pose challenges as well, yet Katey sees that as a positive. While a student athlete at UNH, Katey described, "I had great experiences but I felt owned." At Harvard, Katey appreciates the fact that "these kids are not being paid to play for me. They come to the rink because they want to come to the rink. And I keep them here because I want to keep them here, not because I've already shelled out $25,000 for them to come here."

Katey enjoys working with the young women on her team, helping each of them grow as an athlete and develop as a person. Her coaching philosophy sounds light years away from the stereotypical win-at-all-costs, no-pain-no-gain, style of coaching. "I think the thing that drives me the most," Katey said, "is to provide

Katey Stone

an opportunity that's competitive and challenging but yet an opportunity to have a tremendous amount of fun."

High-powered competition was definitely what Katey and her players faced in the 1999 collegiate ice hockey championship game. Their opponent was Katey's alma mater, perennial hockey powerhouse the University of New Hampshire, coached by Karen Kay, whose team had won last year's championship. When Katey Stone's team won by one goal in overtime, "It was almost like I couldn't believe it happened," Katey described. She was, she thought, still a young coach fairly new to college coaching, and now she and her team had just won a national championship. Katey and her assistant coaches exchanged hugs, and Katey cried tears of joy along with her players and was mobbed by excited players out on the ice. The victory was so overwhelming, that Katey can't remember many more details of what happened then. But she hasn't forgotten the feeling she had. "Wow, this is amazing," she thought at the time.

Katey is positive not only about that national championship

but about the future for women's ice hockey. "It's a great time to be a hockey coach for women," she commented, "because everything's very new, very fresh. Kids are doing it for the right reasons. It's not about money. It's because they love the game."

Although Katey Stone was only 34 in September, 2000, about three years younger than Coach Karen Kay, just as they do to Karen, people sometimes tell Katey that she's a pioneer for the sport. In Karen's own view, women coaches who came before her, "those that have identified the inequities in college athletics, are really pioneers for women's athletics." But as part of that history now, Katey is committed to helping her sport continue to grow. At the young age of 32, she became president of the American Women's Hockey Coaches Association, a position she held for two years. As president, she and others worked to encourage schools to support their hockey programs. And as one of a still small number of women ice hockey coaches, Katey is a proponent of more women hockey coaches at the college level. While she isn't opposed to qualified men coaching women's teams, she wants to see women coaches succeed.

In the spring of 2000, Katey Stone had a vision of what she hoped would be the future of women's college hockey. She attended the women's basketball Final Four, an event she had never been to before. When Katey walked into the sold-out arena in Philadelphia, she immediately noticed the high level of fan support. "I saw 20,000 people watching this women's basketball game."

"Can you imagine if women's hockey ever gets to this point," Katey thought. "It would be unbelievable." And yet, she reminded herself, "that's exactly what the women's basketball coaches probably thought 15, 20 years ago."

In June, 2000, Angie Taylor, then 35 years old, was just finishing her first season as head women's cross country and track and field coach at George Mason University. Since the year had also been her first ever as a head coach, it wasn't surprising that she described it as a "learning experience." But it was also an experience for which Angie had been well prepared.

Growing up in Chicago Heights, a Chicago area community, in high school Angie received the traditional female opportunity of being a cheerleader, but she also ran track and cross country, played basketball and volleyball. Although her father worked as a laborer in a steel mill, the athletic scholarship Angie received to Illinois State University, where she starred as an All-American hurdler, led Angie on an upwardly mobile path to the coaching profession. After college, she competed in the heptathalon for U.S. national teams and at the 1992 Olympic trials, where she was a finalist.

Before she came to George Mason, Angie paid her coaching dues and received valuable experience by serving as a volunteer coach at Illinois State University, and an assistant coach at Southeastern Louisiana State University, the University of Minnesota and Princeton University. During both her own athletic career and as an assistant coach, Angie can point to both male and female coaches who were teachers and mentors for her. The women coaches she had or worked under, Angie commented, never let her believe that "because you're a woman you can't achieve certain goals."

As an African-American woman, Angie is well aware of the very limited number of other African-American women who are head coaches of track and field at Division I colleges. And in spite of her own extensive experience as an athlete and assistant coach, Angie is also well aware that someone might question why she received her position at George Mason. "Is it because she's a woman, because she's African-American?" Angie could imagine someone asking. Her response was simple. "Honestly I think I was the best candidate."

That positive outlook has stood Angie in good stead as she combines the demanding job of head coach with the equally demanding job of being a single mother of a two-year-old daughter whom Angie described optimistically as being "in those terrific two stages." How does Angie do it all? "It's tough, but I've been able to manage," she commented, mentioning the help she receives from family and friends, her daughter's father at times,

Angie Taylor

and even the young women on her team, who often offer to babysit for Angie's daughter.

Being a mother as well as a coach has actually helped Angie with recruiting. To parents of potential recruits, she seems like someone who will understand their feelings about sending their daughters away from home. "You're a mother, so you understand," one mother told Angie. "Well, she's two," Angie demurred, making it clear that there was a whole lot she hadn't yet experienced as a parent. "But still, you have that motherly instinct," the mother responded.

Being a mother also provides part of Angie's coaching inspiration. "Hey, look at my mom," she can envision her daughter, Noell, saying. As a coach who is also a mother, Angie feels, she provides a good role model for the athletes on her team. "Wow, I can't believe the fact that you're a head coach and you're a mom," her athletes will say. "I welcome the challenge," Angie responds. As with many younger coaches, her own competitive spirit was honed by her past experiences as an athlete. "I don't see things as being an obstacle," she stated. "I see them as, hey, I want to get to the finish line first."

Angie remains aware that she's in the debt of the many older women who entered the coaching field before her. "If they didn't fight for certain things, it would still be just the good old boys' network, I think," Angie commented. She's in the debt of pioneering athletes such as former track star Wilma Rudolph, Angie added. In 1993, at the world championships in Stuttgart, Germany, Angie met Wilma Rudolph and can still remember the way she "just had a presence about herself." When Angie and her friend Jackie Joyner-Kersee sit and talk, Angie described, they both agree how lucky they are to have received numerous athletic opportunities.

As a coach herself now, Angie Taylor is glad to have the chance to pass on those opportunities. Watching her athletes achieve both in the classroom and on the track motivates her to continue coaching. "I did it," an athlete might say to Angie after running a personal best in a race. When the young women on her team don't perform as well, Angie described herself "taking them by the hand or talking to them and still encouraging them to go out there and try it again."

———❖———

Connections between younger and older women coaches remain an important part of the coaching experience. Shortly before the college softball season began, Erika Blanco, a brand new assistant softball coach at Cal State-Fullerton, was on a recruiting trip when she spotted a familiar face among the coaches there watching the tournament and checking out potential players. It was Fresno State head softball coach Margie Wright, the charismatic coach for whom Erika had played four years of college softball.

Coaches typically wear school colors to promote their colleges when out recruiting, yet Erika felt a little strange to be wearing her blue Cal State Fullerton sweatsuit with orange insignia, rather than the red and blue Fresno State sweatsuit worn by Margie Wright. Of course, Erika didn't let that role reversal stop her from going over to say hello to her former head coach. Margie, for her part, greeted Erika with a hug and joked with her "about being a traitor" to her former team. She also introduced Erika to Patty Gasso, head coach of national softball champion the University of Oklahoma. It was a memorable moment for Erika. Here she was in her very first year of college coaching, and she was sitting in the stands together with Margie Wright and Patty Gasso, "two icons of softball."

Erika worked at bridging that huge experience gap by picking her former coach's brain as the two women sat watching the tournament. What qualities would Margie look for in a player?

If she watched a small but talented high school sophomore, how could she guess that the girl would grow big enough for college ball? Margie talked about looking at a girl's hands, about considering how coachable she appeared to be. Although Fresno State would compete against Fullerton in the upcoming season, the conversation between Margie and Erika had a comfortable rather than a competitive quality. It was, in fact, a continuation of the young coach-veteran coach mentoring relationship that had begun a few years ago, and the veteran coach-young player relationship that had started years earlier. "I definitely wouldn't be where I'm at today if it weren't for her," Erika summarized.

Growing up in a small town near Fresno, Erika was only 12 years old when her parents brought her to a Fresno State summer softball camp led by Margie Wright. With Erika a promising young player, both Margie and the other camp staff encouraged Erika to think of herself as a future Fresno State Bulldog. All through high school, Erika told her friends, teachers and family that Fresno State was where she planned to play college softball, and she did go on to have a successful four years as a player for the Bulldogs.

In 1996, Erika accepted her first coaching position at Bullard High School in Fresno. Only 22 years old at the time, she'd be coaching players not much younger than herself. Right away, Erika called up her former head coach, the woman she often still refers to simply as "Coach," to ask for her advice. Margie "opened her files and gave me tons of information, just really gave me a good pep talk and motivation to do it," Erika recalled. Margie suggested practice strategies ways to plan out her coaching year and more. Margie also gave Erika an intangible gift—the fact that Margie felt that her former player was up to the job of being a coach.

At Bullard High School, Erika modeled her own coaching style after that of her former head coach. Boosters from Fresno State who took in a high school game often noticed the resemblance. "Oh my gosh, you totally resemble Coach Wright," they might say to Erika. Margie, for example, taught her team to "walk on the field with authority" at the start of a game, with uniforms looking sharp. Erika copied that approach and used numerous other coaching strategies which she'd learned from Margie.

In the spring of 2001, after her four years of high school coaching had included winning four league championships and recognition as North Yosemite League Coach of the Year, 27-year-old Erika Blanco was in the middle of her first season of college coaching as an assistant softball coach at Fullerton, a job that the recommendation she received from Margie Wright had undoubtedly helped Erika to obtain. The head coach Erika worked under, Michelle Gromacki, was someone Erika liked and respected and felt she was learning from. Yet Erika continued to describe Margie Wright as her primary coaching role model.

There's a definite edge of heroine-worship in Erika's glowing descriptions of her former coach and a clear sense of the generation difference between the two women. "She's so elite to me, she's just the top, I can't put myself in her league," Erika commented. Margie, Erika described, is a coach who can "motivate" her players so well before games "that you would run through a brick wall for her, " and a coach who has "this aura about her."

Erika knows that not everyone shares her evaluation of Margie, mentioning the "people who are quitting on her," players who have chosen to leave the Fresno State program within the last couple of years. "You have to fit her style of coaching and her program," Erika admitted, adding that Margie as a coach is "really tough." During Erika's time as a player at Fresno, since she was among the players who had to watch their weight, half an hour before their practice officially began, she and some other players would run through the fields of grapevines across from their stadium. But Erika and the other players didn't have to run alone. With Margie there to lead them in their run, Erika felt inspired to push herself to continue. "It was like coach can do it, I can do it, because she's like 40 years old and I'm 21, and I'm not gonna stop."

When the Fresno players did aerobics as part of their fall conditioning program, Margie led them through a vigorous routine with so much energy that her players would sometimes wonder how their coach could push herself so hard. When the

Erika Blanco

players lifted weights, on occasion Margie showed her players that she could pump iron as well as them. "You respect somebody like that," Erika commented. "You don't want somebody to tell you to run or to lift weights if they can't."

As Erika describes it, the lessons Margie taught her players went well beyond softball, ranging from using correct table manners to how her players should maintain good relationships with their parents. As a coach, Erika tries to continue that approach, working to convince her players that their actions on the softball field tie into their overall approach to life. "If you're not motivated and dedicated to softball," Erika will tell her players, "You're not gonna be that way in your relationship with your partner or school " Still new to coaching, Erika is keenly aware of the change in her personal perspective, such as the way she now recognizes that a player who cuts classes might also skip out on a scheduled weight lifting session. "I see that now," Erika added, "but I don't think I saw that as an athlete." She laughed about the way she's adopted a coach's point-of-view.

That sea change in Erika's life situation—the move from player to coach—was hammered home to her on Tuesday, March 27, 2001, when Fullerton played an evening doubleheader at Fresno State. It was the first time Erika had ever coached against her former head coach, and going into the game, Erika had a mix of feelings. It felt strange to enter the Fresno State stadium but to represent an opposing team, strange to wear a different color of uniforms, to feel the opposition rather than support of the Fresno fans. While "The Star Spangled Banner" played before the game began, Erika had tears in her eyes. As she looked at the flag and the scoreboard, she could remember herself as a college player and the first time she stood together with her Fresno State teammates before a game while the national anthem played. Today, Erika had a sense of just how far she had come.

"It has been a long journey to get to where I am today," Erika explained about her feelings at that moment. Her position as a first year college assistant coach still seemed somewhat surprising. "Who'd a thought I'd be coaching softball all day and get paid for it," Erika commented enthusiastically. "What a dream!"

Throughout the game at Fresno State, Erika remained aware of her former coach. "I absolutely watched her. My eyes were on her the whole entire game," Erika described. Of course, as the dugout coach for her team, with the responsibility for prepping batters for what they might face from the Bulldog pitcher, Erika also watched the game with a coach's eyes. However, the game action itself didn't go the way Erika had hoped. Fresno State ended up winning the first game 6 to 3, and then took the second game as well 1 to 0.

Unlike their relaxed, conversational interaction prior to the season, at the March doubleheader, as coaches in a game day situation, Erika and Margie hardly talked. Both of them, Erika knew, were competitive, both wanted their own teams to win. In addition to the nervousness she felt about coaching against Margie Wright, Erika also sensed the need to keep a proper coaching distance, to acknowledge the "game time ... ready to compete" focus of her former coach.

After the game, Erika and Margie exchanged only a few words. "Great job, Erika," Margie commented, continuing her mentoring relationship. "Good game," Erika responded, not saying anything about the disappointment she personally felt about the doubleheader's outcome. It was a moment in her coaching career that Erika seemed likely to long remember. "I would never put myself at her level at all," Erika commented about Margie Wright. "But at that moment we were coaches."

Karen Smyte

As coaches, younger and older women share a strong interest in the impact they have on their athletes beyond the playing field. University of Michigan assistant women's rowing coach Karen Smyte, who was 34 years old in August, 2000, described coaching as "feminism in action." The physical and mental challenges she experienced during her own rowing career, Karen believes, have influenced "the strong sense of self I have." As a former head rowing coach at Mills College and now as an assistant at Michigan, Karen has the chance to pass that positive impact on to her athletes. "A lot of my job is to believe in (the athletes)," Karen commented, "and to say that, 'I know that you can go faster.' 'I know you're going to be stronger.' It's such an incredibly powerful thing to help someone discover."

Like many women coaches older than herself, Karen sees the need for women in the coaching profession. During her own rowing career, she had almost exclusively male coaches, which is why she thinks that initially she didn't consider coaching as a career option for herself. "I do think there is some power in having a female role model," Karen concluded, expressing enthusiasm for increased numbers of women rowing coaches.

While coaching at Mills College, Karen found the "feminist, active" atmosphere there a good fit for herself. She's more outspoken about political ideas than are some older coaches, including being willing to openly discuss the still difficult subject of homosexuality and sports. While working for a journalism degree at Columbia University, Karen wrote an article on homophobia in women's athletics. At Mills College, she led workshops with athletic director Helen Carroll on topics including homophobia and racism. In the mid-'90s, Karen proposed a presentation on homophobia in women's athletics for a U.S. Rowing convention and was one of the presenters to a packed house of coaches. And as an assistant coach at Michigan, continuing with the "proactive" approach Karen believes in, she'll take the time to discuss the homophobic comments athletes sometimes make, or the fact that rowing is obviously a historically very white sport. Her goal, Karen described, is to create a safe atmosphere where "people can be who they are."

In addition to her political concerns, Karen wrestles with how to combine the varied interests and future possibilities she sees for herself. She pictures herself as both a coach and a mother in the future, but she's aware that many women leave the coaching profession because of the conflict they experience between their multiple roles. The abundant physical and mental energy Karen has—which seems to be a characteristic of many coaches—helps her to combine coaching with her interest in writing. She's working on both an MFA and a novel about a woman rowing coach, but wonders if ultimately she'll be able to do it all.

"I'm not sure if I have the energy to coach the way I want to coach, and to write the way I want to write, and still have friends and family," Karen commented. She loves coaching, a profession she feels "passionate about," yet she feels that her writing as well as her coaching is "a way for me to work in the world to try to effect change."

Soccer coach Stephanie Gabbert, who is slightly younger than Karen Smyte, shares Karen's political awareness as well as her willingness to speak her mind and her passion for the coaching profession. And like many older coaches, Stephanie Gabbert has a strong interest in equity for women's athletics.

In early June of 2000, Stephanie had just returned home to Ames, Iowa, from one recruiting trip and would soon be on the road recruiting again. The search for new players—a time consuming and vital part of most coaches' lives—had a special significance for Stephanie, since only a few months before, in February, 2000, she had accepted a job as head women's soccer coach at Iowa State University. After building a women's soccer program from the ground up at her previous coaching job, at the University of Iowa, Stephanie had moved on to the new challenge of continuing to build a top notch soccer program at Iowa State. In the fall of 2000, Stephanie would begin her first full soccer season at Iowa State.

At the ripe young age of 33, with her collar-length brown hair so far unmixed with gray, Stephanie Gabbert was used to the level of responsibility her coaching jobs involved. Prior to her head coaching positions at Iowa State and the University of Iowa, she'd been an assistant coach at the University of Wisconsin, a head coach at Truman State, and an assistant at the University of Missouri-St. Louis, where she played varsity soccer from 1986–1990. Stephanie spoke positively about her position as head soccer coach—"You're pretty much your own boss, most of the time, I like that," she commented—and equally positively about the present and future of women's college soccer. In recent years, she pointed out, the sport has seen "an incredible amount of growth" and has moved toward being "a premiere sport" for women in college athletics.

Although Stephanie is young enough to have benefitted from Title IX in her own athletic career, she's old enough to have a personal perspective on the changes in women's sports. Growing up in St. Louis, she started playing soccer at the age of 7 or 8, and had the opportunity to compete in other sports as well through high school. But when she played soccer at the University of Missouri-St. Louis from 1986 to 1990, a time period that is not exactly ancient history, she experienced conditions that were very different from the treatment enjoyed by collegiate soccer players today.

When Stephanie's college soccer team travelled, they typically played three games in as many days—to get their money's worth out of their small travel budget—and ate at McDonald's or other fast food restaurants to stretch their limited meal money. They did stay in hotels but slept four players to a room, unlike today, Stephanie commented, where "more than two or three (players) to a room is living in squalor." Although Stephanie received a scholarship to play for the University of Missouri, it was only a partial scholarship, providing far less money than players would normally receive today. Nevertheless, she did receive a far fuller shot at competition than was true for many older women in coaching. During her years as a defender on the University of Missouri women's soccer team, Stephanie was honored as her team's MVP, an all-region player, and in 1988, as a first-team All-America player.

At only 24 years old Stephanie took her first head coaching position at Truman State, a Division II program where Stephanie's budget as well as salary were low. When Stephanie moved on to an assistant coaching position at the University of Wisconsin, she was also moving to a much more upscale program, with Wisconsin one of the top women's soccer programs at the time. After four years at Wisconsin, by the time Stephanie accepted the position of head coach at the University of Iowa, Title IX had continued to radically change the conditions for women's college sports. And yet Stephanie's experience at the University of Iowa illustrates how, like older women in coaching, coaches of Stephanie's age have also had to work for improved treatment.

In her four years at the University of Iowa, Stephanie built a strong women's soccer program. Due to the gender equity requirements of Title IX, more and more universities were adding women's soccer programs and competition was increasingly high-level. In only their third year of competition, Stephanie's team was ranked 23rd in the nation and ended the season third in their conference. Stephanie herself was honored by being named the Big Ten Conference Coach of the Year in 1999.

However, there were definitely things that bothered Stephanie about coaching at the University of Iowa. In her first year there, she only had one assistant coach. In her second year, she was allowed to add a second assistant, but that assistant only received a part-time salary. When she had taken her position at the university, she'd been promised a new soccer field and a new stadium, but neither materialized. Although she needed to recruit top players to build a top-notch program, the soccer field these players would play on was no better than the kind of field most of the players had used during high school. In the new, more competitive, post-Title IX era, all of that mattered. "Your facilities can be a real indicator of how much sup-

Stephanie Gabbert

port your department has for that sport," Stephanie commented.

Stephanie asked for more, just as women coaches have done for years, but received neither the new facilities she'd been promised or the kind of budget she felt she needed to compete effectively with other Big Ten conference schools. Frustrated by the lack of support, looking around for other coaching options, Stephanie was ready to listen when Iowa State contacted her about the head coach opening there.

For Stephanie, leaving the soccer program she'd built at the University of Iowa wasn't easy. It was especially tough for Stephanie to leave the first class of players she'd recruited. Because of an upcoming signing date, Stephanie talked to her players early on. "I've been interviewed for a job and I might take it, so I might not be back next year," she told her team. Many of her players cried, yet they also understood, Stephanie felt. They had seen, for example, their coach's frustration when the team would be asked to leave the university recreational field they used because they didn't have a practice field of their own.

In spite of the inevitable challenges of starting a new job, Stephanie appreciated the plusses of coaching at Iowa State University. Her team had their own practice field and game field, would soon enjoy a new grandstand with a press box, and all in all had what Stephanie described as "a top notch facility." Her new athletic director was supportive of the women's soccer program, and with two full-time assistant coaches and the NCAA limit of 12 full scholarships, not to mention a decent salary, Stephanie felt that both she and her program were fairly treated.

Moving to Iowa State and the tree-lined, Midwestern town of Ames, Iowa, had proved to be a good career move for Stephanie. Looking beyond her personal situation, she felt optimistic about the career opportunities for other women coaches created by the expanding number of women's soccer programs. In contrast to the approximately 60 Division I programs when Stephanie played college soccer, by February, 2000, when Stephanie took her new job at Iowa State, those numbers had exploded upward into over 250 Division I women's soccer teams. However, Stephanie understood that the soccer coaching field posed certain unique challenges for women.

In spite of the large numbers of girls playing soccer across the country, soccer coaching has so far remained a male-dominated field. Stephanie herself had only had male soccer coaches, a fact of soccer life that had never bothered her, and she was likewise used to being one of a very small number of women at coaching schools or clinics. But what did very much concern her was the blatant sexism often directed at women coaches. At a typical soccer clinic for coaches, Stephanie described, "they'll make derogatory comments about women, tell sexist jokes ..." Stephanie was used to asserting herself, a personal trait she'd been encouraged in by her family. As a girl in St. Louis, when she was refused permission to play on the boys' baseball team, her family took the issue to the school board. "I don't mind speaking my mind ... in a male-dominated atmosphere," Stephanie remarked. But some other women soccer coaches, she added, chose to stay away from soccer coaching classes "because they've heard horror stories from others."

Sexual harassment was not at all uncommon at soccer coaching training sessions, Stephanie explained. At night, for example, a male instructor might come by the dorm room of a female coach. Or a male instructor might make his hostility perfectly clear to any women in his class. "Well, hey, Stephanie and so and so (other woman's name)," a male instructor in a coaching course said to Stephanie and another woman, "since you're the women college coaches making all the money now, why don't you tell us how this gets done."

At another coaching clinic, when Stephanie was out on the soccer field along with other coaches, the male instructor noticed that Stephanie was the only woman in the group. The instructor replaced Stephanie with a male, since he was sure that a mere female wouldn't be able to handle a soccer ball. Considering Stephanie's high-level playing experience and skills—she had competed in several U.S. Olympic Festivals and also in a women's semi-professional soccer league—the instructor's action was, to say the least, inappropriate. When Stephanie protested to him, his lame excuse was to say that he'd thought she'd been injured.

In spite of experiences like these, Stephanie remains openminded on the subject of male and female coaches. "I would never say that men shouldn't coach women," she explained. "I think there are some great (male) coaches out there." But she also realizes the importance of having female coaches out there for female athletes. "My players know that I played at a pretty high level, and they respect that," she commented. "I think sometimes for girls and young women to look at a guy doing something ... always gives them the out to say 'Well, he's a guy, it's easier for him.' But if I can do something and show them, then I think it makes it more attainable."

Stephanie herself was raised by a mother active in the women's movement—her mother had been president of the Missouri ERA chapter and also was involved with the National Organization of Women—and Stephanie's mother made sure that her daughter appreciated that she was receiving the benefits of Title IX and sports opportunities which had been unavailable to older women. Stephanie described herself as "an independent person who acts on my own beliefs and believes in the empowerment of young women." As a soccer coach, she aims to "empower" her players "as people rather than just make them great soccer players." And she can envision that training making waves beyond the game of soccer, beyond the players' college years, as they enter the workforce as strong, competitive, self-reliant women.

Stephanie has already received evidence that exactly that is happening. Five years after a former player had graduated from college, the young woman, now running her own business, came to see her former coach. "There's no way I ever would have been able to do this," the former player told Stephanie, "if I didn't play on this team and you didn't make me feel that I could do anything I wanted to."

———◆———

Just as numerous current and former female athletes have expressed similar feelings to their coaches, women coaches such as Stephanie Gabbert, Karen Smyte, and many others have talked about their goals of personal development for the young women athletes on their teams. Numerous women coaches have both nurtured and inspired their female athletes. Younger women coaches today, just as coaches always have, wear the diverse hats of role models and listening ears, supportive mentors and demanding taskmasters.

Today's women college coaches enjoy much stronger financial support than their predecessors, yet also face stronger pressures to produce winning teams. "It's just such a different arena now, and a lot of it has to do with the media exposure and the money involved," commented former women's basketball coach Stephanie Gaitley. "It's so competitive and so win-at-all-costs," she added, giving her critical perspective on the recent changes in women's college athletics.

Although Rutgers University hired female coach C. Vivian Stringer for the highest salary given to any Rutgers coach, which also made her the most-well paid woman coach in the country, most women coaches don't earn anything like the annual $1.2 million dollar salary package received by University of Washington football coach Rick Neuheisel in September, 2001, and some women coaches question whether such high salaries are even a good thing for college athletics. On the other side of the coin, younger coaches especially, Vivian Acosta and Linda Carpenter explained, are likely to coach with the tenuous job security of one year contracts, which, Linda Carpenter described, are "the greatest tool of oppression that has found its way into athletics." Younger coaches, such as Dana Kusjanovic, formerly head soccer coach at Portland State University, and Noleana Woodard, formerly assistant softball coach at San Jose State, can find themselves instantly unemployed, as can the many women college coaches of all ages who lack adequate job protection.

While older women coaches, in years past, sometimes had to teach athletic fundamentals to female athletes with a relatively poor background in sport, today coaches usually recruit and coach female athletes already highly skilled in their sport. Today, when the level of competition of women's college sports has never been higher, women coaches are key figures in this women's sports success story who may themselves, depending on their sport and university, receive a fair amount of public recognition. Yet women coaches and their female athletes still encounter negative attitudes about female athletics and a public ambivalent about women's sports.

As the University of Iowa's Christine Grant eloquently described in the thought-provoking, "Equity: What Price Equality?" she co-authored with Charles F. Darley, many challenges remain for women's collegiate sports. "The precarious circumstance for women" within intercollegiate sports has to do with the fact that women's college sports today take place within a largely male-run power-structure where the historically female model of sport "that incorporates the ideals of nurturance, cooperation and broad participation" is seriously threatened. Nowadays, almost all collegiate athletic directors are male; many of the coaches who lead women's teams are male as well; the AIAW, which formerly led the charge for women's collegiate sports, is a defunct institution; the NCAA, which formerly controlled only male college sports, now dominates the intercollegiate sports arena; and more prominent women's sports are involved in the high-finance of TV deals. Surely all of these are reasons why Christine Grant and Charles Darley concluded that "those women still holding positions of influence in intercollegiate athletics must operate within a structure they did not create and with which most philosophically disagree."

Such a dilemma must be especially apparent to older women like Christine Grant, a former AIAW president, and other older coaches who remember the loss of the AIAW, the last collegiate sports governing body run solely by women. Younger women coaches, in contrast, often seem to generally accept today's NCAA control of most women's college sports as simply the way things are. Yet many younger women coaches as well as older women reject the model of sports Grant and Darley and deny the claim that "winning and making money" are the main objectives. Women coaches of all ages describe winning as something they enjoy, but also as essentially a byproduct of the hard work they do to develop individual athletes as strong people and teams as cohesive groups which have the power to teach valuable lessons.

In today's post-Title IX era for women's sports, the new generation of women coaches may at times simply accept the increased support for women's sports as the norm, and as a group very likely do have less awareness of the history of struggle behind those advances than older coaches do. Certainly the younger women coaches haven't lived through the struggles in the same way. Yet younger as well as older women coaches continue to work for positive treatment for themselves and their athletes, and in general to advance the interests of women in sports.

"I'm passionate about what I do," said 37-year-old Lori Dauphiny, rowing coach at Princeton University. What's especially rewarding for her about coaching is the personal growth she both fosters and witnesses in the young women she coaches. "Sometimes, by the end of their (college) career," Lori described, "I see a totally different woman walking out of the boathouse. One who understands more about what limits really are, and pressing harder, and drive, and taking challenges, and failing and picking up." Other women coaches of all ages make similar statements about the coaching profession.

Women college coaches stand behind team benches full of helmet-wearing ice hockey players or shout instructions from the sidelines of soccer fields or instruct both male and female tennis players. They listen to young women struggling in many ways to define themselves as adults, often witnessing these women's tears or other strong emotions. They speak to community groups, plug their programs to athletic directors and testify in courts of law. They celebrate athletic victories that may remind them of their own personal triumphs as athletes, help their athletes hang tough through difficult losses, and inspire their athletes to reach their full potential both within and beyond the sports arena. Women college coaches are strong individuals who have fought long and hard to make a difference for women.

Notes on Sources

Most of the information for this book, including the numer-ous quotations, comes from in-person, telephone, and e-mail interviews with over 60 coaches, and others with special expertise, that I conducted between January, 2000 and September, 2001. Throughout, what I describe as current ages and positions of individuals is as of the time I interviewed them. In some cases, I also made use of personal materials, such as letters and résumés, which coaches furnished me. Although I do not specifically list each, I often drew on the general biographical information about coaches found in media guides and athletic department web sites. Listed below are my other sources of information, in the order in which they appear in the book.

Hard Fought Victories

The image of Bev Kearney celebrating her team's win comes from the University of Texas's videotape of a CBS broadcast on 6/20/00 of the 1999 NCAA Outdoor Track and Field Championships.

The information about high school girls' sports participation is from the author's previous book, *Playing in a New League* (Indianapolis: Masters Press, 1998). The women involved in college sports is given in a Donna Lopiano letter to the editor, published in the *Oregonian* on 4/22/01; the original source cited is "Gender Equity: Men's and Women's Participation in Higher Education," December 2000, the United States General Accounting Office. For numbers of women coaches, most information is from "Women in Intercollegiate Sport: A Longitudinal Study - Twenty Three Year Update, 1977–2000" by R. Vivian Acosta and Linda Jean Carpenter. However, the numbers of women coaches in 1972 comes from *Whatever It Takes: Women on Women's Sport* by Joli Sandoz and Joby Winans (New York: Farrar, Straus and Giroux, 1999).

The Donna Lopiano quote about women coaches is from "Attracting Women to the Coaching Profession: Recruiting, Education and Retention" by Donna Lopiano, released by the Women's Sports Foundation.

Additional information about Beverly Kearney's background comes from the *Dallas Morning News* article by Chip Brown, "UT track coach overcame life's hurdles," 5/26/00.

Long Time Coming

The quote about males vs. females in sports, along with general information about women's sports history, is from *Coming on Strong: Gender and Sexuality in Twentieth-Century Women's Sport* by Susan Cahn (Cambridge, Massachusetts: Harvard University Press, 1994). "The Story of Women's Athletics: Manipulating a Dream, 1890-1985" by Joan Hult, from *Women and Sport: Interdisciplinary Perspectives*, by D. Margaret Costa and Sharon R. Guthrie (Champaign, Illinois: Human Kinetics, 1994) provided additional helpful background about earlier attitudes toward women in sports, values held by early women physical educators, and sports days and play days, as did Susan Cahn for the latter subject.

Regarding the AIAW and its unsuccessful battle with the NCAA, the Susan Cahn book and Joan Hult chapter already cited provided valuable information, as did *College Sports Inc.: The Athletic Department vs. The University*, by Murray Sperber

(Henry Holt: New York, 1990). Additionally, *Playing Nice: Politics and Apologies in Women's Sports* by Mary Jo Festle (Columbia University Press: New York, 1996) provides a very helpful section on the AIAW, including the quotes from Peg Burke and Christine Grant on the takeover.

The quote from Donna Lopiano about "doubly special" coaches is from "Attracting Women to the Coaching Profession."

The information on Marlene Piper's total number of wins in relation to other coaches was provided by an e-mail from Stephanie Schleuder on 4/11/01.

L. Leotus Morrison's statement about the AIAW is included within her chapter titled "The AIAW: Governance by Women for Women" in *Women in Sport: Issues and Controversies*, by Greta Cohen (Newbury Park: Sage Publications, 1993).

The section on Marian Washington in *Celebrating Women Coaches: A Biographical Dictionary* by Nena Rey Hawkes and John Seggar (Westport, Connecticut: Greenwood Press, 2000) provided helpful data on her honors and awards.

The quote about Judi Garman hiring out a dynamite job is from *Celebrating Women Coaches*.

Teachers, Role Models and Mentors

The material about women surgeons is from *The Woman in the Surgeon's Body* by Joan Cassell (Cambridge, Massachusetts: Harvard University Press, 1998).

Linda Bird Francke's book, *Ground Zero: The Gender Wars in the Military* (New York: Simon and Schuster, 1997), provided helpful information about female cadets and midshipmen.

The research about male and female basketball players, and their attitudes toward coaching comes from "Gender differences in preferences for coaching as an occupation: the role of self-efficacy, valence, and perceived barriers" by C. Bonnie

Everhart and Packianathan Chelladuria, in *Research Quarterly for Exercise and Sport*, June 1998.

The story about Vivian Stringer is from *Are We Winning Yet? How Women Are Changing Sports and Sports Are Changing Women* by Mariah Burton Nelson (New York: Random House, 1991).

Dorothea Stillman's description of macho coaches came from her article "What's Wrong with Playing Like a Girl?" published in *Newsweek*, 3/22/99.

The information on Marianna Freeman's reputation in recruiting is from the Syracuse Athletic Department web site.

The Donna Lopiano quote is from the Women's Sports Foundation position paper she authored, "Do Female Athletes Prefer Male Coaches?"

The John Wooden quote is from *Wooden: A Lifetime of Observations and Reflections On and Off the Court*, by John Wooden with Steve Jamison (Lincolnwood, Illinois: Contemporary Books, 1997); the following quote from Mike Krzyzewski is from *Leading with the Heart: Coach K's Successful Strategies for Basketball, Business, and Life* by Mike Krzyzewski with Donald Phillips (New York: Warner Books, 2000).

The discussion of and quotes from the 1988 survey is from an article by R. Vivian Acosta and Linda Jean Carpenter, "Perceived Causes of the Declining Representation of Women Leaders in Intercollegiate Sports," 1988 Update.

In the Limelight

The information about and quotes from Jody Conradt's induction into the basketball Hall of Fame comes from a video made of the "1998 Naismith Hall of Fame Enshrinement," 10/2/98, supplied me by the University of Texas. The headline about her initial Austin salary was quoted in "She's Stealing the Heart of Texas," by Skip Hollandsworth who also provided the perspective on need for a Texas coach, in

Women's Sports and Fitness, 2/87. The quote about women's basketball is by David Salter from *Crashing the Old Boys' Network* (Westport, Connecticut, 1996). The quotes from Donna Lopiano are from my e-mail interview with her on 3/6/01. The quote about a pyramid scheme is from "She Raised her Game" by Chip Brown in the *Dallas Morning News*, 10/3/98. The information about the return to Austin in 1986 is from the video "The Perfect Season" by the University of Texas at Austin. The quote about Jody's reason for resigning as athletic director is from "Conradt Steps Down from AD's Position" on www.TexasSports.com.

Mel Greenberg, Andy Geiger and Dawn Staley were quoted in "Winning Ways" by David Early, in *SV*, the magazine of the *San Jose Mercury News*, on 1/14/01. The quotes and background information from Tara's book are from *Shooting from the Outside: How a Coach and Her Olympic Team Transformed Women's Basketball*, by Tara VanDerveer with Joan Ryan (New York: Avon Books, 1997). Pat Summitt's quote about the championship is from "Stanford's title fulfills coach's preseason vision," by Dwight Chapin, the *San Francisco Examiner*, 4/20/90. Other quotes about the championship are from "Stanford Women Win It All" by Gary Swan, *San Francisco Chronicle*, 4/2/90, and from "Stanford takes its first title" by Debbie Becker, *USA Today*, 4/2/90. The information about flowers received is from "Stanford Women: It's a trip" by Keith Peters, *Times Tribune*, 4/16/90. Kate Paye's perspective is from the author's previous book, *Playing in a New League*. The perspectives on expectations for Stanford come from "The Comeback Bid" by Michelle Smith, in *Real Sports*, December 2000/January 2001 and from "Expectations put heat on Stanford" by Ed Guzman, in the *Oregonian*, 2/6/01.

The numbers of basketball and hockey programs are from the 2000 update of the Acosta/Carpenter study. Quotes from and descriptions of Shannon's talk on April 11, 2000 are from a videotape provided by the Tucker Center for Research on Girls and Women in Sport. Background about women's hockey and Shannon's support for a girls' team is from *On the Edge: Women Making Hockey History*, by Elizabeth Etue and Megan Williams (Toronto: Second Story Press, 1996). Shannon's quote about pay is from "Her Border Crossing is History for Miller," by Barbara Huebner, *Boston Globe*, 3/22/00. Nancy Theberge's comment on women's Olympic hockey is from her book *Higher Goals: Women's Ice Hockey and the Politics of Gender* (Albany: State University of New York Press, 2000). The critical comments on Shannon are from "Historic Gold: U.S. wins and women's hockey grows up" by C.W. Nevius, *San Francisco Chronicle*, 2/18/98, and Shannon's comments on media coverage afterwards are from "'Frozen Four' Coaches" in the *Boston Globe*, 3/22/00. The critical comments after the Olympics are from "Miller shoulders loss for Canada," by Steve Simmons, 2/18/98, www.canoe.ca/SlamNaganoHockeyWomen. The coverage of Shannon's new contract is "Miller gets new contract—coaching deal through 2004 matches salary of men's coach," by Kevin Pates, *Duluth News Tribune*, 7/13/00. Shannon's comments about the championship are from "UMD wins national title" by John Gilbert, *Duluth Budgeteer News*, 3/26/01 and from "UMD women win national title" by Christa Lawler, *Duluth News Tribune*, 3/26/01.

Fighting for Equity

The Stephanie Schleuder contract proposal mentioned dates from June 30, 1993. The quotes about people being a priority and her years of coaching are from "Stephanie Schleuder and the Challenges of Coaching" by Cynthia Scott, *Melpomene Journal*, Autumn, 1994. Stephanie's writing on coaching philosophy is from "Cap Level 1, Coaching Philosophy: for the USA Volleyball Coaching Association. The quote re pay equity battle is from "U halts contract talks," by Charley Hallman, *Saint Paul Pioneer Press*, 8/94. The commentary about Stephanie's firing is from a *Star Tribune* article by Jay Weiner on 12/10/94; a *Saint Paul Pioneer Press* article by Jim Caple, "Schleuder's dismissal puts Voelz under fire"; "Voelz's firing of 'U' volleyball coach is vicious, uncalled for" by Patrick Reusse, *Star Tribune*, 12/11/94; the "Letters to the Sports Editor" section in the *Pioneer Press*, and "Carlson: Voelz should reconsider decision," Jay Weiner, *Star Tribune*, 12/14/94.

The history on Marianne Stanley's legal battle, although widely reported, was from "Procedural History" from the United States District Court for the Central District of California.

Stephanie Schleuder's comment about justice is from "Coach slot left in limbo," *The Minnesota Daily*, 2/3/95, by Ian Morris and Jennifer Niemela. The information and comments about the legal settlement are from "'U' and Schleuder settle; fired coach is to receive $3000,000, drop all claims" by Jay Weiner, 4/7/95; and "Winning, losing, and how the game is played" by Doug Grow, *Star Tribune*, 12/29/95. The AVCA comment is from "AVCA Board of Directors Takes a Stand Regarding Coach's Recent Dismissal," *American Volleyball*, January/February 1995. The report on the new coach hired is from "Minnesota lures away Illinois volleyball coach" by Nolan Zavoral, *Star Tribune*, 12/28/95. Stephanie's own article, "Commentary: Beware the latest attempt to subvert Title IX," was published in the *Star Tribune* on 2/25/00.

Regarding compensation equity for coaches, the WBCA salary survey, "Basketball Coaches Survey Report, 1999, was quite helpful. The comment on wage discrimination is from "Recognizing and Remedying Individual and Institutional Gender-Based Wage Discrimination in Sport," by Andrea

Giampetro-Meyer, in *American Business Law Journal*, Winter, 2000. Additional information was provided by "Uneven Progress for Women's Sports" by Welch Suggs, in the *Chronicle of Higher Education*, 4/7/00.

Information about the trial verdict involving Joann Wolf is from "University found in violation of Title IX" from CNN Sports Illustrated, 12/7/99.

Other Battles

The history of Brown University's legal battle related to Title IX is from the University of Iowa's extremely helpful website, "Gender Equity in Sports," provided by Mary Curtis and Christine H.B. Grant, www.bailiwick.lib.uiowa.edu/ge. The same web site provided an excellent source of general information in other equity battles, including Joann Wolf's, Stephanie Schleuder's and Marianne Stanley's.

The opinions of athletic administrators on why fewer women are coaches are from "Perceived Causes of the Declining Representation of Women Leaders in Intercollegiate Sports," by R. Vivian Acosta and Linda Jean Carpenter, 1988. Mary Jo Kane's discussion on the same subject is from "Structural Variables That Offer Explanatory Power for the Underrepresentation of Women Coaches Since Title IX: The Case of Homologous Reproduction," Jane Marie Stangl and Mary Jo Kane, *Sociology of Sport Journal*, 1991.

Doing It All

The information on numbers of women in the workforce and their home responsibilities comes from *Balancing Act: Motherhood, Marriage, and Employment Among American Women*, by Daphne Spain and Suzanne Bianchi (New York: Russell Sage Foundation, 1996).

The description of the extra burden on working women is from *The Second Shift: Working Parents and the Revolution at*

Home, by Arlie Hochschild with Anne Machung (New York: Viking, 1989).

The comment about professional women prioritizing their children is from *Getting It Right: How Working Mothers Successfully Take Up the Challenge of Life, Family, and Career*, by Laraine T. Zappert (New York: Pocket Books, 2001). The Gaitley's denial of guilt was quoted in "St. Joseph's Fires Women's Hoops Coach Gaitley," 4/3/01, www.cbs.sportsline.com. The description of Stephanie's post-firing press conference is from "Gaitley fired as St. Joe's coach," by Bill Bergstrom, Associated Press, 4/3/01, sports.yahoo.com.

The comment about the home speedup is from *The Second Shift*.

The descriptions of Kristy Curry and Muffet McGraw at the championship game, quote from Kristy's pre-game talk to her team, and Muffet's thanks afterwards were from the ESPN broadcast on 4/1/01. Muffet's post-game comment about "euphoria" is from "No, it's not football, but Irish win anyway," Chuck Schoffner, *Oregonian*, 4/2/01.

A Question of Attitude

The figures on and thoughts about low numbers of African-American women coaches are from "Progress? Not for Black Women Coaches" by Greg Garber, *Hartford Courant*, 3/16/00.

The comments on women executives are from *Men and Women of the Corporation* by Rosabeth Moss Kanter (New York: Basic Books, 1977).

The numbers of minority athletes versus coaches is from the "Racial and Gender Report Card," The Center for the Study of Sport in Society at Northeastern University, 1998.

The Donna Lopiano quotes are from her Women's Sports Foundation article "Attracting Women to the Coaching Profession: Recruiting, Education, and Retention."

The quotes on homophobia in the military are from *Ground Zero* by Linda Bird Francke and from *In the Men's House: An Inside Account of Life in the Army by One of West Point's First Female Graduates*, by Captain Carol Barkalow with Andrea Raab, (New York: Poseidon Press, 1990).

Pat Griffin's thoughts about how sexual orientation affects coaches overall and their strategies are from her book *Strong Women, Deep Closets: Lesbians and Homophobia in Sport* (Champaign, Illinois: Human Kinetics, 1998).

Beth Bricker's profile in *The Advocate* is "Hoop schemes: as long as the bouncing ball is leading to the bank, many women are choosing to play from the closet," by Susan Biemesderfer, 8/18/98.

Additional information for Jenny Allard's profile is from "Speakers Discuss Gay Experience in Athletics," by Daniel E. Fernandez, 2/20/01, www.thecrimson.com.

The quote on labeling and homophobia is from "Homophobia in Women's Intercollegiate Basketball," by Susan Wellman and Elaine Blinde, *Women in Sport and Physical Activity Journal*, 9/30/97.

Ways of Coaching

Anson Dorrance's thoughts are from *Training Soccer Champions*, with Tim Nash (JTC Sports Inc., June 1996).

The Donna Lopiano quote is from her Women's Sports Foundation position paper, "Do Female Athletes Prefer Male Coaches?"

The information on Bobby Knight is from "Indiana fires 'defiant' Knight," *Oregonian*, 9/11/00, by Joe Drape.

The Pat Summitt quotes are from *Raise the Roof: The Inspiring Inside Story of the Tennessee Lady Vols' Undefeated 1997-98 Season*, by Pat Summitt with Sally Jenkins (New York: Broadway Books, 1998).

The comment about women's basketball coaches is from "Coaching turnover shows increasing pressure in women's game," Chuck Schoffner, Associated Press, 4/1/00, and Mariah Burton Nelson's quote is from *Are We Winning Yet?*

The perspective on female athletes is from "Competition: Perceived Barriers to Success," by Mimi Murray and Hilary Matheson, in *Women in Sport: Issues and Controversies.*

The information about Micki King is from *The Quiet Storm: A Celebration of Women in Sport,* by Alexandra Powe-Allred and Michelle Powe (Indianapolis: Masters Press, 1997).

Challenges and Rewards

Teri Mariani's comment about her thousandth game comes from "1,000th game a winner for PSU's Mariani," by Abby Haight, *Oregonian,* 3/26/01.

A New Generation of Coaches

The information on Vivian Stringer's salary is from "New women's basketball coach commands attention," by Douglas Frank, *Rutgers Focus,* 12/1/95.

The Christine Grant quotes are from "Equity: What Price Equality?" by Christine Grant and Charles F. Darley, in *Women in Sport.*

Index

6173